BK 820.9   M828   1969
MORALITY OF ART

1969   .00   FR   /

30
St. Louis C

D0848984

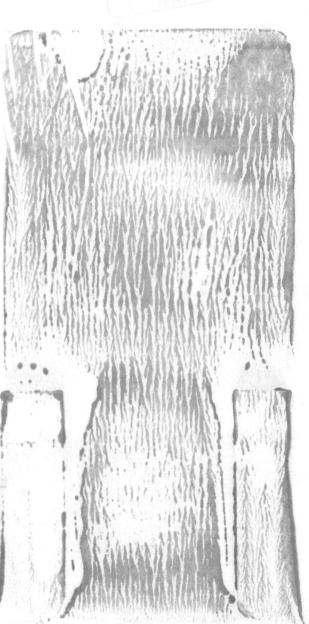

INVENTORY 98

INVENTORY 1985

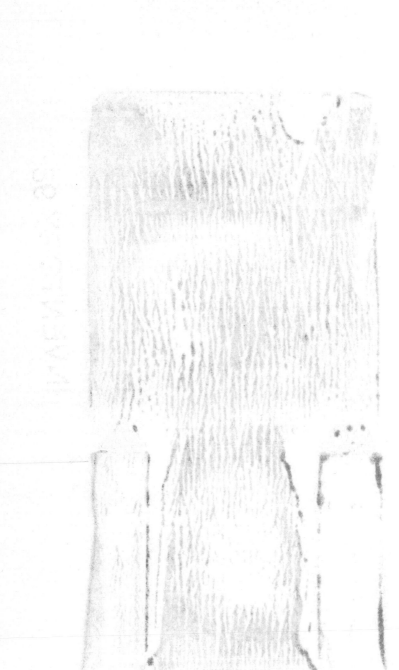

The Morality of Art

G. WILSON KNIGHT

John Goodman: Exeter

THE MORALITY
OF ART

Essays Presented to G. Wilson Knight
by His Colleagues and Friends

Edited by

D. W. JEFFERSON

Whether in art of life, submission and control
are necessary: technique is the morality
of art, just as morality is the technique
of life. *The Christian Renaissance (1962 ed. p. 31)*

NEW YORK
BARNES & NOBLE, INC.
Publishers & Booksellers since 1873

First published in Great Britain
by Routledge & Kegan Paul Ltd, 1969.
Published in the United States of America 1969
by Barnes & Noble, Inc., New York, N.Y.
© *Routledge & Kegan Paul 1969*

Printed in Great Britain

Contents

v

Contents

Note: In all Shakespeare articles the line references are given from the Globe edition, but in many cases a different text is used for the passages quoted.

Illustrations

Preface

Wilson Knight at Leeds

It was a little after the Second World War that Wilson Knight came to Leeds. The appointment, to a readership in English Literature, was one of Bonamy Dobrée's very happy strokes, none the less characteristic in that it gave the Department an outstanding personality strikingly different from his own. Wilson's great contribution to the teaching was his two-year course on Drama, in which English drama was seen as part of world drama from Aeschylus onwards and Ibsen was frequently chosen for detailed study. Shakespeare was then taught by Kenneth Muir, until he became the professor at Liverpool in 1951; the Novel by Dobrée himself, who gradually handed it over to Arnold Kettle, a new arrival in 1947; and Poetry by a poet, Wilfred Childe, a gentle and much-loved colleague who died in 1952. The mention of these names will convey a sufficient impression of diversity. The environment was one in which diversity could be cherished, a good setting for Wilson's powerful originality. In these years he established the role, not only as a teacher but also as an inspirer of dramatic activity in the university, which he maintained with unflagging energy until his retirement in 1962. He was appointed to a personal Chair in 1956. Bonamy Dobrée's retirement had come in the previous year, and with A. Norman Jeffares as head of the Department (from 1957) English in Leeds entered upon a new phase.

The pleasure and privilege of being Wilson's colleague was an experience that never lost its freshness; and this was partly because freshness was of the essence of his personality and thought. He was incapable of making routine statements about literature. However deeply versed he was in the text, his remarks on the great master-pieces always had the air of a spontaneous working out of an inter-pretation with his hearers, whose participation he would often invite with an engagingly friendly and humble: 'Do you see what I mean?' Profoundly convinced though he was of the values and patterns of meaning that he saw in the works before him, these insights had to be lived through again every time he shared his thoughts with an audience. Over a period of years it was customary for Wilson Knight to give a Shakespeare lecture for the benefit of the whole university; and it was part of one's enjoyment, after one came away, to hear the satisfied comments of scientists and technologists. His viewpoints were sometimes daring and unusual, but never remote. He never gave the slightest impression of trying to captivate an audience, but by being at ease with them he made them at ease with him. A former student writes: 'His lectures, seemingly created on the spur of the moment from a question or a few lines of text, were exciting and stimulating. Never didactic or dogmatic, for I feel that Wilson enjoyed his teaching not as an opportunity to dictate but to discuss. He drew full houses, his qualities as an actor having something to do with this. . . . In the lecture room, after a brief reference to his text on the lectern, he moved into open space, and his movements and gestures became complementary to his words. He had great presence, despite a lack of any great physical stature . . .' The element of acting in his lectures has been recalled by many, but it was quite unstudied. He was committed to his theme and completely free from the vanity of the performer.

In his first year at Leeds he produced for the students' Theatre Group a truly memorable *Agamemnon*, in Macneice's translation. This was followed in 1947 by Racine's *Athalie*, in Kenneth Muir's translation, and in 1948 by *Timon of Athens*, with himself in the leading role. His well-known view of *Timon* may not be acceptable to all, but it came across on the stage with remarkable wholeness and power. By way of contrast he played in the same year the part of Private Meek in Shaw's *Too True to be Good*. In 1951 he played Lear in a staff-student 'Festival of Britain' production directed by John Boorman. Other productions in which he played the lead were *Othello* in 1955 and *The Merchant of Venice* in 1959. His career in acting and production, in relation to the views on these matters

developed in *Shakespearian Production*, will certainly be the subject
of full treatment some day. His *Dramatic Papers*, lodged in the
Shakespeare Memorial Library of the Birmingham Reference
Library, refer to his earliest part, that of Vanya in one scene from
Chekhov's play presented by the Cheltenham Operatic and Dramatic
Society about the year 1926 or 1927. His performance as Nym in a
production of *The Merry Wives of Windsor* by the Cheltenham
Amateurs was described by the *Gloucestershire Echo* as having 'a
sort of staccato quaintness. The "humour of it" was something of a
creation.' During his period as professor in the University of Toronto,
in the nineteen-thirties, he enjoyed some striking successes as a
director and actor at the Hart House Theatre, productions of *Hamlet*,
Romeo and Juliet and *Antony and Cleopatra* being among those that
aroused considerable interest and discussion. It was during these years
and the earlier part of his time at Leeds that he was able to practise
most fully what he has always believed concerning the inseparability
of academic study of drama and the experience of it in the theatre.

Before Wilson Knight's arrival the Theatre Group at Leeds had had
the advantage of Kenneth Muir's skill and sensitiveness as a producer. Later it was to draw much stimulus and inspiration from the
work of John Boorman; and there were other members of the
teaching staff who made their contribution as producers and actors.
During a large part of Wilson Knight's Leeds career there was indeed
no lack of colleagues ready to participate in these activities. When it
became a matter of policy to encourage the student producer, the
role of the teaching staff became, of necessity, less prominent. To
many former students who never saw him in action on the stage he
was known as a wise Chairman of the Theatre Group over many
years. He was known also as the generous, sympathetic supporter of
innumerable dramatic ventures, staff and student, some of which
needed all the sympathy they could get. Wilson's complete lack of
snobbery about levels of ability or technique was one of the qualities
that will be remembered with most affection. He would attend the
rehearsals of productions that were sick unto death (for Leeds could
achieve the very bad as well as the very good), and would frequently
find the opportunity to inspire some actor with fresh confidence, by
taking a generous view of his possibilities, in addition to making
suggestions of bedrock usefulness. He regularly attended first nights
where his presence was always a great source of pleasure to the cast.
With colleagues he could be the most comforting of companions.

Preface

In his room on the ground floor of No. 2 Virginia Road (now a Language Laboratory)* he always kept, in the drawer of his desk, a supply of sweets, which he offered to his visitors. One visited him to relax. He had a philosophical, humorous gift for making problems seem less dreary. But there were some situations in which he did not relax. Though he had no strong interest in administration, he was meticulous in all matters where the claims of his students were concerned. If he disagreed with colleagues over an examination candidate, he supported his estimate with chapter and verse from the written papers, and pressed strongly for generous recognition of everything that seemed to him evidence of insight into the topic in question. To him it was natural that students should make discoveries, and it was characteristic of his teaching that it produced interesting work where no one else would have expected it.

The regulations relating to retirement were not designed for people like Wilson, and the various farewell gatherings that were held during his last year are remembered as occasions when he was on his best form. At the dinner of the staff and student English Society his reply to an address of appreciation consisted largely of the reading of an extremely funny version of the story of Hamlet so worded as to contain as many familiar sayings and colloquial formulae as possible. The farewell dinner of colleagues took place at the Bridge Inn, near Wetherby, selected partly because it had been visited by Byron on his wedding night, though it proved to have other merits too. It was happily possible for his brother, the late W. F. Jackson Knight, also to be present. A more charmingly friendly and sociable party could hardly be imagined. Wilson has visited Leeds at regular intervals during the last few years, sometimes to give a lecture, but otherwise to see old friends. On his last visit he was a remarkably youthful seventy.

* No longer time since the School of English moved into new quarters in 1968.

1

Timon of Athens

L. C. KNIGHTS

ONE of the most interesting problems in Shakespeare criticism —as indeed in the criticism of all great literature—is the problem of divergent interpretations. I do not refer to shifts of emphasis and approach inevitable as times change, or to the mysterious power of works of art to reveal *more* meaning in the course of centuries, but to radically incompatible accounts of 'the meaning' of a work among readers who respect each other's standards and general powers of judgment. A glance at the history of opinion about Shakespeare's *Timon of Athens*[1] suggests that the critic who chooses to write on this most puzzling of Shakespeare's plays must take especial care to expose the grounds of his judgment. An attempt to do this is my tribute to the author of *The Wheel of Fire* and *The Imperial Theme*, works which, more than any others available at the time, helped my generation in the arduous and endlessly rewarding task of reading Shakespeare for themselves.

There seems no doubt that *Timon of Athens* is an unfinished play: not in the sense that it lacks a formal conclusion, but in the sense that it has not been finally worked over for presentation on the stage.[2] It is, however, very much more than a mere draft; it is a play moving towards completion; and although the great variety of critical opinion

[1] A full account is given in Francelia Butler's *The Strange Critical Fortunes of Shakespeare's 'Timon of Athens'* (Iowa State University Press, 1966).

[2] The evidence of incompleteness is fully presented by H. J. Oliver in his Introduction to the New Arden edition of the play, which I have used for all quotations from the text.

1

warns us that it is not easy to get at the meaning, there is no reason why we should not trust our impression that Shakespeare is saying something important, and use our wits to determine what that something may be. Our best course, as usual, is to trust our immediate sense of dramatic power, to begin by concentrating on those parts where our minds and imaginations are most fully engaged, and to ask ourselves how these are related to each other and to the remainder of the play—to those parts of lesser intensity that serve to reinforce, to modify or to cast a fresh light on what is more prominent. I am not advocating simple concentration on dramatic highlights: all I am saying is that understanding has to start somewhere, and we run less risk of going astray if we start with whatever it may be that most engages us.

Timon is no exception to the rule that Shakespeare's plays are always superbly well planned. When we look back on *Timon*, after directly experiencing it, we recall three episodes or phases of great dramatic effectiveness. The first is the presentation of Timon in his prosperity, surrounded by suitors, friends and parasites. This begins about a third of the way through the first scene and continues throughout the second (that is to say, to the end of the first Act). The second is the scene of the mock banquet (III.vi), where Timon serves covered dishes of warm water to the friends whose utter falseness has been exposed, denounces them for the fawning parasites they are ('Uncover, dogs, and lap'), beats them, and drives them out. The third is the exhibition of Timon's misanthropy: this consists of the tirade of IV.i, and the tirades and curses of IV.iii, when Timon is confronted, in turn, with Alcibiades, Apemantus, the bandits, and other intruders on his solitude. There is in addition a kind of prologue, when Poet, Painter, Jeweller and Merchant congregate at Timon's house, and the Poet describes the common changes and chances of Fortune's Hill; and a kind of epilogue, where the cowed Senators of Athens submit to Alcibiades, Timon's death is reported, and Alcibiades speaks a formal valediction.

All these major scenes, and all but one of the intervening scenes, concentrate on Timon with an unremitting attention. The question that any producer, like any reader, must ask himself is, how is Timon presented? how are we to take him? Now it is obviously possible to take him as a truly noble man, ruined by his own generosity—'Undone by goodness', as the Steward says—someone, quite simply too good for the society that surrounds him. Roy Walker, in an interesting review of the Old Vic 1956 production, says, 'it was presumably the poet's intention to show how selfish society drives out true generosity'.[3] And another critic writes as follows:

In the first part of *Timon of Athens* Timon appears as a man full of warmth, geniality and overflowing humanity. He is the incarnation of charity and hospitality, and believes in the supreme virtue of friendship, which his generosity is intended to foster. Gold plays an immensely important part throughout the play, but for Timon, before his fall, it is completely the servant of 'honour' (another key word) and of brotherly love. In the great feast of I.ii. he comes very near to enumerating an ideal of benevolent communism in which money merely provides the opportunity for men to express charity towards one another: 'We are born to do benefits; and what better or properer can we call our own than the riches of our friends? O what a precious comfort 'tis, to have so many, like brothers, commanding one another's fortunes' (I.ii. 105–9).[4]

Of remarks such as these I can only say that they seem to me completely to miss the point of the opening scenes. Timon is surrounded by the corrupt and the self-seeking: this is made very plain, and he must have been rather stupid or else possessed by a very strong emotional bias to have had no glimmer of it. Of course it is good to use one's money to redeem a friend from a debtor's prison or to enable a poor serving-gentleman to marry the girl of his choice. But it is not good to engage in a perpetual potlatch.

> No meed but he repays
> Seven-fold above itself: no gift to him
> But breeds the giver a return exceeding
> All use of quittance.   (I.i. 288–91)

Gifts, to be meaningful and not part of a ritual of exchange or display, must be person to person. Timon, who does not pause to look at the Painter's picture or to glance at the Poet's book, hardly *attends* to anyone: in the words of one of the Lords, he simply 'pours it out' (I.i. 287). When, therefore, he voices the incontrovertible sentiments we have had quoted as an expression of his magnanimity—'We are born to do benefits. . . . O what a precious comfort 'tis to have so many like brothers commanding one another's fortunes'—it is not moral truth that we recognize but self-indulgence in easy emotion. As for the significance of the great feast, Apemantus has already told us what to think of it:

[3] Roy Walker, 'Unto Caesar: a Review of Recent Productions', *Shakespeare Survey*, 11; reproduced in part in Maurice Charney's edition of *Timon* (Signet Classics), p. 212.
[4] R. P. Draper, '*Timon of Athens*', *Shakespeare Quarterly*, VIII, 2, Spring, 1957.

3

That there should be small love amongst these sweet knaves,
And all this courtesy! (I.i. 258-9)

And it is not long before the honest Steward sheds light retrospectively on the nature of Timon's hospitality:

> When all our offices have been oppress'd
> With riotous feeders, when our vaults have wept
> With drunken spilth of wine, when every room
> Hath blaz'd with lights and bray'd with minstrelsy. . . .
> (II.ii. 167-70)

Compared with those who have idealized the early Timon for his generosity, the eighteenth-century critic, William Richardson, surely came nearer to the truth when he wrote:

> Shakespeare, in his Timon of Athens, illustrates the consequences of that inconsiderate profusion which has the appearance of liberality, and is supposed even by the inconsiderate person himself to proceed from a generous principle; but which, in reality, has its chief origin in the love of distinction.[5]

Tragedy of course takes us beyond bare moral judgment. But moral judgment necessarily enters into our experience of tragedy: and it is worth remarking how sharply, in this play, Shakespeare seems to insist on the moral issue, even to the extent of using techniques reminiscent of the morality plays. In the first part of the opening scene (in what I have called the Prologue) Timon's situation is presented with a formal simplification that suggests a moral *exemplum* rather than any kind of naturalistic portrayal. As the parasites gather—Poet, Painter, Jeweller, Merchant, and then certain Senators—the audience is invited (by one of them) to observe:

> See,
> Magic of bounty! all these spirits thy power
> Hath conjur'd to attend! (I.i. 5-7)

In the Poet's fable of Fortune's Hill we are given due warning of what to expect

> When Fortune in her shift and change of mood
> Spurns down her late beloved . . . (I.i. 84-5)

It is against this background that Timon appears and displays his undiscriminating, and ruinous, bounty; and it is here that the

---

[5] William Richardson, *Essays on Some of Shakespeare's Dramatic Characters*, Fifth edition (1797), p. 313. So too Dr. Johnson: 'The catastrophe affords a very powerful warning against that ostentatious liberality, which scatters bounty, but confers no benefits, and buys flattery, but not friendship'. Johnson however thought that 'in the plan there is not much art'.

producer can help us a good deal, if he will let himself be guided by
the hints that Shakespeare provides. The stage directions—both the
explicit ones that seem to come direct from the author's working draft
and those that are implicit in the text—are pretty clear indications of
the intended theatrical effect. Timon's first entry is to the sound of
trumpets. The 'great banquet' of the second scene is heralded by
'hautboys playing loud music'. And after the masque of Ladies as
Amazons 'the Lords rise from table, with much adoring of Timon'.
Throughout, there is much elaborate courtesy—'Serving of becks
and jutting out of bums', as Apemantus puts it—and as the glittering
pomp (which we now know can't be paid for) comes to an end,
Timon calls for 'Lights, more lights' (I.ii. 234). All this obvious
showiness serves the same purpose as similar elements in ballad or
morality play: it tells us in straightforward visual terms that what we
have before us is an example of vanity and pride of life decked out in
tinsel. The last words of the scene are given to Apemantus:

> What needs these feasts, pomps, and vain-glories? . . .
>   O that men's ears should be
>   To counsel deaf, but not to flattery.
>   (I.ii. 248 ff.)

What we seem to be dealing with, then, is a play that, in some
important ways, comes close to the Morality tradition. There is no
attempt at characterization; many of the figures are simply representative types. When Timon, in need, appeals in turn to each of his
false friends, all heavily indebted to him, what we watch is a *demonstration* of how right Apemantus had been when he said, at the feast,

> I should fear those that dance before me now
> Would one day stamp upon me. 'T'as been done.
> Men shut their doors against a setting sun.
>   (I.ii. 148–50)

When Timon retires to the woods, naked and abandoned, he is
Misanthropos, and his railings refer not to some sharply realized
individual plight but to the human situation in general.

Now it is of course true that the tradition of didactic simplification
was still active in Shakespeare's lifetime. A rather dull little morality
called *Liberality and Prodigality* was revived and acted before the
Queen in 1601. As in our play Money is shown as in the gift of
Fortune; Prodigality gets rid of Money with something of Timon's
unthinking ease—

B   5

L. C. Knights

Who lacks money, ho! who lacks money?
But ask and have: money, money, money!

—and when Virtue hands over Money to 'my steward Liberality'—
Prodigality having proved unworthy—her servant Equity preaches
the golden mean ('Where reason rules, there is the golden mean')
in the manner of Apemantus moralizing to Timon about 'the middle
of humanity'. But we have only to put *Timon of Athens* beside *Liberality and Prodigality*, or beside a more sophisticated play in the same
tradition such as Ben Jonson's *The Staple of News*, to see how inappropriate, here, any kind of Morality label would be. For myself
I think we get closer to Shakespeare's play by recognizing the didactic
elements than by a too ready responsiveness to Timon as the disillusioned idealist. But to see the play as straight didactic moralizing
directed *at* Timon as Prodigality—as though he were merely an illustration of a moral thesis—that too feels inadequate. The verse is often
too powerful to allow us that kind and degree of detachment as we
judge.

We are still, then, left with the question on our hands: How is
Timon conceived and presented? how are we to take him? Our
answers so far have been mainly negative ones. If we want something
more positive we must take a closer look at the play, paying special
attention—as we always need to do—to those parts where we most
find ourselves in difficulties of interpretation. There are various
difficulties in *Timon*: and I mean more substantial ones than the
identification of Timon's false friends, the name of the loyal Steward,
or Shakespeare's confusion about the value of a talent.[6] One substantial difficulty concerns the dramatic function of III.v, where
Alcibiades, failing to persuade the Senators to spare the life of his
friend who has killed a man in hot blood, plans revenge against
Athens. But this, together with the counterbalancing scene at the end,
where Alcibiades is readmitted to the city, I want to put on one side
for the moment in order to concentrate on Timon's invective, his
display of satire and misanthropy in the fourth act.

The invective, of course, is largely about the power of money: and
it has a superb force.

> O blessed breeding sun, draw from the earth
> Rotten humidity; below thy sister's orb
> Infect the air! Twinn'd brothers of one womb,

[6] See Terence Spencer, 'Shakespeare learns the value of money', *Shakespeare Survey*, 6.

Whose procreation, residence and birth
Scarce is dividant—touch them with several fortunes,
The greater scorns the lesser. Not nature,
To whom all sores lay siege, can bear great fortune,
But by contempt of nature.
Raise me this beggar, and deny't that lord,
The senator shall bear contempt hereditary,
The beggar native honour.
It is the pasture lards the brother's sides,
The want that makes him lean. Who dares, who dares,
In purity of manhood stand upright,
And say this man's a flatterer? If one be,
So are they all, for every grise of fortune
Is smooth'd by that below: the learned pate
Ducks to the golden fool . . .

(IV.iii. 1–18)

Then, as Timon digs for roots and discovers gold:

What is here?
Gold? Yellow, glittering, precious gold?
No, gods, I am no idle votarist.
Roots, you clear heavens! Thus much of this will make
Black, white; foul, fair; wrong, right;
Base, noble; old, young; coward, valiant.
Ha, you gods! Why this? What this, you gods? Why, this
Will lug your priests and servants from your sides,
Pluck stout men's pillows from below their heads.
This yellow slave
Will knit and break religions, bless th'accurs'd,
Make the hoar leprosy ador'd, place thieves,
And give them title, knee and approbation
With senators on the bench. This is it
That makes the wappen'd widow wed again:
She whom the spital-house and ulcerous sores
Would cast the gorge at, this embalms and spices
To th' April day again . . .

(IV.iii. 24–41)

All this has an obvious relevance to the England of the late sixteenth and early seventeenth centuries. Professor Laurence Stone, in his recent book on the Tudor-Stuart aristocracy,[7] documents very fully indeed the scramble for rewards at Court, the lavish expenditure on all forms of conspicuous display, the heavy dependence on credit and lucky breaks, the intense greedy competitiveness of those for

[7] Laurence Stone, *The Crisis of the Aristocracy, 1558–1641*.

whom Fortune's Hill was a vivid symbol for a very present reality. There is no difficulty here. *Timon of Athens*, in so far as it is a direct satire on the power of money, can be seen as Shakespeare's response to certain prominent features in the economic and social life of his own day. And the satire, as we have just seen, has the kind of bite that makes it relevant to *any* acquisitive society, our own as much as Shakespeare's. (It was almost inevitable that Karl Marx should quote Timon's denunciation of 'gold . . . this yellow slave' in an early chapter of *Capital*.)

But—and here comes the difficulty—when Timon first gives expression to his outraged feelings and curses Athens, in forty lines of invective the only reference to money is short, incidental and indirect (IV.i. 8–12). He does, on the other hand, have a lot to say about sexual corruption; just as in encouraging Alcibiades to destroy Athens his catalogue of the city's vices, after a brief mention of usury, plunges into a lengthy diatribe against an anarchic sexuality. Nothing in the play has prepared us for this (apart from the dance of the Amazons in I.ii, Timon seems to have lived in an exclusively masculine society). And although Timon does of course denounce money, and although he subsequently gives some of his new-found gold to Alcibiades to pay troops levied against Athens, and some to the harlots to encourage them to spread diseases, it is not money-satire, or satire on ingratitude, that forms the substance of the long dialogue in the woods with Apemantus. In short, given the obvious data of the play, and given the obvious grounds for Timon's rejection of a society shown as corrupt and usurous, there is nevertheless something excessive in the *terms* of his rejection, just as there is something strange (and, if you see the play solely in terms of a *saeva indignatio* directed against society, even tedious) in the slanging match with Apemantus in the woods. What, then, is Shakespeare up to?

I suggest that as in all the greater plays Shakespeare is using the outward action to project and define something deeply inward. I do not mean simply that in *Lear* or *Macbeth* or *Othello* Shakespeare observes character with a rare psychological penetration, though he does of course do this. I mean that in a variety of ways he uses the forms of dramatic action, external conflict and event, to reveal inner conflicts and distortions, basic potentialities for good and evil, at a level where individual characteristics take second place to human nature itself. In short he demonstrates precisely what T. S. Eliot meant when he wrote:

A verse play is not a play done into verse, but a different kind of play: in a way more realistic than 'naturalistic drama', because, instead of clothing nature in poetry, it should remove the surface of things, expose the underneath, or the inside, of the natural surface appearance.[8]

In *Timon*, as in *Lear* and *Othello*, Shakespeare is revealing what is 'underneath . . . the natural surface appearance'—sometimes in a naive Morality way (as when the mock feast of steam and stones instead of nourishment shows us what the earlier feast really was— not a feast at all), sometimes with the force and subtlety of the great tragedies.

In *Timon* the surface appearance is lightly sketched in the suggestions of a corrupt society, where the business of individuals is very much to feather their own nests: more firmly, though in a rather schematized way, in the presentation of Timon's friends and parasites. But the surface appearance on which, in the first Act, attention is most sharply concentrated is Man in Prosperity, the ego sustained in a fixed posture by an endless series of reflections which show it just as it thinks itself to be:

> All those which were his fellows but of late,
> Some better than his value, on the moment
> Follow his strides, his lobbies fill with tendance,
> Rain sacrificial whisperings in his ear,
> Make sacred even his stirrup, and through him
> Drink the free air.
>
> (I.i. 78–83)

That this picture—of what the Steward, allowing himself a touch of satire, calls 'Great Timon, noble, worthy, royal Timon'—has to be drawn again and again betrays a compulsive need. What supports Timon in his self-idolatry, what buys him reassurance ('You see, my lord, how amply y'are belov'd'), is of course his wealth. But the wealth is secondary in dramatic importance to what it serves: means to the same end could have been extorted professions of filial affection, as in *Lear*, or any of the familiar tricks that we use to cut a fine figure in our own eyes. Towards the end of Act II the Steward points the action:

> Heavens, have I said, the bounty of this lord!
> How many prodigal bits have slaves and peasants
> This night englutted! Who is not Timon's?
> What heart, head, sword, force, means, but is Lord Timon's,

[8] T. S. Eliot, Introduction to S. L. Bethell, *Shakespeare and the Popular Dramatic Tradition.*

Great Timon, noble, worthy, royal Timon?
Ah, when the means are gone that buy this praise,
The breath is gone whereof this praise is made,
Feast-won, fast-lost . . .

(II.ii. 173–80)

At virtually one stroke the props to Timon's self-esteem are removed, and he is reduced to 'unaccommodated man'. He is stripped, so to speak, of his protective covering, and, as in *Lear*, his physical appearance reflects an inner state. 'Nothing I'll bear from thee But nakedness, thou detestable town!' (IV.i. 32–3).

There, I think, you have the central interest of the play. In a world such as the men of great tragic vision have always known it to be, a world where you clearly cannot remove all the threats—the inner and the outer threats—to your security, how, quite simply, do you keep going? Life only allows a limited number of choices. Either you live by some kind of integrating principle through which even potentially destructive energies can be harnessed, stability and movement combined; or, plumping for security—for 'a solid without fluctuation', like Blake's Urizen—you seek artificial supports for a fixed posture. Unfortunately the concomitant of a fixed posture is unremitting anxiety to maintain itself; and it is in the nature of artificial supports, sooner or later, to break down. This is what happens to Timon. When his supports are removed, 'when the means are gone that buy this praise', he is left, like Lear, with 'nothing'—nothing, that is, but a vision of a completely evil world that partly, of course, reflects a social reality, but is also an expression of his own self-hatred and self-contempt:

> . . . . and his poor self,
> A dedicated beggar to the air,
> With his disease of all-shunn'd poverty,
> Walks like contempt, alone.

(IV.ii. 12–15)

It is this, surely, that explains the nature of Timon's first great speech of invective, where there is very little about money and nothing about ingratitude, but much about sexual incontinence and general anarchy.

> Let me look back upon thee. O thou wall
> That girdles in those wolves, dive in the earth
> And fence not Athens! Matrons, turn incontinent!
> Obedience fail in children! Slaves and fools,

10

Pluck the grave wrinkled senate from the bench,
And minister in their steads! To general filths
Convert, o'th' instant, green virginity!
Do 't in your parents' eyes! Bankrupts, hold fast;
Rather than render back, out with your knives,
And cut your trusters' throats! Bound servants, steal!
Large-handed robbers your grave masters are,
And pill by law. Maid, to thy master's bed;
Thy mistress is o' th' brothel! Son of sixteen,
Pluck the lin'd crutch from thy old limping sire;
With it beat out his brains! Piety and fear,
Religion to the gods, peace, justice, truth,
Domestic awe, night-rest and neighbourhood,
Instruction, manners, mysteries and trades,
Degrees, observances, customs and laws,
Decline to your confounding contraries;
And yet confusion live! Plagues incident to men,
Your potent and infectious fevers heap
On Athens ripe for stroke! Thou cold sciatica,
Cripple our senators, that their limbs may halt
As lamely as their manners! Lust and liberty
Creep in the minds and marrows of our youth,
That 'gainst the stream of virtue they may strive
And drown themselves in riot!   (IV.i. 1–28)

It is a little like what Conrad's Marlow glimpsed on his voyage up the river to the heart of darkness, though perhaps more specifically realized. Timon's horror is of anarchic impulses that he knows within himself when the picture of noble Timon is destroyed. It is true of course that Timon presently denounces the inequalities bred by fortune, the corruption caused by money; and throughout the scenes in the woods, when he is visited by Alcibiades and the harlots, the bandits, and various former hangers-on who have heard of his newly discovered wealth, the satire on money-lust continues. All this is clearly very near the dramatic centre of the play. But to treat it as *the* controlling centre, *the* dominant theme, is to see things entirely from Timon's point of view, from the point of view of a man who feels unjustly treated by others,—as of course he is. But the play only makes sense as a whole when we see him as self-betrayed, his revulsion against the city as equally a revulsion against himself.[9] Midway in the indictment of money that I quoted from the opening of IV.iii Shakespeare drops the necessary clue:

[9] John Wain speaks of the 'neurotic and self-feeding' nature of Timon's tirades—*The Living World of Shakespeare*, p. 195.

> . . . all's obliquy;
> There's nothing level in our cursed natures
> But direct villainy. Therefore be abhorr'd
> All feasts, societies, and throngs of men!
> His semblable, *yea himself, Timon disdains.*
> Destruction fang mankind!
>
> (IV.iii. 18–23)

If Shakespeare's intention was in fact, as I suppose, to portray self-revulsion, the shattering of an unreal picture and the flight from hitherto concealed aspects of the self that are found insupportable, this would also explain the drawn-out exchanges with Apemantus in the woods. In the opening of the play Apemantus, as professional cynic, is not an attractive figure. But he is no Thersites. It is from him, almost as much as from the Steward, that we get a true picture of Timon's 'bounty' and its effects:

> That there should be small love amongst these sweet knaves,
> And all this courtesy!
>
> (I.i. 258–9)
>
> What a sweep of vanity comes this way.
> They dance? They are madwomen.
> Like madness is the glory of this life,
> As this pomp shows to a little oil and root.
> We make ourselves fools, to disport ourselves . . .
>
> (I.ii. 137–41)
>
> Thou giv'st so long, Timon, I fear me thou wilt give away thyself in paper shortly. What needs these feasts, pomps, and vain-glories?
>
> (I.ii. 246–8)

But if Apemantus is not Thersites, neither is he Lear's Fool, the disinterested teller of unwelcome truths: the emotional bias, like the ostentatious poverty, is too marked. It is this that explains his dual and ambiguous role in the later scene. On the one hand he is the objective commentator, a mentor that Timon ignores at his peril; and since this is so clearly intended it is a mistake to play him simply as the abject and railing cynic. His pronouncements have authority:

> This is in thee a nature but infected,
> A poor unmanly melancholy sprung
> From change of fortune [F. future]
>
> (IV.iii. 202–4)
>
> If thou didst put this sour cold habit on
> To castigate thy pride 'twere well; but thou
> Dost it enforcedly. Thou'dst courtier be again
> Wert thou not beggar.
>
> (IV.iii. 239–42)

The middle of humanity thou never knewest, but the extremity of both ends.

(IV.iii. 300–1)

And th'hadst hated meddlers sooner, thou shouldst have loved thyself better now.

(IV.iii. 309–10)

On the other hand, and simultaneously, he is a kind of mirror image of Timon. His first words on his reappearance are,

I was directed hither. Men report
Thou dost affect my manners, and dost use them, (IV.iii. 198–9)

and not only is Timon's general manner identical in tone with that of Apemantus in the opening scenes, each echoes what, at another time, the other has said.[10] Geoffrey Bush remarks: 'Apemantus is what Timon becomes. . . . Even in the first three acts, though Apemantus and Timon are opposites, they are oddly drawn toward each other, as if they found a peculiar importance in each other's company. They go together . . . they are, as it were, two aspects of a single self, the extremes between which the personality of a human being can alternate'.[11] And it is not only cynicism about the world that they share. At the beginning of the play Apemantus was described as one 'that few things loves better than to abhor himself' (I.i. 59–60). Timon's echo of that we have already heard: 'His semblable, yea himself, Timon disdains' (IV.iii. 22). The final exchange of insults between the two, before Apemantus is driven off with stones—

—Would thou wert clean enough to spit upon!

—A plague on thee, thou art too bad to curse. . . . (IV.iii. 364 ff.)

reads like a monologue of self-hate.

Some of this, perhaps, is matter for dispute. What is abundantly clear is that Timon's misanthropy is in no essential way an approach to reality; it is primitive rage at the destruction of an ego-ideal, horror and hatred at what is revealed when support for that ideal picture is withdrawn. Denied the absolute and one-sided endorsement that he had claimed, the self-esteem that his wealth had enabled him to buy, he refuses to see his claims for what they were. Instead he projects onto the world at large his own desire to get what he wanted by means that were essentially dishonest. He has been, in effect, a thief. Confronted with the bandits, he declaims:

[10] See the New Arden notes at IV.iii. 279 and 394.
[11] Geoffrey Bush, *Shakespeare and the Natural Condition*, p. 62.

13

> I'll example you with thievery:
> The sun's a thief, and with his great attraction
> Robs the vast sea; the moon's an arrant thief,
> And her pale fire she snatches from the sun;
> The sea's a thief, whose liquid surge resolves
> The moon into salt tears; the earth's a thief,
> That feeds and breeds by a composture stol'n
> From gen'ral excrement; each thing's a thief . . .
>
> (IV.iii. 438–45)

Shakespeare, who expected his audience to recognize a bad argument when they heard one, knew that each of the elements mentioned here in fact repays, or gives to another, what it takes. Timon, in becoming nastier, has become sillier. But by now there is scarcely any pretence on Timon's part that he is denouncing real corruption in a real world: he is satisfying an emotional animus that can exhaust itself only in death.

> Come not to me again; but say to Athens,
> Timon hath made his everlasting mansion
> Upon the beached verge of the salt flood,
> Who once a day with his embossed froth
> The turbulent surge shall cover . . .
> Lips, let sour words go by and language end:
> What is amiss, plague and infection mend!
> Graves only be men's works and death their gain;
> Sun, hide thy beams, Timon hath done his reign.
>
> (V.i. 217–26)

I am of course aware that this unfavourable view of Timon has against it not only the opinions of many critics but, more important, certain pronouncements within the play itself—pronouncements that, unlike the eulogies of the parasites, are disinterested, and must therefore be given due weight. There is the unwavering loyalty of the Steward, for whom Timon is

> Poor honest lord, brought low by his own heart,
> Undone by goodness . . .
>
> (IV.ii. 37–8)

and there is the eulogy by Alcibiades that virtually concludes the play:

> Though thou abhorr'dst in us our human griefs,
> Scorn'dst our brains' flow and those our droplets which
> From niggard nature fall, yet rich conceit
> Taught thee to make vast Neptune weep for aye
> On thy low grave, on faults forgiven. Dead
> Is noble Timon . . .
>
> (V.iv. 75–80)

But I do not think that either substantially modifies the account that I have given. The Steward, playing Kent to Timon's Lear, reminds us in his devotion that love and loyalty see further than the eye of the mere spectator; there is no need to doubt the potentiality of goodness that is in Timon. But in the play it remains unrealized. The most that his old servant's undemanding devotion can wring from Timon is the recognition that his undiscriminating condemnation of mankind must allow of one exception:

> You perpetual-sober gods! I do proclaim
> One honest man. Mistake me not, but one,
> No more, I pray . . .
> > (IV.iii. 503–5)

The current of his feeling remains entirely unchanged:

> Go, live rich and happy,
> But thus conditioned: thou shalt build from men;
> Hate all, curse all, show charity to none,
> But let the famish'd flesh slide from the bone
> Ere thou relieve the beggar . . .[12]
> > (IV.iii. 532–6)

As for Alcibiades, the fact that his role is only roughly shaped forces us back on intelligent guessing. But the general intention seems clear. The point of the central scene in which he pleads unsuccessfully with the Senators for the life of the soldier who has killed a man in a brawl is partly to emphasize the greed and corruption of society (that much of Timon's indictment is true):

> . . . I have kept back their foes,
> While they have told their money, and let out
> Their coin upon large interest; I myself
> Rich only in large hurts. All those, for this?
> Is this the balsam that the usuring Senate
> Pours into captains' wounds?
> > (III.v. 106–11)

[12] I find myself in complete agreement with Mr. H. J. Oliver when he writes in the Introduction to the New Arden edition (pp. 1–1i): 'The presence of the Steward among the characters, then, so far from being the puzzle or contradiction that Chambers found it, is essential to the meaning of the play and expressly forbids us from identifying *our* judgment (or Shakespeare's) with Timon's. . . . Timon's misanthropy, like everything else in Shakespeare's plays, is part of a dramatized situation and is in no sense a lyrical statement of the poet's own belief; and Timon's invective for which the play has received most of such praise as has generally been given it, is all the more remarkable when one pauses to reflect that it states an attitude from which, through the presence of the Steward, Shakespeare has dissociated himself completely.' All I would add is that, as we have seen, it is not only the presence of the Steward that 'places' Timon's misanthropy.

But there is more to it than this. Both Alcibiades and the Senators are right in the *general* truths they enunciate:

> *Alcibiades*   For pity is the virtue of the law,
>   And none but tyrants use it cruelly.
>
> *First Senator* He's truly valiant that can wisely suffer
>   The worst that man can breathe,
>   And make his wrongs his outsides,
>   To wear them like raiment, carelessly . . .
>   (III.v. 8–9, 31–4)

What we are forced to question, by Alcibiades' special-pleading and the Senators' complacency, is the reliability of the speakers. Alcibiades' claim that his friend acted 'in defence' (l. 56), with 'sober and unnoted passion' (l. 21), is undercut by his own admission that the man 'in hot blood Hath stepp'd into the law' (ll. 11–12), and this not in self-defence but, 'Seeing his reputation touch'd to death' (l. 19). And although the Senators profess to stand for law and the virtues of restraint there is something very disagreeable in their legalistic morality.

> *First Senator*   My lord, you have my voice to't; the fault's
>   Bloody; 'tis necessary he should die;
>   Nothing emboldens sin so much as mercy.
>
> *Second Senator* Most true; the law shall bruise 'em.
>   (III.v. 1–4)

Neither side is trustworthy. In this respect, then, the scene is a variation on the main theme. Much of what a man says may be true, as much of what Timon says is true; but what really matters is the integrity and self-knowledge, or the lack of these qualities, in the person speaking. If the Senators are clearly untrustworthy, Alcibiades does not represent an acceptable norm.

It is the recognition of this that prevents us from taking the last scene of all with the moral earnestness that both Alcibiades and the Athenians would like to impart. These eighty-five lines raise far more questions than they answer. Some of our perplexities may be due to the play's unfinished state. But if we take the scene in conjunction with III.v—the previous confrontation of Alcibiades with apparently representative Athenians—it suggests a world of hazy verbiage. (What right has Alcibiades to reproach Athens with being 'lascivious'? When last seen he was trailing about with a couple of mistresses. As for the Senators, anything goes, so long as they can save their skins and plaster the situation with appropriate platitude.) And this does not only contrast with Timon's blazing hatred, it offers a parallel. Men set themselves up for judges, when the underlying attitudes, from which their judgments spring, are distorted by evasions, self-exculpations, and lack of self-knowledge. All that is said in this final scene is, for Alcibiades and the Senators, an easy way out—the world's way when confronted with any kind of absolute, of negation or affirmation. In this context, 'Dead is noble Timon' suggests a bitter irony. Timon's self-composed epitaph was not noble; and his wholesale condemnation of the world, though not an easy way, was easier than the pain of self-recognition.

Presumably we shall never know when *Timon of Athens* was written, nor why it was not finally completed. The best of the verse puts it firmly in the period of Shakespeare's great tragedies. There are very many parallels—verbal and substantial parallels—with *King Lear*. Coleridge jotted down that it was 'an after vibration' of that play.[13] But why should a man try to repeat an unrepeatable master-piece? My own guess, for what it is worth, is that *Timon* was drafted when *Lear* was already taking shape in Shakespeare's mind. Both plays are about a man 'who hath ever but slenderly known himself', who tries to buy love and respect, who has genuine reason to feel wronged, and whose sense of betrayal releases an indictment of the world that can't be shrugged off as 'madness' or 'misanthropy', but a man also whose sense of betrayal by others masks a deep inward flaw; in both the stripping away of all protective covering reveals with fierce clarity a world of evil. But there the major resemblances cease. *Timon of Athens* contains a loyal and decent Steward; it does not contain a Cordelia. Timon goes almost as far in hatred and revulsion as Lear; there is nothing in his mind that corresponds to Lear's gropings towards self-knowledge. And it is the active presence in *King Lear* of positive and affirmative elements that, paradoxically, makes its presentation of pain and evil so much more deeply disturb-ing. You can disengage from *Timon of Athens*, for all its power: you have to live with *King Lear*. And when the greater theme took possession of Shakespeare's mind, the more partial one could be abandoned: Timon had 'done his reign'.

---

[13] Coleridge, *Shakespearean Criticism*, ed. T. M. Raysor (Everyman edition), Vol. I, p. 211.

2

'The True Conduct of Human Judgment': Some observations on *Cymbeline*

GEOFFREY HILL

WHEN Queen Elizabeth was dead they cut up her best clothes to make costumes for Anne of Denmark's masques.[1] These performances,

especially after the advent of Inigo Jones in 1607, became the rage of Jacobean London. The Vision in *Cymbeline* was clearly designed in response to this taste. . . .[2]

Shakespeare's actual working-brief is unfortunately not so clear. One cannot conclude that *Cymbeline* was created for the Court or even specifically for the Blackfriars. Evidence, which is extremely tenuous, seems to indicate a performance at the Globe (*c.* 1611). It is of course true that, even if the play were designed primarily for the public stage, its author was a servant of the royal household 'taking rank between the Gentlemen and Yeomen'.[3] The king, though not a niggardly patron, was easily bored and preferred hunting. On the other hand, if the King's Men were employed as purveyors of *divertimenti*, they were no worse off than, say, Monteverdi at Mantua and probably more highly favoured. In terms of the dignity of art this is not saying much but 'since princes will have such things'[4] it is possible for serious artists to elicit a private freedom from the fact of not being received as they deserve.

[1] E. K. Chambers in *Shakespeare's England* (1916), I, p. 105.
[2] J. Dover Wilson —prefatory note to *Cymbeline*, ed. J. C. Maxwell (1960), p. ix.
[3] F. E. Halliday, *The Life of Shakespeare* (1961), p. 178.
[4] Francis Bacon, 'Of Masques and Triumphs'.

18

It has been suggested that *Cymbeline* was a 'dual purpose' play,[5] adaptable to either public or private production. It may, in that case, have said different things to different audiences. A Court or Blackfriars audience could have seen what it expected, 'an unlikely story . . . an exhibition of tricks'.[6] In daylight, at the Globe, the 'tricks' just might have appeared as critiques, oblique metaphors or moral emblems. The supposition that a private audience was necessarily more sophisticated than a public one is questionable. There is an edgy watchfulness to the play's virtuosity which might indicate Shakespeare's reluctance 'to commit himself wholly to the claims of his material'.[7] No such reluctance need be deduced. Even so, an element of reserve about the claims of orthodox mystique, or about the eloquence of current political mythology might be demonstrable. Imogen sees Britain's relation to the world's volume as being 'of it, but not in't' (III.iv. 141), an enigmatic phrase which might equally well describe *Cymbeline's* capacity for private nuance in its unfolding of the supreme theme of national regeneration and destiny.[8]

Myths were things of utility to Tudor and Stuart politicians. They were also, though more sensitively, things of utility to the dramatist. The thought of Shakespeare hamstrung and humiliated by his own sycophancy is obtrusive but not inescapable. In the light of a recent well-documented essay[9] it would be unwise to ignore the relevance of Stuart myth to our understanding of this play. Henry VII was the saviour of his people; his great-great-grandson James VI and I, the unifier and pacifier, was 'the fulfilment of the oldest prophecies of the British people'.[10] To the medieval chroniclers Kymbeline was a man of peace whose reign coincided with the birth of Christ. Shakespeare could have read this in Holinshed and sensed the connotations.[11] Milford Haven, where the secular redeemer had landed in 1485, was a hallowed place celebrated in Tudor and Stuart patriotic verse. Such numinous power is not unknown even in the twentieth century. A modern author voices his emotions about Stalingrad:

---

[5] J. M. Nosworthy, *Cymbeline* (New Arden Edition 1955), p. xvi. This text is used for quotations. A more recent investigator, R. T. Thornberry, in *Shakespeare and the Blackfriars Tradition* (Ohio State University Dissertation 1964) rejects the dual-purpose theory and regards *Cymbeline* as a play composed specifically for the Globe.

[6] H. Granville-Barker, *Prefaces to Shakespeare* (2nd Series: 1930), p. 244.

[7] Maxwell, *op. cit.* p. xxxix.

[8] So well described by G. Wilson Knight, *The Crown of Life* (1947), ch. 4.

[9] Emrys Jones, 'Stuart Cymbeline', in *Essays in Criticism*, XI (1961), pp. 84–99.

[10] *op. cit.* p. 90.

[11] R. Moffet, '*Cymbeline* and the Nativity', in *Shakespeare Quarterly*, XIII (1962), pp. 207–18.

I felt that Stalingrad was in the middle of the world, a place where the final conflict between good and evil was fought out . . .[12]

Holy and awesome places do exist, and there is propriety in Imogen's being 'Magnetized to this, enchanted, spot',[13] 'this same blessed Milford' (III.ii. 60), and in the contrivance of the play's denouement there. It is less easy to concede, however, that the political myth provides

a kind of interpretative key to events on the stage which, without such a key, appear insufficiently motivated, almost incoherent.[14]

To suggest this while concluding that the play is finally guilty of 'a central fumbling, a betrayal of logic'[15] is to say in effect that one still finds it incoherent. The symptoms have merely been associated with a different cause, with over-caution induced by the play's 'being too close to its royal audience'.[16]

One's own case would be put rather differently. It would be that Shakespeare's involvement with the claims of his material is full and unqualified while, in his view of extraneous and imposed value-judgments, he remains singularly open-minded. The play's virtuosity is manifested in the association of committed technique with un-committed observation. The play is aware of the fact of compromise but it is in no sense compromised. Recognizing the aims and expec-tations of such a company as the King's Men, who were undoubtedly popular at the Jacobean Court, one also admits the reasonableness of the suggestion that Shakespeare may have had James in mind when writing *Cymbeline*. Scepticism should be directed not so much against an extremely plausible hypothesis as against a number of moral and aesthetic conclusions which have been drawn from it. Even if it were an established fact that a royal audience actually attended a per-formance of this play,[17] the proposition that Shakespeare therefore 'officiously' protected his royal protagonist from 'the consequences of his weak nature and ill-judged actions'[18] would still be open to debate. It could be argued that *Cymbeline* is more subtly and sen-

[12] Alan Sillitoe, *Road to Volgograd* (1966 edition), p. 40.
[13] Knight, *op. cit.* (1948 ed.), p. 155.
[14] Jones, *op. cit.* p. 98.
[15] *op. cit.* p. 97.
[16] *op. cit.* p. 97.
[17] It is on record that the play was acted at Court in 1634, but that is not quite the same thing.
[18] Jones, *op. cit.* p. 97.

sitively handled than the objection allows and that the play shows considerable openness in places where its metaphysics have been assumed to be nothing if not 'transcendental'. One of these is the love of those 'two supremely excellent human beings'[19] Imogen and Posthumus; the other is the theme of the king's peace. Since one accepts that the strands of personal and national destiny are interwoven, to debate these elements is to study the crucial implications of the play. In each case, one would suggest, Shakespeare 'stands back' not through timidity or unconcern but in order to obtain focus. His concern is with nearness and distance, with adjustment of perspective; in his handling of character and situation he makes a proper demonstration of that concern.

In recent years it has begun to be possible to understand Imogen in terms proper to the dramatic context. For so long, and for so many admirers, she had been simply 'one of the great women of Shakespeare or the world'.[20] There were, of course, dissenting voices. Shaw's reaction to the adulatory tradition was rough but not impertinent:

All I can extract from the artificialities of the play is a double image—a real woman *divined* by Shakespear without his knowing it clearly . . . and an idiotic paragon of virtue produced by Shakespear's *views* of what a woman ought to be . . .[21]

The antithesis is arbitrary, the premiss invalid, the naturalistic criterion misleading. Shaw supposes the dramatist to be merely intuitive when he is, in fact, quite deliberate. Shakespeare has shaped his play to procure the reality of the woman from the romance of her setting. Shaw's comments have considerable value however. He perceives a dichotomy and his suggestion of a double image is very relevant. It could be said that *Cymbeline* involves the realization of double images, not as Donne's visualization of the spirit of mutual regard ('My face in thine eye, thine in mine appeares') but as we might refer to double exposures in photography: accidental or contrived palimpsests that come from one view having been superimposed on another. Does the supremely excellent Imogen commit a breach of natural propriety when she speaks of Posthumus, after his departure, to his servant Pisanio? She wishes that she had made him.

---

[19] Moffet, *op. cit.* p. 208.
[20] Mark Van Doren, *Shakespeare* (1941), p. 309.
[21] Letter cited by A. M. Eastman and G. B. Harrison, *Shakespeare's Critics* (1964), pp. 172–3.

swear
The shes of Italy should not betray
Mine interest, and his honour.   (I.iv. 28–30)

These words are said to be 'quite out of character'[22] but the objection
rests on a preconceived notion of what this character comprises.
Imogen's remark is not a happy one and it is difficult to see how, in
the circumstances, it could be. Shakespeare's interest is in certain
kinds of immaturity and in the inaccuracy and imbalance affecting
relationships. Imogen wishes, when she meets 'Polydore' and 'Cad-
wal', that

they
Had been my father's sons, then had my prize
Been less, and so more equal ballasting
To thee, Posthumus.   (III.vi. 76–8)

'Ballasting' could mean 'freight' or 'stabilizing weight'. Imogen seems
to mean that a male heir to the throne would have reduced her own
status to a level nearer that of Posthumus. Her words acknowledge
how Posthumus' conquest of her must have appeared to some
observers—as a piratical act—and imply a fear that those who fore-
saw disaster in such inequality may have been right. In the play's
opening scenes the breach of convention and the strained court
relations create the original milieu for inflationary panegyric and
protestation. The love-cries of Posthumus and Imogen are a lyrical
defiance of circumstance and a breeding-ground of error. The
courtiers involve themselves in partisan polemic. A 'perfect' Posthumus is necessary to their own self-respect. What they say of him is
bound to seem 'too good to be true'[23] but to suppose that Shakespeare
is himself off-balance is to miss the point of the situation. It has been
suggested that 'Shakespeare intends us to accept the First Gentleman's estimate of [Posthumus'] virtue'.[24] That Shakespeare intends
nothing of the kind has been well argued in a recent essay.[25] The
wager-plot reveals

beneath Posthumus' apparently perfect gestures an essential meanness in
the man himself and in the conventional virtue that he embodies.[26]

[22] Nosworthy, *op. cit.* p. 17.
[23] Maxwell, *op. cit.* p. xxxix.
[24] Nosworthy, *op. cit.* p. 4.
[25] Homer D. Swander, '*Cymbeline* and the "Blameless Hero",' *E.L.H.* XXXI (1964),
pp. 259–70.
[26] *op. cit.* p. 260.

This is perhaps overstressed. Meanness is not intrinsic to Posthumus' nature and can be eradicated. Nevertheless, the point is taken. He survives and matures in grace, but from a condition in which he was possibly more like Iachimo or the despised Cloten than his admirers could have credited. Iachimo, at least in the wager-scene, is not so much a villain as a catalyst for Posthumus' own arrogance and folly. At the end of the play both men express personal remorse in terms that bear comparison. Iachimo feels that guilt 'takes off [his] manhood', the air of Imogen's homeland 'enfeebles' him (V.ii. 2–4). Posthumus' conscience is 'fetter'd' (V.iv. 8). One man regards his honours as but 'scorn' (V.ii. 7), the other thinks of himself as debased coin (V.iv. 25). Posthumus, in forgiving Iachimo, is in a sense forgiving himself. Implied comparisons between Posthumus and Cloten are also to be discerned. The suggestion has indeed been made that 'the two characters, never on stage together, should be played by a single actor'[27] and the significant visual pun, whereby Imogen is convinced that Cloten's body is her husband's, has frequently been noted. It is more significant that Posthumus is not Cloten and one sees that the irony reflects as strongly upon Imogen as upon her husband. What kind of man did she imagine him to be? Did she truly know him at all? The double irony is beautifully released in her mistaken tears.

At such points Shakespeare is treating ideas of false assumption, false connection. Dr. Leavis' objection that Posthumus' jealousy 'has no significance in relation to any radical theme, or total effect, of the play'[28] seems without real foundation. When the husband recoils from his wife's supposed infidelity the play focuses, not in any simple way upon character, but upon the experience of relationship:

> Me of my lawful pleasure she restrain'd,
> And pray'd me oft forbearance: did it with
> A pudency so rosy, the sweet view on't
> Might well have warm'd old Saturn; that I thought her
> As chaste as unsunn'd snow.   (II.v. 9–13)

Mr. Traversi rightly points to the 'sensual poison'[29] at work here. Are we, though, to regard this merely as the extravagance of Posthumus' contaminated imagination? The paragon of romantic love

---

[27] Homer D. Swander, *'Cymbeline*: Religious Idea and Dramatic Design' in *Pacific Coast Studies in Shakespeare* (1966), p. 251.
[28] *The Common Pursuit* (1953), p. 176.
[29] *Shakespeare: The Last Phase* (1965 edition), p. 62.

now sees his marital function, somewhat obtusely, as the taking of
'lawful pleasure', yet his words, unlike those of Claudio or Leontes,
do seem to imply a degree of genuine recollection rather than of
purely fanciful diatribe. The recollection is of a somewhat vulnerable
awkwardness on both sides. These are, after all, wedded lovers and
not two virginal puppets from *The Faithful Shepherdess*, to whose
theoretical exacerbations phrases like 'A pudency so rosy' and 'As
chaste as unsunn'd snow' seem more properly to belong. In spite of
what has been called 'the puritanical emphasis on pre-nuptial purity
in *The Winter's Tale* and *The Tempest*'[30] the tone of Perdita's 'But
quick, and in mine arms' seems the real heart of innocence whereas
this admittedly second-hand description of Imogen's nuptial modesty
does not. Conversely, Imogen and Posthumus have a grim actuality
of separation to contend with; a problem that other young lovers in
the Romances do not have to face. It is perhaps worth remarking
that the very fact of their marriage renders them exceptional. When
Cymbeline starts they are already beyond the conventional romantic
denouement. As Imogen imagines her husband's ship sailing further
and further away and the figure of Posthumus becoming smaller and
smaller, the language with which she tries to grasp her loss has a
touch of that extravagance displayed by the courtiers who try to force
Posthumus into attitudes of perfection. We are not unmoved by the
human credibility of this but we should recognize that, between such
over-refinement of invention and the bitter grossness later displayed
by Posthumus, there is a moral and emotional hiatus. It is true that
there is no 'deep centre'[31] here, because there is loss or failure of contact. This would seem to be, more than anything else, evidence of
Shakespeare's psychological accuracy.

The state of the relationship here is a state of tactlessness, meaning
'the absence of the keen faculty of perception or discrimination' or,
more simply, 'being out of touch'. There is a vice which, according to
Bacon,

brancheth itself into two sorts; delight in deceiving, and aptness to be deceived; imposture and credulity; which, although they appear to be of a
diverse nature, the one seeming to proceed of cunning and the other of
simplicity, yet certainly they do for the most part concur . . . as we see it
in fame, that he that will easily believe rumours, will as easily augment
rumours.[32]

[30] Knight, *op. cit.* p. 149.
[31] Leavis, *op. cit.* p. 174.
[32] *Advancement of Learning*, 1605 (Everyman edition), p. 28.

A feasible corollary might be that there is a kind of naiveté which asks to be devoured and a natural and partly-unconscious collusion between the deceived and the deceiver: between, for instance, Posthumus and Iachimo, Imogen and Iachimo, Cymbeline and the Queen. There is a language surrounding this collusion, a two-fold idiom of inflation, on the one hand fairly innocent and spontaneous, on the other a matter of policy. Of the First Gentleman's gush of praise for Posthumus' qualities it could be said, in a phrase used of Shakespeare's royal master, that 'the sums he gave away so easily were not his to give'.[33] This adds some point to Posthumus' later reference to himself as 'light' coin. As though sensing the folly of former inflation, he recoils to the other extreme of debasement.

The question of the play's rhetorical patriotism is more problematical. Cloten's 'tactlessness', the juxtaposition in him of oafish petulant inadequacy and outspoken nationalistic fervour, has been discussed by Wilson Knight. There is possibly a slight oversimplification in the description of Cloten's rudeness to the Roman envoy as

British toughness and the islanded integrity . . . Cloten . . . is for once in his element without being obnoxious.[34]

One would suggest that, on the contrary, Cloten is obnoxious, and so is the Queen; their patriotism is an exacerbation rather than an amelioration of this. It is somewhat reminiscent of the old ranting of *Locrine*. The fact that a proportion of Shakespeare's audience would undoubtedly identify itself with Cloten's xenophobia and thus be trapped in an emotional cul-de-sac makes for an interesting piece of dramatic ambivalence. Television audiences suffer the same kind of dilemma when torn apart by the antics of Mr. Alf Garnett.

The Britons defy Troglodytes, Aethiopians, Amazons and 'all the hosts of Barbarian lands', if these 'should dare to enter in our little world'.[35]

Finally, Cymbeline admits that his resistance to Rome had been instigated by his 'wicked queen' (V.v. 463). In view of James' self-appointed task as European peacemaker, Shakespeare's portrayal of such erroneous and ferocious insularity might be regarded as a tenable risk; but the question is boldly treated and taken further than mere diplomacy would have required.

[33] D. H. Willson, *King James VI and I* (1956), p. 261.
[34] *op. cit.*, p. 136.
[35] L. C. Knights, *Drama and Society in the Age of Jonson* (1962 edition), p. 205: a reference to *Locrine*.

There is, in fact, little indication of any desire on the part of the dramatist to make discreet alignments with official Jacobean policy, and the suggestion that 'the character of Cymbeline . . . has a direct reference to James I',[36] in so far as this implies a commitment to eulogy, is not convincing. One would accept, however, that Shakespeare caught, accurately and retentively, a certain tone of Jacobean mystique and that an oblique awareness of royalist views and demands can be detected. It is as though, in the play's finale, we were presented with a completely open situation. A British king is seen for what he is: uxorious, irrational, violent when prodded, indulgent, of absolute status and ultimately invulnerable. This might be taken as a disinterested view of the 'law' of Prerogative. The concluding atmosphere of transcendental peace has been found appealing. The king reiterates the word 'peace' three times in eight lines (V.v. 478–85) and also speaks of 'my peace' (V.v. 459). One is reminded that

some earlier editors were so offended by the apparent megalomania of '*my* peace' that they emended to 'by'.[37]

The editorial procedure may have been questionable but the original suspicion may not have been entirely groundless. Cymbeline's evocation of peace is a happy combination of the cursory and the opulent. To his daughter he admits his 'folly' (V.v. 67); politically, the guilt is laid upon a defunct secondary cause. There is a passage in *The Trew Law of Free Monarchies* (1603) which simultaneously concedes and vetoes possible monarchical deficiencies. The people, writes James, should look to the king:

fearing him as their Judge, loving him as their father; praying for him as their protectour; for his continuance, if he be good; for his amendement, if he be wicked; following and obeying his lawfull commands, eschewing and flying his fury in his unlawfull, without resistance, but by sobbes and teares to God.[38]

Such a thesis, many-faceted and unanswerable, destroys objections by assimilation. Critics who object to the plodding inadequacy of the verse spoken by the 'poor ghosts' of the Leonati (V.iv) may not have considered that the play needs an element of formal pleading which is quite distinct from the eloquent magnanimity of confirmed majesty. Their wooden, archaic clichés are like an emblem of old and

[36] Jones, *op. cit.* p. 96.
[37] Moffet, *op. cit.* p. 215.
[38] C. H. McIlwain, *The Political Works of James I* (1918), p. 61.

rather weary sincerity, whereas Cymbeline's concluding oratory is the reaffirmation of the mystique of status.

Shakespeare is in accord with the *Trew Law* to the extent that he brings the play to an end 'without resistance'. It is neither adulatory nor satiric, but observes what is there. Altogether, one feels that *Cymbeline* betrays nothing, is eminently logical and does not fumble. To be left, at the end, with things inexplicable and intractable is a perennial hazard for all artists; but in Shakespeare's last plays an acceptance of this seems to be at the heart of his dramatic vision. It is hardly scepticism, rather a kind of pragmatism, a necessary counterpoise to the thoroughly pragmatic 'myths' of the Stuarts. It has been said that 'the ending of *The Tempest* is very moving, not least because it is so reticent'.[39] Reticence about things that cannot be reconciled is a characteristic of the last plays. In *Henry VIII* this tacit recognition is itself reduced to a formula as the two conflicting obituaries of Wolsey are presented in sequence by Queen Katherine and Griffith. The play sounds a note of political quietism while in *Cymbeline* the tension of paradox is persistently felt. In each case, however, we are involved in a dualistic acceptance of things as they are. Such dualisms seem to avoid the chain of cause and effect which drives the tragedies. They avoid, also, the formal concept of Tragedy in which 'hamartia'[40] indicates the irreparable severing of tragic experience from the normal conduct of life; the start of the irreversible slide down the scale of act and consequence. In the late plays hamartia appears as something integral to the human condition, innate, to be lived with.

Admittedly, this observation might be little more than a truism stretched awkwardly between time-serving cynicism, lazy nostalgia and altruistic resilience. There are comments of a relatively simple kind, spanning the range of Elizabethan-Jacobean chronology, which could qualify as any one of these. John Lyly argued, sometime in the 1580s, that

If wee present a mingle-mangle, our fault is to be excused, because the whole worlde is become an Hodge-podge.[41]

---

[39] David William, '*The Tempest* on the Stage' in J. R. Brown and B. Harris, *Stratford on Avon Studies 1* (1960), pp. 135.

[40] A term covering a gamut of flaws from 'simple error' to 'sin'. For a full description see G. F. Else, *Aristotle's Poetics: the Argument* (1957), esp. pp. 376–99. One is aware that Shakespeare may not have known the *Poetics*.

[41] I am indebted to the discussion by R. Weimann in *Shakespeare in a Changing World*, ed. A. Kettle (1964), pp. 36–7.

One finds a reminiscent explanation, prefaced by the composer Thomas Tomkins to his *Songs* of 1622. These, he hopes, are

> suitable to the people of the world wherein the rich and poor, sound and lame, sad and fantastical, dwell together.[42]

Uncomplicated observations of this nature are possibly imitated in Hamlet's

> the age is grown so picked that the toe of the peasant comes so near the heel of the courtier, he galls his kibe.   (V.i. 151–3).

Such an aphorism is far from representing the mood caught in Shakespeare's so-called Romances. Their spirit is altogether more complex and has been excellently described.[43] Even so, Lyly and Tomkins are not alone in their persuasion that the world of common observation is one which disobeys at every turn the world of over-riding mythology and that such contradictions affect the nature of art and the ways in which people respond to it. A sense of mundane fallibility is stated with characteristic authority by Bacon. Of the false appearances imposed by words he writes:

> it must be confessed that it is not possible to divorce ourselves from these fallacies and false appearances, because they are inseparable from our nature and condition of life.[44]

He adds, however, that 'the caution of them . . . doth extremely import the true conduct of human judgment', thereby converting what might have been a merely passive acceptance into something active and therapeutic. The last act of *Cymbeline* reveals a possibly analogous attitude, particularly as the play's major dilemma has been brought about largely by false appearances imposed by words. Just how far Shakespeare is from an indulgence in flaccid geniality is shown by the summary disposal of Cloten and the crazed death of the Queen. One might say of the final gallimaufry, mirroring in so many ways the sad and fantastical, that it avoids instruction, whether comic or tragic, but is, in Bacon's sense of the term, 'cautionary'.

It has been suggested that 'there is more Baconism in late Shakespeare than is normally recognized'.[45] This is clearly a challenging suggestion; it would perhaps not be possible to establish 'Shakespeare's Bacon' on the same basis of documentary evidence as is

[42] cited by J. Kerman, *The Elizabethan Madrigal* (1962), p. 26.
[43] Notably by Charles Barber, '*The Winter's Tale* and Jacobean Society' in Kettle, *op. cit.*, pp. 233–52.
[44] *op. cit.*, p. 134.
[45] Barber, *op. cit.*, pp. 247–8.

available for Shakespeare's Plutarch or Shakespeare's Montaigne. It is arguable, however, that *Cymbeline* turns on an awareness of experiment or experiential knowledge. Imogen's cry:

> Experience, O, thou disprov'st report! (IV.ii. 35)

which is, in some senses, the *leit-motif* of the play, is uttered at a point where the threads of the action are interwoven: the marriage-story with that of the lost children and the theme of Britain. Its facets illuminate all areas. 'Experimentation had long had its connections with magic',[46] and the Queen who possesses, or imagines she possesses, 'strange ling'ring poisons' (I.v. 34), 'mortal mineral' (V.v. 50), is a practitioner of Bacon's 'degenerate natural magic'.[47] Shakespeare twists and exaggerates one side of Bacon's casuistical dichotomy between lawful and unlawful investigation. Wilson Knight speaks of the Queen's 'instinctive' support of her son;[48] a perceptive epithet suggesting that element of unregenerate energy which also inspires her murderous cunning and her evil exploitation of natural resources. The two lost princes are also seen, in some of their acts, as housing 'primal nature in its ferocious aspect'.[49] There is, however, a major difference between the Queen's nature and theirs. Guiderius kills Cloten with what seems an untroubled animal reflex but the princes' moral intelligence partakes of 'rehabilitated Nature'.[50] They are moved by that sense of proportion which is a requirement of true relationship. When Arviragus says:

> We have seen nothing:
> We are beastly: subtle as the fox for prey,
> Like warlike as the wolf for what we eat:
> Our valour is to chase what flies. (III.iii. 39–42)

this is not, as it might seem, emblematic fatalism. It was a Renaissance understanding that 'Man had learned about his own nature from his observance of animals'[51] and Arviragus' self-reproach has an experiential emphasis. The scene provides a significant departure from orthodox commonplace. Belarius' truisms about Court *v.* Country are a point of departure rather than a place of rest and have dramatic relevance as revealing the force of an obsession rather than

---

[46] Hardin Craig, *The Enchanted Glass* (1952 edition), p. 75.
[47] *op. cit.*, p. 101.
[48] *op. cit.*, p. 130.
[49] *op. cit.*, 159.
[50] cf. Basil Willey, *The Seventeenth Century Background* (1953) ch. 2.
[51] Craig, *op. cit.*, p. 99.

the truth of an ideal. His values are questioned by the two princes who argue, in effect, that *a priori* value must be submitted to, and substantiated by, experience.

Cymbeline has been called an experimental drama mainly because of its competitive awareness of the new Jacobean stage-fashion for Romance. The term could be applied in other ways, since the play is significantly experimental with its characters, values and situations. One simple essential in an experiment is time. Philario says of Posthumus, with unintentional irony:

> How worthy he is I will leave to appear hereafter, rather than story him in his own hearing. (I.iv. 33–5)

The events of the play perform what the First Gentleman admitted he could not: they 'delve' Posthumus 'to the root' (I.i. 28). To say that the realization of character involves the realization of situation is to be guilty of proclaiming the obvious. Such an emphasis is necessary, however, for *Cymbeline* is above all a study of situation, relationship, environment and climate of opinion. If we are 'on occasion . . . content to forget the play and concentrate on its heroine'[52] very great harm is in fact done. Again, the question of possible dramatic bias may be raised. If Cymbeline himself, who is both character and 'climate', seems to elude the extremes of scrutiny one need not infer evasiveness on the dramatist's part. The king's decision, though victorious, to pay his 'wonted tribute' after all (V.v. 462) invites us to take it seriously, as a gesture of deep humility and the play's moment of truth. It might be taken more appropriately as a token of considerable ambivalence. Its solemnity exists for the participants in the immediate situation while the play itself contains a reserve of irony. Cymbeline's magnanimous gesture is also one of Shakespeare's supremely comic moments. If it is a moment of truth this is because it lays bare the absurdity of the original mouthing and posturing and pointless antagonism.

> Laud we the gods,
> And let our crooked smokes climb to their nostrils
> From our blest altars. (V.v. 476–8)

The poetry is both plangent and jagged. 'Should not the smoke of an acceptable sacrifice rise undeviously to the heavens?'[53] It is a proper

---

[52] Nosworthy, *op. cit.*, p. lxii.

[53] B. Harris, '*Cymbeline* and *Henry VIII*' in *Stratford on Avon Studies 8* (1966), p. 228.

question. Cymbeline's command makes an uncontrollable element appear deliberate, converting the accidental and the thwart into a myth of order and direction. Such a myth reflects a royal sense of occasion and the mystique of status but one recognizes that the phrase has the kind of resonance which could bring more distant connotations into sympathetic vibration. This evocation of majestic aplomb belongs, as it were, partly to Cymbeline the 'character', partly to Shakespeare the dramatist: on the one hand 'Business as usual', on the other 'This is what the reality of Prerogative is like'. Such a double-take would be quite in accord with the play's feeling for compromise. *Cymbeline*'s sense of finality, seen in this light, resides in its capacity to annul, through time, exhaustion and sleep, the business of the wicked and arrogant and the impetuosity of the immature. 'Crooked smokes', considered as the dramatist's 'own' metaphor is like silent music, a visual rendering of the favourite Jacobean musical device known as 'chromatic tunes'.[54] What this means is embodied in a line of Pisanio's:

Wherein I am false, I am honest; not true, to be true. (IV.iii. 42)

This is the taming of 'false relation'[55] to a new constructive purpose. Dissonance is the servant preparing the return of harmony. In the words of John Danyel's lute-song of 1606:

> Uncertain certain turns, of thoughts forecast,
> Bring back the same, then die and dying last.[56]

Cymbeline, which 'aims at effecting the gratification of expectancy rather than the shock of surprise',[57] brings back the same in both grace and mediocrity. It brings back husband to wife and tribute to Rome. It also reaffirms the king in the dualism of his selfhood and his prerogative. Shakespeare is perhaps ready to accept a vision of actual power at cross-purposes with the vision of power-in-grace; 'the real world', in fact, 'in which the life of the spirit is at all points compromised'.[58]

[54] P. Warlock, *The English Ayre* (1926), p. 57. 'Chromatic tunes' is a phrase from a poem set by John Danyel. Warlock analyses the chromaticism of Danyel's setting on pp. 58–61.

[55] False relation is one of the key-themes in *Cymbeline*, implying false conjunction and false report. For a description of false relation in Jacobean music see the essay by Wilfred Mellers, in B. Ford, *The Age of Shakespeare* (1956), p. 394.

[56] Warlock, *op. cit.*, p. 57.

[57] H. S. Wilson, '*Philaster* and *Cymbeline*' in *English Institute Essays 1951* (1952), p. 162.

[58] D. William, *op. cit.*, p. 135.

To make such a suggestion is not to push Shakespeare into placid cynicism or angry satire but it is to feel that he at least knew the difference between acceptance and indulgence. *Cymbeline* has been called 'enchanted ground'.[59] If it is, then that ground is

drenched in flesh and blood, civil history, morality, policy, about the which men's affections, praises, fortunes do turn and are conversant;[60]

steeped, that is, in those knowledges which men generally 'taste well'.

[59] Nosworthy, *op. cit.*, p. xlviii.
[60] *Advancement*, p. 122.

3

How to Edit Shakespeare

BONAMY DOBRÉE

A THOUGH many years ago I had the temerity to edit a Shake-speare play, I would not for that reason lay down the law on how to conduct so tricky an undertaking, since at that time I was not aware of the happy freedom opened up by Thomas Edwards in *The Canons of Criticism*, the sixth edition of which (1758) I happen to possess, and is the edition from which I shall quote.

From the first the eighteenth century was passionate for Shake-speare—in criticism, as appears from the writings of Steele, Addison, Dennis and others; and from the fact that actors made their reputa-tions from taking leading parts in his plays (which were more often acted than any others). Also the ball was set rolling for editions of his plays, though it was not until the end of the century that his poems were included. The first edition was that of Rowe in 1709, if edition it may be called, rather than a reprint of the fourth Folio, for he did no more than vaguely consult and compare the earlier Folios, and one or two Quartos. Pope followed in 1725, taking Rowe as his text, putting in the margin passages that he regarded as spurious—he was the first 'disintegrator'—but at least performing 'the dull duties of an editor' as he regarded them, by giving a few variorum readings from some of the Quartos, and making emendations, some of which are still accepted. His brushing into the margin passages that he did not like (mainly because they were so improper), and casting out *Pericles* together with most of *Love's Labours Lost* and *Twelfth Night*, infuriated Lewis Theobald, who in 1726 produced the indignant

Shakespeare Restor'd, to be followed in 1734 by a considered edition. Though Pope, himself a veritable 'slashing Bentley', might dismiss him as 'piddling Tibbald', Nichol Smith was able to say of him that in spite of his collation not being so 'deep and laborious' as he claimed, he was 'the first of our Shakespeare editors, and for these reasons. He respected the readings of older editors, and did not give full rein to his taste . . . he did not emend at first sight.' In 1734 he was followed by Sir Thomas Hanmer, and in 1747 by Warburton, with whose edition we shall here be confronted. Other editions followed in each decade, till, at last, Shakespeare himself, it would seem, was becoming tired of the whole affair. Coleridge tells us in *Anima Poetae* of an occasion when pundits were discussing who should next edit Shakespeare, and a voice from the cellarage (so to speak) was heard to 'exclaim in the dread and angry utterance of the dead, "No! no! Let m'alone".' So, 'inexorable boobies', as the spirit called them, they let Malone.

But to return to our muttons. In 1747 Warburton published his edition with a pompously pretentious preface. In his immature years, he tells his readers, he had read Shakespeare, and made some notes. These, he stated, 'were amongst my younger amusements when, many years ago, I used to turn over these sort of Writers to unbend myself from more serious applications', more becoming, no doubt, to the future Bishop of Gloucester. Out of the kindness of his heart he had lent these notes to Pope and Theobald, and allowed those aspiring editors to make use of them; but Hanmer had plundered them without permission! Rowe, Warburton stated, had been employed by the printers on the 'silly maxim' that 'none but a poet should meddle with a poet'; and though Pope had been selected for the same reason, he had 'by the mere force of an uncommon genius', been able to separate the genuine from the spurious plays or passages: but, alas! 'dear Mr. Pope' was no critic, and, realizing his own shortcomings, had been very willing that his edition should be 'melted down' into Warburton's, who presented it as a combined effort. Of Hanmer, 'the Oxford editor', as Warburton preferred to call him, he had no opinion whatever. Theobald, he conceded, had his points, but though he could transcribe what he read, and his 'punctilious collation of the old books was of some value . . . what he thought, if ever he did think, he could but ill express'. Clearly it needed someone like Warburton to do the job properly! So he proceeded to do it, putting Shakespeare right, correcting him on all sorts of points, and doing his best to damp down what he considered the improprieties—the indecencies were clearly interpolations—and in short did exactly what Theobald had objected to Bentley's doing when he 'improved' Milton, the 'chief turn' in Bentley's criticism having been 'plainly to show the world, that if Milton did not write as he would have him, he ought to have wrote so'.

When Warburton's edition appeared, it was read by a certain Mr. Thomas Edwards, a member of Lincoln's Inn, who, not being a practising lawyer, had the leisure and the inclination to read. He was profoundly irritated by Warburton's pretentious Preface, horrified by what the D.N.B. calls his 'grotesque audacities', finding that his emendations were often 'arbitrary, fantastic, and wanton'. How could he expose this monstrous mangling of Shakespeare? Luckily Warburton himself had suggested the means, having said in his Preface 'I once intended to have given the reader a *body of canons*, for literal criticism, drawn out in form'; and that he had also intended to provide 'a general alphabetic glossary'. Well, as he hadn't done so, Edwards himself would do it for him, basing his rules on Warburton's practice. So in 1748, he produced his *Canons of Criticism*, a really devastating attack, of which Isaac D'Israeli remarked in his *Quarrels of Authors* that it was 'one of the very best pieces of facetious criticism, of which our literary history may boast a few.[1] The work of Edwards is decisive in its purpose of 'laughing down Warburton to his proper rank and character'.

Edwards obviously enjoyed himself hugely as from Warburton's treatment of Shakespeare's text he turned over possible Canons in his mind, discovering a great many, of which a selection must here suffice:

Canon I. A Professed Critic has a right to declare, that his Author wrote whatever he thinks he should have written, with as much positiveness as if he had been at his elbow.

II. He has a right to alter any passage, which he does not understand.

VII. He may find out obsolete words, or coin new ones; and put them in place of such, as he does not like, or does not understand.

IX. He may interpret this author so as to make him mean directly contrary to what he says.

XV. He may explane a difficult passage by a word absolutely unintelligible.

[1] Vol. 1. pp. 86–8.

There are twenty-one Canons in the first edition, of which the last reads:

> It will be proper in order to shew his wit; especially if the Critic be a married man, to take every opportunity of sneering at the Fair Sex.

Edwards was serious about this work; as much as anybody he wanted a reliable edition of Shakespeare, and he prefaced his fun with an Introduction illustrating the grounds of his objections to Warburton. For instance:

> In *King Lear*, Act III. Sc. 3. the fool says,
>   'I'll speak a prophecy, *or* e'er I go'
> which Mr. Warburton alters to
>   'I'll speak a proph'cy, *or two*, e'er I go'
> where the word *prophecy* is, with great judgment, I cannot say melted, but hammer'd into a dissyllable, to make room for the word *two*; and you have the additional beauty of the open vowels, so much commended by Mr. Pope in his *Art of Criticism*; which make a fine contrast to the agreeable roughness of the former part of the line.

Warburton also declared that *or e'er I go* was not English. Edwards has no difficulty in showing that, *e'er* being a contraction of *ever*, when preceded by *or* is often used as meaning *before* as in 'Or ever, the silver cord be loosed'. One more instance from the Introduction may be given:

> In *Othello*, Act III. Sc. 7. the common editions read,
>   'Farewell the neighing steed, and the shrill trump,
>   The spirit-stirring drum, th' *ear-piercing* fife.'
> This epithet of *ear-piercing* a poet would have thought not only an harmonious word, but very properly applied to that martial instrument of music; but Mr. Warburton says, I would read,
>   'th' fear-spersing fife'
> which is such a word, as no poet, nor indeed any man who had half an ear, would have thought of; for which he gives this reason, which none but a Professed Critic could have thought of; that piercing the ear is not *an effect on the hearers.*

Edwards adds a footnote on 'I would read':

> To do Mr. W. justice, I would suspect this is a false print; it should be, I would *write*; for no man can *read* such a cluster of consonants.

It will be seen from these examples that the Introduction is designed largely to show up Warburton's claim that it needs a critic rather than a poet to edit Shakespeare as Shakespeare would have wished.

Only a man who really did take the business seriously would have done the immense amount of work the *Canons* entailed. Edwards was clearly very familiar with the plays, and resented any tampering with the text, though he could endure the correction of obvious printers' errors. We can take an example under Canon I.

Examp. VIII. Vol. 2. P. 250. LOVE'S LABOR'S LOST.
 'It insinuateth me of *infamy*,'
 Mr. Theobald had corrected this to *insanie*; (from *insania*) Mr. Warburton's note is, 'There is no need to make the Pedant worse than Shakespear made him; who *without doubt* wrote insanity.' WARB.
 But why, without doubt? Shakespear understood the characters he drew; and why might not this Pedant, as well as others, choose to coin a new word; when there was an old one as good? In short, why might not Holofernes take the same liberty, as Mr. Warburton so frequently does?

Modern editors accept 'insanie', as Holofernes' words would indicate was right: 'This is abhominable, which he would call abominable, it insinuateth me of insanie: *ne intellige domine?* to make frantic, lunatic.'

What got Edwards' goat, as we would say, was Warburton's insufferable assurance; *he* really knew where others merely fumbled. And we can hardly be surprised when we read four of his previous comments:

Examp. V. Vol. 4. P. 133.
 'So many thousand actions *once* a foot'
'Shakespear *must have* wrote,' *Anglicè* written;
 "*t once* a foot, i.e. at once.' WARB.
 Yet I doubt, Mr. Warburton cannot shew an instance, where *at* has suffered this apostrophe; before his edition in 1747.

 Examp. VI. Vol. 2. P. 444. We must read, as Shakespear *without question* wrote,
 'And *thyself*, fellow Curtis.' WARB.

Examp. VII. Vol. 5. P. 8. 2 HENRY VI.
 Certainly Shakespear wrote, *East*.

This presumably refers to 'west' in the lines (Sc. 1):

> Had Henry got an empire by his marriage
> And all the wealthy kingdoms of the west . . .

Warburton's suggestion was silly; they are not all so; but at all events the *certainly, must have, without doubt,* with their arrogant assurance, were such as to irritate any reader.
 It will have been seen that Edwards is not easy to follow unless

you know every line of Shakespeare. He expects you to have Warburton's edition on the table beside you, for though he usually gives the play, he does not tell you the Act or scene. However, let us take an example from the *Canons* referred to. Under Canon VII:

Examp. III. Vol. 6. P. 214. TIMON OF ATHENS.
   'With all th' abhorred births below crisp heaven. We should read *cript*, i.e. vaulted; from the latin *crypsa*, a vault.' WARB.
   Mr. Warburton should have shewed by some authority that there is such a word as *cript*, for vaulted; which he seems to have coined for the purpose: but, if there is, it should have been spelt *crypt*, not *cript*; as it comes from *crypta*, not *crypsa*; which indeed would give *cryps*, and that might easily be mistaken for *crisp*; as Mrs. Mincing says, 'so pure and so *crips*'.

Edwards is being almost as pedantic and solemn as Warburton himself, but it is amusing to find the reference to Congreve.
   Or we may take an example under Canon VI:

As every Author is to be corrected into all possible perfection, and of that perfection the Professed Critic is the sole judge. He may alter any word or phrase, which does not want amendment, or which *will do*; provided He can think of any thing which he imagines *will do better*.

Examp. V. Vol. 7. P. 233. CYMBELINE.
   'The very Gods—
The *very* Gods may indeed signify the Gods themselves, immediately, and not by intervention of other agents or instruments; yet I am persuaded, the reading is corrupt: and that Shakespear wrote,
   —the *warey* Gods—
warey here signifying, *animadverting, forewarning*, and *ready to give notice*; not, as in its more usual meaning, *cautious, reserved*.' WARB.
   Here again it were to be wished, that Mr. Warburton had given some authority for using the word in this sense; which if he had looked for, he might have found at least how to spell it.

Edwards was able to make play with the glossary too. He gives no references to Shakespeare, but that is hardly necessary.

OATS, 'a distemper in horses.' Vol. 2. P. 442.
   '—— the *oats* have eat the horses,'
I hope Mr. Warburton takes care to keep his horses from this dangerous distemper.

Applicable to Warburton here, as in many places, is Humpty Dumpty's remark to Alice: 'When *I* use a word . . . it means just what I choose it to mean—neither more nor less.'
   Warburton was extremely annoyed by the *Canons*, and wrote an attack upon their author, then simply known on the title-page as 'A

Gentleman of Lincoln's Inn'. Warburton declared that the author can have been no gentleman; and at any rate what business had a lawyer to meddle with Shakespeare? In later editions, which bear his name (at any rate the sixth does), Edwards amusingly answers Warburton's complaints. Why should he be deprived of his gentility? And

> Who is Mr. Warburton? what is *his* birth, or whence his privilege? that the reputations of men both living and dead, of men in birth, character, station, in every instance of true worthiness, much his superiors, must lie at the mercy of his petulant satire, to be hacked and mangled as his ill-mannered spleen shall prompt him. . . .

Evidently Warburton had considerably riled Edwards, who nevertheless managed to answer the Bishop very effectively. As to Warburton's declaration that this man who wrote the *Canons* was no gentleman, and anyway as a lawyer had no right to read Shakespeare, after some preliminaries he goes on:

> A Gentleman (if I do not mean myself, with Mr. Warburton's leave I may use that word) I say, a gentleman, designed for the severe study of the law, must not presume to read, much less to make any observations on Shakespear; while a Minister of Christ, a Divine of the Church of England, and one, who, if either of the Universities would have given him that honour would have been a Doctor in Divinity; or, as in his preface he decently expresses it, *of the Occult Sciences*; He, I say, may leave the care of his living in the country, and his chapel in town, to curates; and spend his Heaven-devoted hours in writing obscene and immoral notes on that author, and imputing to him sentiments which he would have been ashamed of.

Edwards' purpose had not primarily been to attack Warburton, but to bring common sense, ordinary appreciation of people and of words, into the editing of Shakespeare, recognising the immense labour involved; and he winds up his Preface:

> I shall conclude, in the words of a celebrated author on a like occasion [Middleton, in *Remarks on the Jesuit Cabal*]; 'It was not the purpose of these remarks to cast a blemish on his envied fame; but to do a piece of justice to the real merit of the *work* and its *author*; by that best and gentlest method of correction, which nature has ordained in such a case; of laughing him down to his proper rank and character.'

This he had certainly done, as D'Israeli, we have seen, duly noted.

Poor Warburton! At least he had some imagination; but as Joseph Warton said of Edwards' book, 'All impartial critics allow these remarks to have been decisive and judicious, and his Canons of Criticism remain unrefuted and unanswerable'. No doubt they were of enormous value at the time, as a warning to rash neophytes not to rush in where the learned fear to tread. Now, after two hundred years of assiduous scholarly Shakespeare editing they can have no more than amusement value, an addition, also, to the picture we have of literary activity at the time. And even if, for those who, like Professor Wilson Knight, deeply ponder Shakespeare's vision, they may seem futile wrangling over the wrong thing, since people's mistakes put others on the right path, the brief battle helped to ensure reasonably reliable texts on which they can cogitate.

4

The Hesitation of Pyrrhus

CLIFFORD LEECH

I N this paper I am concerned with the most striking occasion on which Shakespeare remembered Marlowe. Everyone knows the tribute in *As You Like It* (III.v. 81–2);[1] it can be argued that Shakespeare arrived at the notion of a two-part play on the contention of York and Lancaster through the example before him in *Tamburlaine*, especially in view of the wide sweep in that play's Second Part, where the single dominant figure of Part I has come to be seen as only the most forceful, the most eloquent, among a whole series of striving figures;[2] I have urged elsewhere that *Venus and Adonis* was subject to more than a little influence from *Hero and Leander*, Marlowe's subtle comedy about Venus' nun giving a starting-point for the grosser, the flamboyantly decorated treatment of the goddess herself;[3] possibly *The Phoenix and the Turtle* includes memories of Ovid's *Amores*, II.vi. which Marlowe translated;[4] possibly, too, the discussion of 'widow Dido' in *The Tempest* (II.i. 75–101) provides a mirror-image of the story that Marlowe used, a reluctant girl being brought for marriage from Italy to Tunis (mistakenly identified by Gonzalo with the destroyed but near-by Carthage) while in the Virgil-Marlowe story a Carthage queen tried to hold in marriage another stranger, who left her for Italy. In this last instance the

[1] Act-, scene- and line-references to Shakespeare are from the Globe edition; quotations are from *The Complete Works*, ed. Peter Alexander, 1951.
[2] Cf. 'The Dramatists' Independence' *Research Opportunities in Renaissance Drama*.
[3] Cf. 'Venus and Her Nun: Portraits of Women in Love by Shakespeare and Marlowe', *Studies in English Literature*, V (Spring 1965), pp. 248–68. See pp. 259–63.
[4] Cf. A. L. Rowse, *Christopher Marlowe: A Biography*, 1964, p. 38.

association of Dido with Claribel reinforces the anguish of Alonso's daughter and makes the more ironic the stubborn cheerfulness of Gonzalo over the marriage (cf. V.i. 206–9). It may also suggest that Shakespeare remembered Marlowe's play for a decade after *Hamlet*.

For of course it was on an occasion in *Hamlet* that Shakespeare had a piece of Marlowe's writing most strongly in his mind—perhaps indeed open on the table before him, for *Dido Queen of Carthage* was published, as the work of Marlowe and Nashe, in 1594. It may be well, however, to ask why the Pyrrhus speech came into *Hamlet* at all. The players were needed for the acting of 'The Murder of Gonzago', and the discussion of theatre matters, from the popularity of the boy-players to the changing acting-style among the adults, not only links *Hamlet* with those other plays around 1600 that, commonly in inductions, brought before the audience an anatomy of tiring-house affairs[5] but deepens the light on the character of the Prince by relating to his concern with the stage his declared intention to put on an antic disposition. To introduce a player's speech in Act II, however, gave Shakespeare a technical problem. When a play within a play is acted, it must be differentiated clearly in manner from the way the characters of the play proper conduct themselves in word and gesture:[6] we know that all theatrical behaviour is simpler and more emphatic than the way we privately speak and move, so a play within a play must have a second degree of simplification and heightening. One way to achieve this (and the easiest) is by burlesque, and it was this method that Shakespeare used in 'The Murder of Gonzago', where the words are tumid in their circumlocutions and repetitions and the actors' damnable face-making calls forth the Prince's rebuke. Here there was obvious fun at the expense of a popular drama already outmoded but doubtless persisting: when the First Player assures Hamlet that his company has already 'indifferently' reformed its acting-manner, there is some impatience in the Prince's reply: 'O, reform it altogether'. If, however, there was to be a player's speech in the second act, it was clearly out of the question that the simple burlesque of Act III should be anticipated. One can have too much of burlesque, for one thing, and for another the anticipation would dull the effect of the key-moment when Hamlet tests Claudius. An alternative to burlesque is pastiche, a

[5] Cf. J. M. Nosworthy, 'The Structural Experiment in *Hamlet*', *Review of English Studies*, XXII (October 1946), pp. 282–8.
[6] Cf. Thomas De Quincey, 'Theory of Greek Tragedy' (*The Collected Writings of Thomas De Quincey*, ed. David Masson, 1897, X, 344–5).

rendering of a former style which brings it back to mind but does not show contempt. This is far more difficult to achieve with success, and Shakespeare must have had a strong impulsion to include the Pyrrhus speech if it thus entailed a special kind and degree of effort. We must come at a later stage in this paper to the substantial reasons he had for its inclusion.

But first it is necessary to consider more closely whether it is not in fact another exercise in burlesque. Certainly it is frequently taken as such; certainly pastiche can easily slide into burlesque; certainly this speech has an obviousness in its rhetoric, a violence of depiction ('mincing with his sword her husband's limbs') and of imagery ('Now is he total gules', 'Bak'd and impasted with the parching streets'), that have made nineteenth- and twentieth-century readers uneasy.[7] Yet the difference from 'The Murder of Gonzago' is obvious: one need merely ask an actor which of the two he enjoys speaking. Moreover, Shakespeare has elaborately made it plain that here he is not making fun. Although the speech is not Marlowe's, it is sufficiently echoic of the speech in *Dido* for us to have to take Hamlet's tribute to the play it came from as a tribute to Shakespeare's great predecessor. And the Prince's comment is unequivocal:

I heard thee speak me a speech once, but it was never acted; or, if it was, not above once; for the play, I remember, pleas'd not the million; 'twas caviary to the general. But it was—as I received it, and others whose judgments in such matters cried in the top of mine—an excellent play, well digested in the scenes, set down with as much modesty as cunning. I remember one said there were no sallets in the lines to make the matter savoury, nor no matter in the phrase that might indict the author of affectation; but call'd it an honest method, as wholesome as sweet, and by very much more handsome than fine. One speech in it I chiefly lov'd: 'twas Æneas' tale to Dido. (II.ii. 454–68)

He can say it was perhaps 'never acted', for Marlowe's play is only obliquely involved; but the absence of bawdy and affectation, the honesty and wholesomeness and handsomeness, may surely be taken with reference both to *Dido* and to the variant on a *Dido* passage that is now being presented. We cannot believe that Shakespeare is making Hamlet a poor judge: it would go against our accepting his comments on acting in later talk with the players; it would be inconsistent with Ophelia's praise at the end of the nunnery-scene, and

---

[7] Dryden, too, chose this speech (which he thought non-Shakespearian) as one that may 'smell a little too strongly of the buskin' (*Essays of John Dryden*, ed. W. P. Ker, 1900, reprinted 1926, I, 224).

with the persistent image of a man of high intelligence that the play offers. Nor is there need for him to be hypocritical here: he is blunt enough later when he addresses the players, and he never has a good word for 'The Murder of Gonzago' (only the story on which it is based is 'written in very choice Italian'). Moreover, the player is moved by the speech, which suggests it is no fustian.

Shakespeare, then, had Marlowe's description of Priam's death in mind, and made variations upon it for one reason and another. First, it must become more emphatic in manner, so that the differentiation from the general manner of *Hamlet* itself (and that at times can be overtly rhetorical and violent: 'the sheeted dead Did squeak and gibber in the Roman streets', 'in the porches of my ears did pour The leperous distilment', 'Now could I drink hot blood') might be at once evident. Secondly, there must be a variation from Marlowe that lets us see why the speech was there at all.

Marlowe had, of course, used the second book of the *Aeneid* as his source. As in Virgil, his Dido asks for an account of how Troy fell, and in 179 lines we are given the story that in the original took up a book of more than eight hundred lines. (Shakespeare's version was to be only 68 lines.) Marlowe uses the obvious ways to give his actor (a boy, according to the title-page in 1594) time to catch his breath: Dido puts in the occasional exclamation or question; and at the end Aeneas is so moved that the narrative has to be ended by Achates. Nevertheless, this account of Troy's fall is a remarkably detailed summary of the speech in Virgil. We are told that some of the Greeks did really want to go home, that Ulysses turned them aside from that, that he and Epeus and Sinon were responsible for the stratagem of the horse; that Laocoon was killed by the serpents and the horse was brought in through a breach in the walls; that the main body of the Greeks returned and joined those issuing from the horse, while the Trojans slept. There follows a horrible account of the slaughter in the streets, and of how Hector's ghost urges Aeneas to leave Troy. He is protected by Venus from Pyrrhus' wrath, and then comes the passage that fixed itself in Shakespeare's mind: the story of Priam's murder. Here there is a sharp difference from Virgil's account.

In the *Aeneid* Priam puts on his armour, girds on his sword, and advances to die among the enemy. But Hecuba persuades him to take sanctuary with her by the household altar. Pyrrhus finds them there, and kills their son Polites as he flees towards them. Priam utters words of rebuke, contrasting Pyrrhus' savagery with Achilles' moment of humanity when he gave to Priam the mangled body of Hector. The father then weakly throws his spear, which hangs lightly from Pyrrhus' shield. At once the Greek drags Priam to the very altar-stones, winds his left arm in Priam's hair, and gives him a violent death-wound with his sword.

In Marlowe, Priam and Hecuba huddle in an embrace by the altar, and (Polites' death being omitted) Priam begs for life. In response, Pyrrhus cuts off his lifted hands. Hecuba fixes her nails in Pyrrhus' eyelids, but the soldiers pull her away by the heels ('And swung her howling in the empty air'). Priam, aroused, attacks Pyrrhus though without hands to strike:

> Which he disdaining whisk'd his sword about,
> And with the wound thereof the King fell down. (II.i. 253–4)[8]

Here there is a textual point in dispute, for Collier altered 'wound' to 'wind', thus bringing the passage closer to Shakespeare's. He may well have been right to do so, for 'the wound' of line 254 is hardly prepared for by the whisking of the sword, and the misprinting of 'wound' for 'wind' is by no means unlikely in this context of arms and their use: Shakespeare would have read 'wound' if he used the quarto of 1594, but he may also have seen the play acted[9] or read it in manuscript. When the king is down, Pyrrhus rips the body 'from the navel to the throat' and then, having dipped Achilles' flag in Priam's blood, he goes into the crowded streets, finds it hard to move in the throng, and pauses:

> So, leaning on his sword, he stood stone still,
> Viewing the fire wherewith rich Ilion burnt. (II.i. 263–4)

It is a striking moment: what remains in life for a man who has killed Priam King of Troy? The stillness of the murderer was indeed to remain in Shakespeare's mind.

With variations on Virgil that I have discussed elsewhere,[10] Marlowe then returns to Aeneas and narrates how he got to his ships.

We have seen that Shakespeare's account is shorter. First, it deals only with the scene in Priam's palace. And 'it begins with Pyrrhus'.

---

[8] Quotations from and references to *Dido* are from the Revels Plays edition, *Dido Queen of Carthage and The Massacre at Paris*, ed. H. J. Oliver, 1968.

[9] It may be identical with the *Dido and Aeneas* recorded by Henslowe in January 1598.

[10] 'Marlowe's Humor', *Essays on Shakespeare and Elizabethan Drama in Honor of Hardin Craig*, Columbia, Missouri, 1962, pp. 69–81. See p. 72.

The dramatist goes out of his way to emphasise the concentration on Pyrrhus by having Hamlet make a false start as he tries to remember the speech:

> If it live in your memory, begin at this line—let me see, let me see:
>   'The rugged Pyrrhus, like th' Hyrcanian beast,'
> 'Tis not so; it begins with Pyrrhus.
>   'The rugged Pyrrhus, he whose sable arms . . . (II.ii. 469–74)

Moreover, it needs noting that the first lines about Pyrrhus are given to the Prince himself, which of course has a good theatrical effect in contrasting the voices of Prince and player but also brings Pyrrhus into association with Hamlet. Thus the whole description of Pyrrhus, with its especially violent imagery, is not only Shakespeare's addition —for there is nothing corresponding in Virgil and only a brief touch in Marlowe—but is the section given to Hamlet to speak. The exaggerations (e.g., 'With eyes like carbuncles') may be taken as appropriate to the Prince seeing himself as the avenger of his father's death. Then, the player taking over, we learn of Priam fighting ('Striking too short at Greeks') and soon dropping his sword. Here Shakespeare is close to Virgil. And then:

>   Unequal match'd,
> Pyrrhus at Priam drives, in rage strikes wide;
> But with the whiff and wind of his fell sword
> Th' unnerved father falls. (II.ii. 493–6)

If Shakespeare found 'wound', not 'wind', in Marlowe, the grotesque touch is his own. If he found 'wind', he has developed the idea, using 'whiff' to increase the grotesqueness. In any event, here Priam has not yet been touched by the sword: Shakespeare does not include the cutting off of the hands. The death-blow must follow, but Pyrrhus momentarily pauses. The noise of the falling city rings in his ears, and his raised sword is motionless:

>   For, lo! his sword,
> Which was declining on the milky head
> Of reverend Priam, seem'd i' th' air to stick.
> So, as a painted tyrant, Pyrrhus stood
> And, like a neutral to his will and matter,
> Did nothing. (II.ii. 499–504)

Then the sword falls, like the coming of a storm after a waiting stillness in the sky. The speech ends with an exclamation against Fortune and a description, unrelated to Virgil or Marlowe, of Hecuba running frantic in the streets. This passage is given prominence by Hamlet's interruption 'The mobled queen?' and Polonius' praise of these words.

A king, a queen, a revenger of a father's death: these are the elements stressed in Shakespeare's version. He has related Pyrrhus to the Prince who has called for the speech; he has brought in new matter to show Hecuba's devotion (taking away Marlowe's grotesque picture of her clinging with her nails to Pyrrhus' eyelids and then being flung in the empty air, but making her a figure of distraught dignity as, blinded with tears, clothed with a blanket and a clout, she runs barefoot up and down); he has treated Priam with firm respect. Those who argue that Shakespeare is simply exaggerating Marlowe's effects must face the fact that Priam does not lose his hands here; he does not beg for life; he does not leave Hecuba to do the fighting; he is 'reverend Priam'.

The differences between Marlowe and Shakespeare concern us most, but it is instructive to see resemblances as well. I am particularly concerned with Pyrrhus' momentary pause, with the shifting of its position,[11] but it is incidentally to be observed how Aeneas' inability to conclude the story in *Dido* is used by Shakespeare when his player shows signs of emotional disturbance and is therefore begged to cease. It was understandable that Aeneas should be moved, for he was narrating the fall of his own city, the deaths of wife and kinsmen and king. But Shakespeare, though clearly prompted by Marlowe, made a separate point when his player wept: he was reaffirming the principle asserted by Thomas Wilson in *The Art of Rhetorique* (1553): 'He that will stirre affeccions to other, muste first be moved himself.'[12] The actor must have some of the rhetorician's arts, but that does not mean he is a technician.

Hamlet sees himself as Pyrrhus, the revenger who pauses. He is convinced that the pause is only a calm before storm: the deed will be done even if now the sword hangs motionless. Yet in the speech the man to be killed is 'reverend Priam', a true king who, we have seen, is treated with more care and gentleness than Marlowe gave him. And the queen, of course, is Gertrude, but a Gertrude who stays true. 'Mobled' is Hecuba here, for Gertrude is hardly to be recognized in

---

[11] Steevens and Fleay noted the resemblance between the pauses in Marlowe and Shakespeare, but did not comment on the effect of the change in position. See the New Variorum *Hamlet*, I, 183, 186.

[12] Sig. Tlᵛ; quoted in Bernard Beckerman, *Shakespeare at the Globe 1599–1609* New York, 1962, reprinted 1966, p. 119.

this frantic figure. Would she run mad for a dead Claudius? Did she run mad for her dead first husband? We know the answer to the second question; neither Hamlet nor we can ever answer the first. But what emerges clearly enough is that there are two equations contained within the speech: Pyrrhus is both Hamlet and Claudius; Priam is both Claudius and the elder Hamlet; Hecuba in both equations is Gertrude. In transposing the hesitation of Pyrrhus from the end of the affair to the moment before its climax, Shakespeare gives us an image of the hesitation that Hamlet is now practising and of the hesitation that Claudius should have practised but, apparently, did not. Hecuba's grief is the grief Gertrude should have felt at her first husband's death; it may also be the grief, Hamlet suspects, that waits for her when Claudius dies. The tale to Dido has become both a record of Elsinore's immediate past (with ironic inversion in Pyrrhus' hesitation and Hecuba's grief); it is also an exercise in wish-fulfilment as the Prince listens to the account of a revenge accomplished for a dead father. Even so, the revenge is dreadful, and the queen is driven wild. The Prince has thus invited a narration that presents what he later calls a 'horrid hent': when he not only grasps the sword (as in the prayer-scene) but lets it fall (in the last minutes of his life), he will be perhaps not so savage as 'the Hyrcanian tiger', for that was rejected as not truly belonging to the speech, but none the less 'total gules, horridly trick'd With blood of fathers, mothers, daughters, sons'. It turns out to be true enough, if we accept a singular for Hamlet's plural: Polonius, Gertrude, Ophelia, Laertes are to die before the Prince gets to his Priam. We can see why Shakespeare built up the horror of Pyrrhus' appearance: partly it is because Pyrrhus is Claudius, partly because he is also Hamlet; the killing of Priam is more of a catastrophe than the killing of Claudius could be, but there is horror in them both. It was like Hamlet, too, to build up the situations he encountered into world-shaking matters. Gertrude's frailty is a new fall of Woman; his own escape at sea has been specially engineered by Heaven; his thoughts about the deaths around him lead to talk of Caesar and Alexander. Elsinore can, for him, be Troy, and the action of Claudius or himself can bring to ruin what Marlowe called 'the pride of Asia'.

Hamlet has been performed with the Pyrrhus speech played for laughs. Once I saw it with the actor enunciating 'Did nothing' with ludicrous effect: then there was a pause for Hamlet and the rest to show their merriment. Not only does this make nonsense of Hamlet's praise of the speech and the play it was alleged to come from: it also makes nonsense of the actor's final tears and Hamlet's later recognition that the emotional disturbance (though merely for Hecuba, a figure of legend) was genuine. Apart from that, there is too much implied in this speech for a burlesque treatment to be other than butchery. It gives us the clearest indication in the play that Hamlet sensed a relationship between himself and Claudius. He is closer in situation to Pyrrhus than Claudius was, yet Priam was closer to the elder Hamlet than Claudius is. And while Gertrude did not, in the first equation, behave like the mobled Hecuba, Hamlet is impelled to ask himself how a second husband's death will affect her.

Shakespeare has not out-Marlowed Marlowe. While his imagery is more violent and his use of words more inkhorn-like ('his antique sword . . . Repugnant to command'), his incidents are generally more restrained; while Pyrrhus is deeper in blood, Priam and Hecuba are far more austerely presented than in *Dido*. But it is the structural change that is of the greatest significance. In *Dido* the slaughter of Priam works up to a final climax, with Pyrrhus stone-still, leaning on his sword: that is finely imagined; if he uses that sword again, it will be for far lesser work; it is best to have it now only as a prop for a tired man. But in *Hamlet* the climax is central, before the killing of the king: that is where Hamlet himself is, where he will continue to be until the imminence of his own death makes him aware that his 'interim' is approaching vanishing-point. 'Interim' is Hamlet's word in Act V; it was also Brutus' word in *Julius Caesar* a short time before, when he too spoke of what separated 'the acting of a dreadful thing' from 'the first motion'. And dreadful indeed revenge was, even when you saw your father as Achilles.

5

In One Person Many People:
King Richard the Second

A. NORMAN JEFFARES

ichard the Second is one of Shakespeare's most satisfyingly
constructed plays. Filled with pageantry, its subject is essentially dramatic, the fall of one man, the rise of another. The
theme, the deposition of a king, the usurpation of his crown by
another, is one which raised important issues in Elizabeth's reign:
but these transcend the play's own transcending of a piece of earlier
English history. For Shakespeare poses problems in this play which
are perennially pertinent when a man does not measure up to the
demands and responsibilities of a position of power. The play's
structure, on the face of it, might be taken as illustrating a conflict
between two men: one unfitted, the other fitted for responsibility.
But Bolingbroke only appears to fill the role for which Richard is
unsuited (*Henry IV* shows he doesn't fully do so), and the play is
essentially a study of Richard's character. The construction, in fact,
subtly illustrates the complexity of Richard's tragedy, and the
aesthetic appeal of the play depends upon the matching of Richard's
increasing self-awareness with his decreasing power.

Scholars have raised the question of the sources Shakespeare may
have used for his writing of the play. Seven principal sources have
been suggested: Holinshed's *Chronicles*; Daniel's *The First Foure
Bookes of the Civile Warres*; *Woodstock* (an anonymous play, also
known as *1 Richard II*); Froissart's *Chronicle* in Lord Berners' translation; Edward Hall's *The Union of the two noble and illustre famelies*

In One Person Many People: King Richard the Second

of Lancastre and Yorke; *La Chronicque de la Traison et Mort de Richart Deux Roy Dengleterre* (an anonymous French MS chronicle of c. 1400); and Jean Creton's *Histoire du Roy d'Angleterre Richard.* Professor Ure in his admirable Arden edition (1956; paperback 1966) of the play has cast a sceptical eye over the arguments for these sources, and in the course of his survey clearly shows Shakespeare's 'beautification' of the historical material, quoting Marston's phrase describing how he 'enlarged every thing as a Poet'. There is, therefore, justification for taking the play as it unfolds its action and meditation upon the stage, for Shakespeare is exploring an historical situation with a high degree of imaginative insight which does not require a knowledge of the factual basis of his story—nor of his deviations from it. In view of this we can attempt to read the play from, as it were, a position of historical innocence, recording what happens in the text of the play, and attempting to analyse the pattern into which Shakespeare has arranged his material.

The play opens with a scene where Richard is dealing with a quarrel between two of his nobles. Henry Bolingbroke, Duke of Hereford, accuses Thomas Mowbray, Duke of Norfolk, of treason, and also of having murdered the Duke of Gloucester. The King is acting here as a Judge; he is conscious of his duty to be impartial:

> Mowbray, impartial are our eyes and ears . . .
> He is our subject, Mowbray; so art thou:
> Free speech and fearless I to thee allow.
> (I.i. 115, 122–3)[1]

He acts according to protocol in attempting to soothe the two men down; he wants to purge 'choler without letting blood' (I.i. 153) and speaks in medical terms as though his courtiers were his patients:

> Forget, forgive, conclude and be agreed:
> Our doctors say this is no month to bleed.
> (I.i. 156–7)

The two Dukes are too enraged (we have been prepared for this by the King's description of them earlier, I.i. 18–19) to accede to Richard's request. He therefore allows the quarrel to proceed to the chivalrous receipt of single combat:

> We were not born to sue, but to command;
> Which since we cannot do to make you friends,
> Be ready, as your lives shall answer it,
> At Coventry upon Saint Lambert's day . . .

[1] Quottaions are from the Arden edition (ed. Peter Ure, paperback edition, 1966).

51

> Since we cannot atone you, we shall see
> Justice design the victor's chivalry.
>
> (I.i. 196–9, 202–3)

So far, so good. The King has behaved in an apparently regal way: he has tried to compose a quarrel; he has, perhaps, overdone his insistence upon his kingly role without getting his own way. The scene has set an unresolved quarrel before the audience, created anticipation of the event, and shown us Richard acting as a king.

The second scene alters our view of Richard. In it the widowed Duchess of Gloucester appeals to John of Gaunt, Duke of Lancaster and Bolingbroke's father, to revenge the murder of his brother, the Duke of Gloucester. He refers the matter to the will of heaven, since the king is implicated—

> But since correction lieth in these hands
> Which made the fault that we cannot correct.
>
> (I.ii. 4–5)

He further regards Richard as having caused Gloucester's death, but refuses to do anything about it:

> God's is the quarrel—for God's substitute,
> His deputy anointed in His sight,
> Hath caus'd his death; the which if wrongfully,
> Let heaven revenge, for I may never lift
> An angry arm against His minister.
>
> (I.ii. 37–41)

In effect, nothing can be done if God's deputy behaves in an all too human way. This view of the King's inviolability as an anointed ruler was a commonplace view in Tudor times.

The third scene re-introduces the two Dukes, and inevitably the tension is heightened now we realize that John of Gaunt believes Richard caused Gloucester to be murdered (at Calais where Mowbray was in charge). Again Richard behaves correctly. The forms of the rules for challenger and defendant are gone through. Both are called upon to identify themselves, and Richard makes statements fully in keeping with his position as umpire or judge of the contest. To Bolingbroke he says:

> Cousin of Hereford, as thy cause is right,
> So be thy fortune in this royal fight!
>
> (I.iii. 54–5)

And to Mowbray:

> Farewell, my Lord, securely I espy
> Virtue with valour couched in thine eye.
> (I.iii. 97–8)

The trumpets sound, the combatants prepare to advance, and then the tension is unexpectedly interrupted by the King's throwing down his warden or truncheon. He delivers a homily on the evils of civil war and political ambition; he sentences Bolingbroke to ten years' banishment and Mowbray to exile for life. Later he revokes Bolingbroke's sentence to six years because, he says, of John of Gaunt's age.

The fourth scene shows Richard's awareness of Bolingbroke's political ambition, and his realization that temporary banishment may lead to future trouble. The lines Richard addresses to Aumerle

> He is our cousin, cousin, but 'tis doubt,
> When time shall call him home from banishment,
> Whether our kinsman come to see his friends.
> (20–2)

are interpreted by Pollard as an ironical suggestion[2] that 'in spite of this [i.e. Bolingbroke's cousinly relationship with Aumerle] he may not be recalled'. But it would also be possible, and more plausible, to regard Richard as emphasising his own cousinly relationship with Bolingbroke. The speech from ll. 20–36 emphasises 'our', meaning Richard's, using the word four times, in contrast to 'his', meaning Bolingbroke's. Ure suggests that the lines are 'a threatening sneer', but G. L. Kittredge thought that Richard means that he suspects that when Bolingbroke comes back he will return as an enemy not a friend.[3] This seems a more likely interpretation, as the 'friends' are implicitly contrasted with 'the common people' (of I. iv. 24). Bolingbroke's behaviour to the common people and his courtship of them have aroused Richard's suspicions:

> A brace of draymen bid God speed him well,
> And had the tribute of his supple knee,
> With 'Thanks, my countrymen, my loving friends'—
> As were our England in reversion his,
> And he our subjects' next degree in hope.
> (I.iv. 32–6)

---

[2] *King Richard II. A New Quarto* with an introduction by A. W. Pollard (1916), pp. 83–4.
[3] See his edition (Boston, 1941).

Richard's character is further revealed. His coffers

> with too great a court
> And liberal largess, are grown somewhat light,
> We are inforc'd to farm our royal realm.
> (I.iv. 43–5)

He will use the money thus obtained for his Irish wars and if it is not sufficient will use blank charters—a form of levy on the wealthy. When he hears John of Gaunt is seriously ill he shows his designs upon the old man's estate

> Now put it, God, in the physician's mind
> To help him to his grave immediately!
> The lining of his coffers shall make coats
> To deck our soldiers for these Irish wars.
> Come, gentlemen, let's all go visit him,
> Pray God we may make haste and come too late!
> (I.iv. 59–64)

The first act has been a gradual exhibition of the nature of Richard's exercise of power. At first his majesty has dominated the scene. But he has failed to patch up the quarrel between Mowbray and Bolingbroke; after banishing the latter he is not sure that he has done anything but put off trouble. He is revealed as a bad manager of his finances, ruthless in remedying his deficit, by farming out the revenue, by being prepared to make forced levies, and by envisaging taking over Gaunt's money and estates. Paradoxically, it was Gaunt who earlier stressed the fact that Richard is God's anointed.

The second act opens with John of Gaunt, who is dying, discussing with his brother, the Duke of York, Richard's shortcomings. John of Gaunt wishes to admonish him but York advises against this, regarding it as a waste of breath. After John of Gaunt's patriotic speech, which indicates that England must be true to herself and can only be conquered from within, York repeats his advice

> The king is come, deal mildly with his youth,
> For young hot colts being rein'd do rage the more.
> (II.i. 69–70)

Gaunt, however, delivers an old man's hectoring speech to the king. He regards Richard as sick in reputation and describes him as committing his anointed body to the physicians that first wounded him, his flatterers; he attacks Richard for becoming landlord of England rather than its king, implying that like any other mortgagee he is liable to the law. Not unnaturally Richard fires up at this censure, and Gaunt leaves the stage after a fierce exchange. York makes a bumbling, inept attempt to gloss over the situation, pleading with Richard to regard Gaunt's words as caused by illness and age.

> He loves you, on my life, and holds you dear,
> As Harry Duke of Hereford, were he here.
> (II.i. 143–4)

To which Richard replies grimly

> Right, you say true; as Hereford's love, so his;
> As theirs, so mine; and all be as it is.
> (II.i. 145–6)

The news of Gaunt's death follows, and Richard orders the seizure of his plate, coin, revenues, and movables. Even the Duke of York is moved to protest. He has endured the death of Gloucester, Bolingbroke's banishment and the prevention of his marriage (to the French king's cousin), the rebukes administered to Gaunt, his own disgrace, and the wrongs of England, but this seizure of Bolingbroke's inheritance is too much. He reminds the king that he is king 'by fair sequence and succession' and warns him of the thousand dangers he is plucking on his head:

> You lose a thousand well-disposed hearts,
> And prick my tender patience to those thoughts
> Which honour and allegiance cannot think.
> (II.i. 206–8)

Richard, however, pays no attention to York's remonstrances but creates him Governor of England during his own absence in Ireland.

So far the scene has developed rapidly. John of Gaunt has bluntly told the king that his father would have deposed him before he was possessed (of the crown) and that he is now possessed (of the devil) to depose himself (107–8). Richard has openly recognized the mutual dislike of the families (144–5), going further than he did in his earlier comments on Bolingbroke's courting the common people (I.iv. 23–36). Even York now doubts his own capacity to remain loyal (206–8). Richard has so far appeared in a worse light than before, ruthless with Bolingbroke's property, stupid in his choice of York as his deputy, and stupider still in leaving the country after having illegally seized Bolingbroke's property and thus provided an excuse for him to return. The speed and tension have increased, and the closure of the scene increases both further—for some of the court find the seizure of Bolingbroke's property too much for them to accept, and Northumberland reveals the plot that Bolingbroke is ready to land once the king has left for Ireland.

The intensity is built up skilfully. The contrast between Richard, courted by Bushy, Bagot and Greene, and Bolingbroke, who is courting the people, was made earlier. In II.i John of Gaunt complained of Richard's unwillingness to listen to advice, York of his readiness to listen to flattery and to adopt foreign fashions: and John of Gaunt then regarded the 'farming' of the realm as shameful. This was the main point in his attack on Richard, that Richard has wasted the kingdom, become Landlord rather than King, and is thus liable to the provisions of the law. York later takes up this point and points out the dangers of acting wrongfully, the potential loss of allegiance. At this stage the courtiers reinforce the complaints: not only is Bolingbroke unfairly treated but the flatterers are false informants, the commons over-taxed, the nobles fined, and new enactions devised daily. There has not even been any glory resulting from all this expense; and the king is bankrupt.

Shakespeare introduces the incidents of the plot remorselessly; we move steadily up the staircase of his plot step by step. We reach another level in the second scene of this act, the Queen discussing her forebodings with Bushy. Then comes another upward movement, the news that Bolingbroke has landed and Northumberland, Percy and others have defected to him. York arrives on stage to reveal his administrative confusion and incompetence; the caterpillars, Bushy, Bagot and Greene, see ruin coming, disloyally accept defeat in advance, and try to get out of danger while they can.

In the third scene Bolingbroke greets his supporters and defends his arrival in England, replying to York's attack upon him for his act of gross rebellion in returning in arms. York points out that, though the anointed king is in Ireland, he represents him; but he listens to Bolingbroke's argument that he is a subject who appeals to the law, that he has come, in person because attorneys are denied him, to claim his inheritance. York remains neutral, not having sufficient power to do anything about the situation anyway; he regards Bolingbroke and those who aid him as rebels, though Northumberland protests they merely support Bolingbroke's demands for 'his own'. Bolingbroke, however, goes far beyond his original statement that he has come for his rights. Another step in the action is his declared intention of weeding and plucking away the caterpillars of the realm.

The fourth scene reports the withdrawal of Richard's Welsh army, and Salisbury remarks that he sees Richard's glory

> like a shooting star
> Fall to the base earth from the firmament
> (II.iv. 19–20)

The third act opens with Bolingbroke's decision that Bushy and Greene must die for the part they have played in despoiling him of his estate. They have, he says, misled the king and caused him to be unfaithful to the Queen, to whom he sends reassuring messages. The scene ends with his departure to fight Glendower. We see Bolingbroke in action here, tough, brutally efficient. The contrast in character between him and Richard is developed in the next scene, which is Richard's arrival in Wales from Ireland. Richard knows that he is faced with rebellion, but is confident that the native king cannot falter under foul rebellion's arms. Carlisle and Aumerle urge him to action; he makes a speech stressing his divine right—his position as an anointed king, the deputy of God, for whom angels will fight. But the news that the Welsh have left suddenly shatters his confidence

> All souls that will be safe, fly from my side,
> For time hath set a blot upon my pride.
> (III.ii. 80–1)

Aumerle reminds him of his position; he begins to comfort himself with his high position and with the reflection that York has an army. He greets Scroope cheerfully, even flippantly:

> Say, is my kingdom lost? Why, 'twas my care,
> And what loss is it to be rid of care?
> (III.ii. 95–6)

But after he hears that the rebellion is general, that Bushy, Bagot and Greene are dead, he launches into his famous self-pitying speech:

> No matter where—of comfort no man speak.
> Let's talk of graves, of worms, and epitaphs, . . .
> How can you say to me, I am a king?
> (III.ii. 144–77)

'Our lands', he says, 'our lives, and all, are Bolingbroke's'.
He revives again when Aumerle reminds him of his father's (York's)

power; yet when he learns that this hope, too, has gone he gives way to grief completely. He dismisses his followers:

> let them hence away,
> From Richard's night, to Bolingbroke's fair day
> (III.ii. 217–18)

In this scene Richard has exhibited irresolution and a distressingly maniac-depressive see-sawing between ill-founded optimism and well-founded pessimism. He has not the elementary self-reliance, the self-contained self-sufficiency of a successful ruler. The point is underlined by his dismissal of his followers: now he is investigating defeat in solitude:

> A king, woe's slave, shall kingly woe obey.
> (210)

The problems have now been raised. The king is God's deputy. Rebellion and civil war are appalling evils. Yet the king is ruining the kingdom, is flouting the law upon which his power depends through natural law, and therefore is not acting as a king should. He has not acted in the interests of the country; he has rejected the advice of his older counsellors, Gaunt and York; and he has been influenced by self-seeking flatterers, whose loyalty has not given him genuine lasting support and, when measured against Bolingbroke's support from the gentlemen of the south and the northern Castles, is seen to be useless. The function of Act III, Scene II, has been to deepen our understanding of Richard's character as well as the nature of his personality as king-under-test, king-faced-with-difficulties. The problems add together into one large issue: that of the man too small for his post. A small man can fill a big post when things go well, when he can rely on precedent and much can be forgiven a man trying to do his best when he is in difficulties. But the critical test comes when situations become more than merely difficult, when they begin to go seriously wrong. Shakespeare has caught the essential element in such a case, the apparently inexorable telescoping of accident into accident. Richard's return has been caused by his maladroitness in setting off a chain reaction: in breaking the law over Bolingbroke's inheritance he has made a move which sets the other events in motion.

Act III, Scene II, provides a kind of resting place before the climax of the play. In it one man displays his inaction, his passive acceptance of a loss of power. This is made poignantly clear by the contrast between his passivity and Bolingbroke's decisive deployment of power in the preceding short, sharp scene: he does not waste words. *Per se* there is nothing wrong with Richard's long speeches: he likes to talk and he talks well; he has a lively imagination and he analyses situations sensitively. But words alone, are, in the case of a king, uncertain good, however certain they may be in the mouth of a poet. And they can lead an intellectual to worse than indecision.

The centre of the play must be the meeting of the two men; it has a chiasmic, symbolic structure. The men are the two buckets in the well; Bolingbroke's fortune has been at the bottom: his banishment occurs when Richard is at the top of his power. But Richard overbalances in greedily snatching Gaunt's possessions; and Bolingbroke rises as the king goes down. The king has deceived himself in thinking that 'heaven guards the right'. He discards the words once the growth of the rebellion and the support for Bolingbroke is known. As the king's bucket gathers speed in its descent so Bolingbroke's forces increase.

We have been prepared for this height/depth antithesis. Salisbury has seen Richard falling 'to the base earth' and Richard (ironically) sees weak men as 'falling' if angels fight on his side (III.ii. 61–2) and later regards himself as 'high' (III.ii. 88). The crisis scene opens with Bolingbroke aware that the situation is in his favour. After the interlude of York's chiding Northumberland for not calling Richard King Richard, Bolingbroke requests Northumberland to bring what is, in effect, a politician's message to the king sending his allegiance, his readiness to lay his arms and power at his feet *provided* his banishment is repealed and his lands restored; otherwise, he declares, he will make war.

The scene is well devised. Bolingbroke deploys his forces around Flint Castle and makes a show of his power. The king appears on the walls of the castle. He looks like a king, according to York, below. And he speaks like one to Northumberland, reminding him that he is the lawful king, threatening that God will strike those who lift hands against his crown, pointing out Bolingbroke is committing treason with every stride he makes on Richard's land, and that civil war will follow. When Northumberland states Bolingbroke's terms Richard agrees to them:

> His noble cousin is right welcome hither
> And all the number of his fair demands

A. Norman Jeffares

Shall be accomplish'd without contradictions
(III.iii. 122–4)

Having done this he toys with the idea of recalling Northumberland, sending defiance to the traitor and thus dying. He laments having to undo the sentence of banishment and cries out

> O that I were as great
> As is my grief, or lesser than my name!
> Or that I could forget what I have been!
> Or not remember what I must be now!
> (III.iii. 136–9)

There follows the critical speech in which Richard gives way in advance:

> What must the king do now? Must he submit?
> The king shall do it. Must he be depos'd?
> The king shall be contented. Must he lose
> The name of king? a God's name, let it go.
> (III.iii. 142–6)

Richard ends his speech with an ironical query

> Most mighty prince, my Lord Northumberland,
> What says King Bolingbroke? Will his Majesty
> Give Richard leave to live till Richard die?
> You make a leg, and Bolingbroke says 'ay'.
> (III.iii. 172–5)

This is terrifying irony. Richard sees himself as an actor with a pre-destined part: he realizes what is happening. To Northumberland's request that he descend to the base court to meet Bolingbroke he replies

> Down, down I come, like glist'ning Phaeton,
> Wanting the manage of unruly jades.
> In the base court? Base court, where kings grow base,
> To come at traitors' calls, and do them grace!
> In the base court? Come down? Down, court! down, king!
> For night-owls shriek where mounting larks should sing.
> (III.iii. 178–83)

The image of the 'base earth' of Salisbury's earlier speech is caught up and developed. (But, to Northumberland, Richard scorns to speak 'fondly like a frantic man'.) Richard continues to develop the idea when he meets Bolingbroke

> Up, cousin, up; Your heart is up, I know,
> Thus high at least, although your knee be low
>
> (III.iii. 194–5)

We can imagine the king pointing, perhaps, at his crown as he speaks. He continues to play his new role as if sleep walking:

> What you will have, I'll give, and willing too,
> For do we must what force will have us do
>
> (III.iii. 206–7)

The lesson is reinforced in the next short but important scene where Isabel, Richard's queen, overhears the gardeners discussing the state of the country, using the traditional comparison of the state to a garden, and mooting Richard's deposition. The gardener sees the fortunes of Richard and Bolingbroke in terms of vertical movement, but uses the image of scales—the implication of justice is clear. Richard is alone, his vanities make him lighter; Bolingbroke, besides himself, has all the English peers. Fortune is playing its part: the roles of the men are reversed, and Bolingbroke 'weighs King Richard down'.

The fourth act continues the relative movement of the two characters. Firstly we are reminded of the opening scene. Here the drama intensifies, with the nobles bawling at each other, to be stilled by Bolingbroke who declares his intention of bringing Mowbray back from banishment. Unlike Richard in I.i, he is completely in control of the situation; he does not need to protest his power. And then York brings the news that Richard hands over his high sceptre, and tells Bolingbroke to ascend his throne 'descending now from him'. Bolingbroke, continuing the symbolism, replies

> In God's name, I'll ascend the regal throne
>
> (IV.i. 113)

Carlisle then raises the moral problems. He implies that Richard will be tried (for a table of the actual sequences of events in Holinshed, see Ure's comments, *op. cit.*, pp. 124–5 and 134–5).

> What subject can give sentence on his king?
> And who sits here that is not Richard's subject?
>
> (IV.i. 121–2)

> And shall the figure of God's majesty,
> His captain, steward, deputy elect,
> Annointed, crowned, planted many years,

61

Be judg'd by subject and inferior breath,
And he himself not present?

(IV.i. 125–9)

He is promptly arrested for treason. Bolingbroke then answers Northumberland's query as to whether he will grant the commons' suit (e.g. the proposal of 22 October 1399 that Richard should have judgment decreed against him, which is not made clear in the text of the play) with an order for Richard's appearance, so that he can publicly transfer the crown. When Richard enters he sees himself as Christ betrayed, and uses the well image to indicate the complete transference of his power to Bolingbroke, with the visible symbol of the crown handed over:

> On this side my hand, and on that side thine,
> Now is this golden Crown like a deep well
> That owes two buckets, filling one another,
> The emptier ever dancing in the air,
> The other down, unseen, and full of water.
> That bucket down and full of tears am I,
> Drinking my griefs, whilst you mount up on high.
>
> (IV.i. 183–9)

Richard hands over his titles and possessions in a long speech. Northumberland wants to complete the process with a public confession, but this is too much for Richard, who sees those round him in the role of Pilate, though he regards himself as a traitor for taking part in the uncrowning of a king. The process is a kind of Black Mass. With his refusal to go through the last degradation of a public confession and his request for a looking-glass to see what a face he has once it is bankrupt of majesty, Richard's personal tragedy is fully before us in its immensity. He regards the glass as a flatterer, and breaks it. His only request to Bolingbroke for permission to leave is answered by an order for his conveyance to the Tower. The scene closes with the beginning of the conspiracy of the Bishop of Carlisle, the Abbot of Westminster, and Aumerle.

The fifth act continues to develop this personal tragedy of Richard the man. The mirror-breaking had shown his inturning view of his situation; now the enforced parting of king and queen stresses his solitary position; 'doubly divorc'd', as he puts it, from his crown and queen. The second scene again reinforces the contrast between Bolingbroke and Richard, Bolingbroke welcomed by the crowds and returning their salutations (much as Richard had described his courting of the common people in I.iv. 24–37), Richard received with contempt. Aumerle's part in the conspiracy against Bolingbroke is discovered by York, who decides to tell Bolingbroke of it, and some suspense is built up, for Aumerle is urged by the Duchess of York to get to Bolingbroke before his father, confess and seek pardon. In the third scene Bolingbroke shows magnanimity in pardoning Aumerle and swift action in hunting down the other conspirators.

This conspiracy against Henry leads to the brief fourth scene where Exton takes the hint that Henry would be glad to see Richard out of the way. Richard dies in action in the fifth scene, set in Pomfret Castle where he has been detained. Irresolution is thrust from him, paradoxically, at the end of his life. The sixth scene cleans up the problems of the conspiracy, with the secular rebels beheaded, but the Bishop of Carlisle treated with kindness and clemency. At the news of Richard's death brought by Exton Henry decides he will make a pilgrimage to the Holy Land

> To wash this blood from off my guilty hand
> (V.vi. 50)

In a sense, Richard has conquered. The principles upon which he acted towards Bolingbroke rested upon the stability which is based upon the divine right of the ruler. Bolingbroke upset the natural order. Did he commit a greater crime to rid England of lesser? Is being the right man in the role of ruler merely a matter of leadership, strength, and possessing powers of decision? Is it even a matter of possessing the magnanimity he shows to some of the conspirators? Can the wrong means justify the end, if the end itself is wrong? Bolingbroke's treatment of Exton after the murder of Richard certainly condemns the means. But the general problem remains.

The construction of the play can be seen in different ways. Professor Ure divides it into four main parts, four unequal phases. He calls them

(1) Richard as King; his dealing unwisely with crises. Act I to Act II.i.
(2) Bolingbroke's invasion and the transference of power. Act II.i, to III.i.
(3) To the end of Richard's deposition, which Professor Ure calls his passion. III.i, to V.i.
(4) Bolingbroke as King, his mastery of political crises. V.ii to the end of the play.

The structure while it balances one man against the other has deliberately had the issue of contest removed from it. That is to say,

Bolingbroke is used as a foil to Richard with whose story the play is concerned. It is possible, however, to see the play as hinged on one particularly dramatic scene, III.iii, the meeting of the two men and the abandonment by Richard of his position, his power, and his ruler's integrity. This integrity rests, in part, upon his belief in his capacity to be a ruler. In Richard we have a double split in personality. He appears to behave well in the opening scenes. His behaviour as king is gradually revealed. It is when he wishes for Gaunt's death that we first see another, shadier side of his personality. Now we know he is loaded with a past in which Gloucester's death is laid at his door. We see him rejecting the advice of his graver counsellors—we know already that he is under the influence of bad—and finally breaking the law of inheritance. It is obvious at this stage of the play that he is not acting up to his responsibilities; he is carrying out his particular role in life inconsistently as well as imprudently.

The paradox of the play and the mystery of its power rest in the manner in which Shakespeare transfers our interest from the king into the man, into the growth of Richard's spiritual quality. He gains time—perhaps the real suspense of the play centres on this—to make his soul. But he can only do this once he is true to himself, once he sheds the role for which he is not suited. Yet he loses his life because he should have had to shed that role in order to find himself. Behind the chiasmic up-down exchange of positions between Bolingbroke and Richard there is another path of character development to be traced. In the first diagram the characters are less important: the basic story is that of a king unfit for rule replaced by a man who has the qualities necessary for the successful exercise of power. But the essential drama fastens on Richard's spiritual development, his self-knowledge, which is accompanied by his realization that Bolingbroke's usurpation is morally wrong. Richard's end in death is justified by his maluse of means; Bolingbroke's end in power is not justified by Richard's maluse of means.

Shakespeare makes us understand this tragedy in various ways. We are allowed to see into this thought through Richard's speeches. We need not describe him as a poet king because of these, nor as an actor. The contrast with Bolingbroke's economy of words is sharpened by the painful difference between Bolingbroke's deeds and Richard's false economy in them, his inactivity. We need his speeches to fathom the complex nature of his mind, his way of shedding the *persona*, as he has envisaged it, of kingship. He can see himself, to a certain extent, but not sufficiently, in a detached manner. He describes himself as playing in one person many people 'And none contented'. (At times he is like a tired automaton, a figure in a procession, a puppet eager to be rid of his role: 'What must the king do now?' Yet at times he flares up and refuses to act as the stage managers of the revolution wish.)

He realizes the effect he produces on others as, for instance, when he himself introduces the idea of deposition, works out the other roles he could take up, develops the idea that his and Aumerle's tears are fretting them a pair of graves (III.iii. 142–70) and then breaks off, realizing he is indulging his imagination too freely:

> Well, well, I see
> I talk but idly, and you laugh at me. (III.iii. 170–1)

In his prison soliloquy he also breaks off, realizing that he is 'fooling here'. His realization amounts in each case to a painful awareness of the truth. He cannot escape his situation: neither the exchange of the crown for symbols of humility and poverty, nor weeping will answer; his realization when in prison that he wasted time and time now wastes him does not help. Richard knows he has fallen short of what is required of him; he suffers because he cannot become other than a king. Because he has been 'unking'd by Bolingbroke' he strait is nothing.

This, then, is the centre of the tragedy and our attention is directed to the inwardness of it. Even the Queen in her foreboding talks of her inward soul in connection with the unborn sorrow ripe in Fortune's womb (II.ii. 10–12) And Bushy cannot argue her out of her grief:

> It may be so; but yet my inward soul
> Persuades me it is otherwise. Howe'er it be,
> I cannot but be sad . . .
> (II.ii. 28–30)

She continues

> But what it is that is not yet known what,
> I cannot name; 'tis nameless woe, I wot
> (II.i. 39–40)

According to Professor Wolfgang Clemen[4] this is the earliest occurrence of the mood of gloom, of depression, in Shakespeare. There is also a feeling of impending disaster elsewhere in the play.

[4] *Shakespeare Studies*, VI, 1953, p. 30.

York alludes to a 'tide of woes'; the caterpillars, not unreasonably, allude to heart's presages that they three may never meet again; and York has an air of abandonment in II.ii: 'Things past redress are now with me past care'. The Welsh captain lists omens, and Salisbury puts the situation metaphorically with his shooting star image. The parallel prophecies by Gaunt and Carlisle are placed in corresponding positions within the play's very carefully balanced structure. And from Act III onwards Richard himself takes up the notes of warning hinted at earlier (e.g. II.i. 25: 'Reproach and dissolution hangeth over him'): his references to darkness increase and he prophesies grief, care, woe and sorrow.

Various studies have shown the significance of the imagery, the medical terms, for instance. And re-reading the play brings out an insistence on the dangers of flattery. John of Gaunt and York describe the ill effects of Richard's flatterers, and he himself, when he breaks the mirror for its flattery, realizes how deeply he has allowed himself to be misled. (It is, as Professor Ure has pointed out (*op. cit.* p. lxxxi), the most remarkable of Richard's departures from the role set down for him by Bolingbroke, and 'wrenches attention inwards towards Richard' and 'points forward to the solitary and selfcommuning Richard of the prison soliloquy'). He has misled himself by ingenuity, and through weakness; he has flattered himself into thinking he could escape imaginatively into private life. And the breaking of the glass brings into being yet again the contrast between Bolingbroke, the wielder of power, and Richard, the volatile, helpless king who has destroyed his role and with it himself

> Mark, silent king, the moral of this sport—
> How soon my sorrow hath destroy'd my face.
> (IV.i. 290–1)

6

Prince Hal, Henry V, and the Tudor Monarchy

CHARLES BARBER

O NE of the interesting things in Shakespeare's history-plays is the way in which they straddle two ages, managing to deal simultaneously with medieval England and Elizabethan England. The main history-cycle depicts the breakdown of late-medieval English society, and ends with the inauguration of a new era, that of the Tudors; but at the same time the Tudor monarchy is in some ways represented within the cycle, especially by the Lancastrian monarchs Henry IV and Henry V. Both the Lancastrians and the Tudors came to the throne by means of successful rebellions, those of Henry IV and of Henry VII. Moreover, Henry VII's own claim to the throne had been a Lancastrian one, through Margaret Beaufort; and, although the Tudor historians (followed by Shakespeare in *Richard III*) played up the marriage with Elizabeth of York and the union of the white rose with the red, Henry had in fact been careful to get himself accepted as king and crowned before he married Elizabeth—as Shakespeare doubtless knew, since it emerges clearly enough from the Tudor historians that he had read (e.g. Edward Hall). So Shakespeare's Lancastrians resemble the Tudors both dynastically and in being New Men; and, like the Tudors, they are 'modern' men. In *Richard II*, Bolingbroke is the practical, politic man, whose businesslike efficiency replaces the medieval ceremoniousness, formality, and chivalry of the court of Richard II: like the Tudors, he inaugurates a new era.[1]

In the *Henry IV* plays, however, it is Prince Hal rather than his father who typifies the Tudor monarchy; and the whole structure of *Henry IV Part 1* reflects the delicate equilibrium of late sixteenth-century English society. Queen Elizabeth I, ruling a society whose essentially feudal and medieval forms were under increasing pressure from within (from puritans, from capitalist entrepreneurs, from 'new' landed gentry), walked a tightrope: on one side puritans, on the other side catholics; on one side parliament attacking monopolies, on the other side the older nobility jealous of their status and prerogatives. She maintained her position by constant compromise (of which the Church of England is a clear example) and by holding the balance of power between the contending social forces. In the reign of James I the equilibrium was to be destroyed by the increasing economic power of the capitalist gentry, so that the crown was forced to take sides and ally itself with the traditionalists; but in the 1590s the balance of forces was still sufficiently even for the Queen and her court of New Nobility to hold the scales. This is the situation reflected in the structure of *Henry IV Part 1*, in which Prince Hal attempts to strike a balance between the opposed attitudes of Hotspur and of Falstaff, between old-fashioned chivalry and new cynicism. The Hotspur-Hal-Falstaff axis, which is especially emphasized by the contrasting attitudes to honour, is one of the central structural features of the play.

Hotspur stands for the old feudal way of life and for the power of the feudal magnates. He comes from the north (in Shakespeare's day more feudal and more catholic than the south-east), and his rebellion would surely have reminded the original audience of the Rising of the Northern Earls (1569), the last serious rebellion of the reign, which had been led by Thomas Percy, seventh earl of Northumberland.[2] Hotspur's sole concern is with war, and the honour to which he aspires is simply military glory. Warfare is enjoyed for its own sake (he calls it 'sport'), and is valued more highly than either material rewards or personal relationships:

---

[1] On the formality and ceremoniousness of the court in *Richard II* and the way in which it typifies the medieval period, see E. M. W. Tillyard, *Shakespeare's History Plays* (London, 1944), pp. 250–69.

[2] For a full account of the resemblances between the two rebellions see Lily B. Campbell, *Shakespeare's 'Histories' Mirrors of Elizabethan Policy* (San Marino, 1947), pp. 229–37.

> Away, away you trifler, loue, I loue thee not,[3]
> I care not for thee Kate, this is no world
> To play with mammets, and to tilt with lips,
> We must haue bloudy noses, and crackt crownes,
> And passe them currant too.
>
> (II.iii. 93–7)

Kissing is thought of in terms of the tournament ('tilt'), and money is replaced by broken heads ('crackt crownes'). Warfare, moreover, means personal prowess, not strategy or tactics: Hotspur is not a general, but a mere basher; this appears clearly in the dispute with Worcester and Vernon before the Battle of Shrewsbury, when Hotspur, thirsting for action, wants to fight immediately, despite the obvious disadvantages.

Hotspur is the turbulent provincial magnate, and has nothing of medieval courtliness about him. He despises the arts:

> I had rather be a kitten and cry mew,
> Then one of these same miter ballet mongers,
> I had rather heare a brazen cansticke turnd,
> Or a drie wheele grate on the exle tree,
> And that would set my teeth nothing an edge,
> Nothing so much as minsing poetry.
>
> (III.i. 129–34)

Here Hotspur is rejecting the ideals of the humanistic Tudor gentleman, who (the sixteenth-century courtesy-books insist) must be trained in Arms and Arts for the purpose of serving his sovereign. An essential part of the education in Arts, from Elyot's *Governor* onwards, is always the study of Latin and Greek poetry. In rejecting poetry, Hotspur is rejecting the ideals of the new Tudor nobility, and recalling an earlier age when arms were for the knight and arts for the mere cleric. Hotspur seems more 'modern' when he rejects Glendower's magic and insists on a naturalistic explanation of earthquakes (III.i. 27–35); however, this too can be seen as a rejection of Art, but it is perhaps also motivated by a desire in Shakespeare to dissociate Hotspur from the 'Wizard Earl' of his own day (Henry Percy, ninth earl of Northumberland, 1564–1632). Hotspur, as be-becomes an old-fashioned magnate, also despises the citizenry, the 'veluet gards, and Sunday Citizens' (III.i. 261), and exhorts his wife to swear like a lady, not in the puritanical manner of those who never walked further than Finsbury.

[3] Throughout *Henry IV Part 1* is quoted from Q1, *Henry IV Part 2* from Q1, *Henry V* from F1, and *Hamlet* from Q2, but all line-references are to the Globe edition.

The conspirators also exemplify the divisive tendencies of the feudal magnates: they carve up the country between them (at any rate on the map), whereas the monarchy stands for national unity. Their divisiveness of course contributes to their defeat, since Hotspur and Worcester are left unassisted by the others to face the undivided forces of the king; and in *Henry IV Part 2* Northumberland similarly fails the Archbishop of York and his associates.

However, while Hotspur embodies the values of the feudal magnates, and the conspirators represent the divisive and non-nationalist tendencies of feudalism, it is clear that Shakespeare is never merely schematic. The characters are people, not mere social counters. The conspirators form an interestingly diversified group, and Worcester is as much a 'politician' as the king (and in fact a good deal more machiavellian). Indeed, one of the things that contributes to the pathos of Hotspur's death is the audience's feeling that his ardent idealism has simply been used by other people for politic ends. In a world dominated by 'bare and rotten pollicy' (I.iii. 108), the simple-minded military ideals of Hotspur are inadequate, and he is easily utilized by Northumberland and Worcester (just as, in *Hamlet*, the politician Claudius has no difficulty in diverting or manipulating Fortinbras and Laertes). Hotspur is an anachronism.

At the other extreme from Hotspur is Falstaff, their polarity being underlined by Falstaff's soliloquy on honour (V.i. 130–40), which contrasts with Hotspur's 'By heauen me thinkes it were an easie leape' (I.iii. 201–7). Military glory, which for Hotspur is the most important thing in life, is to Falstaff a 'meere skutchion'. I have suggested that, in the pattern of the play, Falstaff stands for anti-traditionalist attitudes. Plainly, however, he is neither a puritan nor a capitalist, but rather a brigand; the virtues of thrift and hard work are hardly ones that he cultivates. In any case, he is a rich and multifarious character, and is made all the more elusive by his constant habit of play-acting, of putting on a turn. Nevertheless, while he may not be an exponent of New Philosophy, he certainly does call all in doubt, and it is the critical, questioning, rather cynical intellect that makes his attitudes those of a New Man. Moreover, in rejecting all traditional ties and values, Falstaff adopts a predatory self-seeking individualism, and this sometimes expresses itself in terms that remind us very much of Shakespeare's Machevils. There is one very interesting passage in *Henry IV Part 2*, when Falstaff in soliloquy reveals his intention of cheating Shallow if he gets the chance:

Well, ile be acquainted with him if I returne, and t'shal go hard, but ile
make him a philosophers two stones to me, if the yong Dase be a baite
for the old Pike, I see no reason in the law of nature but I may snap at him.
(III.ii. 353–7)

Falstaff justifies his actions by the law of nature, a nature in which
predatory creatures like pike devour the weak; it is 'natural' (and
therefore right) to use your wits to prey on others. This is the Nature
of Edmund and of Hobbes, not that of Aquinas or Hooker,[4] and it
clearly aligns Falstaff with the New Men.

Between Hotspur and Falstaff stands Hal, who tries to combine
chivalry with policy. Before the Battle of Shrewsbury he is given a
build-up as a rival to Hotspur in chivalry:

> I saw yong Harry with his beuer on,
> His cushes on his thighs gallantly armde,
> Rise from the ground like feathered Mercury,
> And vaulted with such ease into his seat,
> As if an Angel drop down from the clouds,
> To turne and wind a fiery Pegasus,
> And witch the world with noble horsemanship.
> (IV.i. 104–10)

At the same time his politic qualities—his detachment, his tendency to a
coldly calculating self-interest—are sufficiently obvious, and are exem-
plified in the 'I know you all' speech (I.ii. 219–41); but Shakespeare
softens the impact of these qualities, not only by means of Hal's
bonhomie, but also by giving us a more extreme case for contrast in
Prince John of Lancaster. Hal's hobnobbing with his tavern cronies
suggests the reliance of the Tudor monarchy on popular support (a
theme which is continued in *Henry V* when the king visits his soldiers
in disguise); Hotspur by contrast is contemptuous of the tavern as
well as of the citizenry. (And when it comes to the push, of course,
the tavern cronies support the crown against the rebels.) Hal not only
stands as a mean between Hotspur and Falstaff: he destroys them
both. At the end of *Henry IV Part 1* Hotspur is killed, outfought by
Hal; at the end of *Henry IV Part 2* Falstaff is rejected, overreached by
Hal. Hal triumphs both in war and in policy, and the field is left clear
for the ideal monarch of *Henry V*, though at the price of removing the
real problems from the world of the play: Henry V is the ideal Tudor
monarch as he might be were it not for awkward people like Falstaff
and Hotspur.

[4] Cf. John F. Danby, *Shakespeare's Doctrine of Nature* (London, 1949), Part I.

71

For obvious reasons, the political parallels between Henry IV and Henry VII, between Prince Hal and Elizabeth I, are not commented on in the plays: they are merely implicit. But in *Henry V* the Lancastrian-Tudor parallel is allowed to become more open. It is most clearly emphasized by the insistence on the king's Welsh connection. The Tudors cultivated their Celtic ancestry as part of their mystique, and it was not for nothing that Henry VII's eldest son was christened Arthur. In *Henry V* the king twice refers to the fact that he is Welsh (IV.i. 51, IV.vii. 110), and Fluellen enlarges on the subject (IV.vii. 12 ff., 111 ff.). The parallel can be allowed to become explicit in this way because Henry V is a figure who can represent the aspirations of the Tudor monarchy: a strong king, bringing internal stability and order, a warrior king who can focus national feeling. The ideal of order, so dear to Tudor propagandists, is stated at length in the famous honey-bee speech (I.ii. 183–204), and is enforced in the execution of the traitors Cambridge, Grey, and Scroop. National feeling is played on by the whole military-patriotic theme of the conquest of France, and is very little qualified; there is indeed Michael Williams's vivid and horrifying picture of all the legs and arms and heads chopped off in battle coming together at the Last Judgment (IV.i. 139 ff.), and there is Burgundy's eloquent speech in praise of peace (V.ii. 23–67); but the overall effect of the play is to canalize patriotic feeling, not to qualify it. At the same time, the use of the four captains, English, Welsh, Irish, and Scots, suggests a national unity larger than that of England alone, and supports Tudor aspirations to the overlordship of the British Isles as a whole.

The failure of the play to qualify adequately its rather simple patriotic-military feeling is one reason why, to the modern reader, it is so much inferior to the *Henry IV* plays. But there are other reasons too. In making Henry V into an ideal monarch and allowing the parallel with the Tudors to emerge fairly clearly, Shakespeare was tying his own hands politically. Of course, an advantage of history plays that straddle two periods is that the author can disclaim implications for his own age which are dangerous and embarrassing; but other people may well insist on them, as the use of *Richard II* by the Essex rebellion illustrates. And in fact in *Henry V* Shakespeare plays safe by extensive whitewashing and suppression. It is not only that the contemporary problems embodied in Hotspur and in Falstaff have been killed off; this might be justified on the grounds that Shakespeare is celebrating the Tudor Peace—a peace foreshadowed by the defeat of the rebels (by policy) in *Henry IV Part 2*, whereupon 'Peace puts forth her oliue euery where' (IV.iv. 87). More serious than this, Shakespeare hushes up or plays down facts of which he was well aware (as can be seen from the other plays), and tends to sweep politics under the carpet.

For example, in *Henry V* there is no mention of any politic motives the king might have for a war with France. At the end of *Henry IV Part 2* the dying Henry IV refers to the 'by-paths, and indirect crookt waies' by which he had come to the crown (IV.v. 185), and explains to Hal that his plans for a Crusade had aimed at diverting men's attention, so that they should not look too closely into his title; and he advises his son, when he succeeds to the throne, to 'busie giddie mindes With forraine quarrells' (IV.v. 214–15). In reply, Hal asserts his determination to hold by force the crown which his father had 'won':

> You won it, wore it, kept it, gaue it me,
> Then plaine and right must my possession be,
> Which I with more then with a common paine,
> Gainst all the world will rightfully maintaine.
> (IV.v. 222–5)

In due course he also takes his father's advice about engaging his subjects in foreign wars, but in *Henry V* no mention is made of the motive urged by Henry IV: Hal is shown as being scrupulously concerned with the justice of his claim and with nothing else. The churchmen may have politic reasons for encouraging the war, but for the king all ulterior motives are excluded.

Another case is the treatment of the conspiracy of Cambridge, Scroop, and Grey. The Chorus to Act II, which introduces the subject, asserts repeatedly that the motivation of the plot was simply money ('treacherous Crownes . . . the Gilt of France . . . The summe is payde'). Exeter rubs in the same idea at the beginning of II.ii ('for a forraigne purse'), and so does the king himself when the conspirators are unmasked ('for a few light Crownes . . . for thy vse . . . forraigne hyer . . . the Golden Earnest of Our death . . . sold your King'). Is not Shakespeare protesting too much? Cambridge himself does indeed hint at another motive:

> For me, the Gold of France did not seduce,
> Although I did admit it as a motiue,
> The sooner to effect what I intended.
> (II.ii. 155–7)

73

But he goes no further than this, and the audience is left in the dark. But of course Shakespeare knew perfectly well what other motive Cambridge might have for the conspiracy, for he had expounded the matter in detail in *Henry VI Part 1*: there (II.v. 61–92) Edmund Mortimer, Earl of March, explains to Richard Plantagenet how Richard's father, the Earl of Cambridge, had married Mortimer's sister, and had rebelled against Henry V in an attempt to restore the Mortimers, who had a better lineal title to the throne than the Lancastrians.[5] But this is politics, and brings up the whole question of the Lancastrian usurpation, and so is not to be tolerated in a play which equates Lancastrian with Tudor and holds up Henry as the ideal king. In Henry's long reproach to the conspirators, the whole emphasis is personal, not political: the tone is one of pained astonishment that a personal friend like Scroop, who had seemed a model nobleman, should have plotted against him (and for money too). It is all very eloquent and high-minded and touching, but comes rather oddly from a playwright who had as much insight into political behaviour as Shakespeare had.

Throughout *Henry V*, the whole question of the Lancastrian usurpation and its consequences is hushed up; this is in strong contrast to the *Henry IV* plays, where the subject is discussed and argued about frequently and at great length. The final Chorus or Epilogue to *Henry V* does refer to what happened under Henry VI: the loss of France, and civil war in England; but it attributes these disasters, not to usurpation, but to the fact that too many people had the managing of the state. In only one place in *Henry V* is the usurpation mentioned—in Henry's prayer before Agincourt:

> Not to day, O Lord,
> O not to day, thinke not vpon the fault
> My Father made, in compassing the Crowne.
> I *Richards* body haue interred new,
> And on it haue bestowed more contrite teares,
> Then from it issued forced drops of blood.
> (IV.i. 310–15)

One is reminded irresistibly of the somewhat similar situation in *Hamlet*, written only a year or two later, when the conscience-stricken

---

[5] In Holinshed, Shakespeare's main source for *Henry V*, it is said (just once) that the conspiracy was undertaken for 'a great summe of monie' from the French king; but, Holinshed adds, some people ('Diverse') say that the real motive was to put the Earl of March on the throne, and that Cambridge's story about the money was told to protect March. See G. Bullough, *Narrative and Dramatic Sources of Shakespeare*, Vol. IV (London, 1962), pp. 384–6.

Claudius tries to pray; but Henry is allowed to get away with it, whereas Claudius is not. Admittedly Claudius's guilt is greater, for he is himself the murderer and usurper, whereas Henry merely profits from murder and usurpation. But Claudius goes to the heart of the problem in a way in which Henry does not:

> forgiue me my foule murther,
> That cannot be since I am still possest
> Of those effects for which I did the murther;
> My Crowne, mine owne ambition, and my Queene;
> May one be pardond and retaine th'offence?
> (III.iii. 52–6)

Can one hang on to the proceeds of the crime, and still be pardoned? This is the question that Henry does not ask, that Shakespeare does not ask; for to ask it is to risk undermining the whole purpose of the play. *Henry V* is the one Shakespeare history-play that sets out to give an uncritical glorification of the Tudor monarchy and its ideals. To do this, Shakespeare suppresses aspects of the history of the period of which he was perfectly aware, and holds in abeyance his own powers of moral and political analysis. It is this fundamental dishonesty that makes the play one of the least satisfactory of all Shakespeare's histories.

7

Shakespeare and 'The Theatre of the World'

HAROLD FISCH

I

RECENT scholarship has pointed with ever greater emphasis to the many references to the theatrical profession in Shakespeare's plays. It is obvious that these constitute a major source of imagery in the work of the early, middle, and later periods. Mr. Leonard F. Dean,[1] for instance, has shown how, in *Richard II*, the notion of a player king provides the key to Richard's behaviour throughout:

> As in a theatre, the eyes of men
> After a well-grac'd actor leaves the stage
> Are idly bent on him that enters next . . .
> (V.ii. 24–6)

says York, expressing this recurrent notion. Richard's abdication is a deliberately and elaborately staged performance, literally, 'a woeful pageant'. Richard III in an earlier play is an even more skilled and versatile actor than Richard II. He consciously fools the other characters to the top of his bent, employing an 'antic disposition' that never flags. Most brilliant of all is the magnificent histrionic flair he exhibits in Act III where, a prayer book in his hand, he enters between two divines in an assumed 'act' of devotion. The play within the play is indeed no isolated device in *Hamlet* but a built-in mechanism of Shakespeare's theatre. It provides, according to Mrs. Anne Righter, the essential link between actor and audience,

---

[1] '*Richard II:* the State and the Image of the Theatre', *P.M.L.A.*, LXVII (1952), 211f.

adjusting the reality of the one world to that of the other taking the place of the extra-dramatic address so often found in medieval drama.[2] When Shakespeare's plays are narrowly examined it will be found that few of them lack the element of pageant, masque, or dramatic spectacle. King Lear performs a crazy act in which he brings Goneril and Regan to a mock-trial. Brutus calls upon his friends to wash their hands in Caesar's blood: the deliberately histrionic moment is defined by Cassius in the words

> How many ages hence
> Shall this our lofty scene be acted over
> In states unborn and accents yet unknown!
> (III.i. 111–13)

and Brutus chimes in with:

> How many times shall Caesar bleed in sport,
> That now on Pompey's basis lies along
> No worthier than the dust!
> (III.i. 115–17)

Mrs. Righter does well to point out that words like 'act', 'scene', 'part', 'tragedy', 'pageant', and other words connected with the profession of acting have a persistent frequency in Shakespeare's plays, becoming more functional and organic as his drama proceeds.[3] 'My dismal *scene* I needs must *act* alone' says Romeo before he makes his well-rehearsed entrance into Juliet's tomb. Here is a little performance which goes wrong because one of the actors fails to come in on his cue, and towards the end of Shakespeare's career Paulina stages a fabulous act in *The Winter's Tale*, by unveiling before Leontes the statue of his wife Hermione, and 'we are mocked with art'. In Shakespeare's final play Prospero is nothing other than a great stage-manager, organizing the meetings of Ferdinand and Miranda, keeping his eye on the doings of the various actors, and indeed mounting the whole tempest and its consequences through his theatrical art, the 'insubstantial pageant' which he says resembles the 'great globe itself'. This phrase reminds us that the Globe theatre is said to have carried upon it the legend 'Totus mundus agit histrionem'.

The comparison of the world to a stage and all the people in it to actors is an ancient commonplace, going back, as Curtius has shown, to classical times, and vividly revived in the twelfth century by John

[2] *Shakespeare and the Idea of the Play* (London, 1964), pp. 66, 84.
[3] *ib*. pp. 89–95.

of Salisbury.[4] In the sixteenth century it was a well-established popular notion to be found in song-books, pamphlets, poetry, and plays.

> All the world's a stage

says Jaques,

> And all the men and women merely players,

and Antonio assures his friends at the beginning of Act I of *The
Merchant of Venice*

> I hold the world but as the world, Gratiano;
> A stage where every man must play a part,
> And mine a sad one. (I.i. 76–8)

There is certainly nothing uniquely Shakespearean about this
trope. In the first place, it functions, both for Shakespeare and
other dramatists, as a means of intensifying the reality of the stage
performance by making the actors refer to a world of illusion which
contrasts with the supposed reality of what they are doing. By a system
of mirrors their world is made to seem like a real world and the play
within the play is the illusion. A similar device is used by MacLeish
in *J.B.*[5] But the play image has a parallel function relevant both to
Shakespeare and to the contemporary theatre of the absurd; it is
that of reducing the world *outside* the theatre to the level of the stage.
It suggests, as Mrs. Righter says, that 'elements of illusion are present
in ordinary life'. 'When we are born,' says King Lear, 'we cry that
we are come To this great stage of fools' (IV.vi. 86–7). Such comparisons of the world to a stage are indeed part of a commonplace
reflection on the vanity of the world. The world is Vanity Fair:
what happens in it has the illusory, tinsel quality of a stage performance. 'All the men and women *merely* players.' The word 'merely'
underlines the idea of the eternal sameness of the play. Life is a *mere*
show, a *mere* stage performance. Our life is to that extent artificial
and inauthentic, appearance and reality linked together in an ever-
shifting and uncertain relationship, as in the *La vida es sueno* of

---

[4] E. R. Curtius, *European Literature and the Latin Middle Ages* (trans. Willard B.
Trask, New York, 1953), p. 139 f.

[5] There we have two levels, the 'real' world of J.B. and his family to which we attri-
bute a mode of existence comparable with our own, and the world of Nickles and Mr.
Zuss which is professedly theatrical. As Mr. Zuss says: 'At least we're actors. They're
not actors. Never acted anything.' (*J.B.*, Riverside Press, Cambridge, Mass., 1958,
p. 5.) Here it is quite obvious that the attribution to Zuss and Nickles of a 'mere' stage
existence serves to enhance the degree of real existence which we ascribe to the fate of
J.B. and his family and so causes us to relate their destiny to what happens in our own
world: whilst at the same time the theological or metaphysical aspect of the Job-plot
is treated as relatively unreal. We accept God and Satan as participants in the story
on their own terms, *viz* as 'merely players'.

Calderon where the hero—in a situation resembling that of Christopher Sly—declares,

> What is life? An illusion, a shadow, a story. And the greatest good is little enough: for all life is a dream, and dreams themselves are only dreams.[6]

It seems that these are the agreed interpretations of the trope for the many critics who have concerned themselves with it, and it certainly cannot be disputed that the stage-metaphors and all the associated references and verbal indications do serve to underline the illusory quality of human life as an empty show. Moreover, it has been noted that such imagery 'is scarcely flattering to the theatre . . . [it] expresses not only the hollowness of life, but also the degradation and stupidity of the actor's profession'.[7] Now I am going to suggest that this whole reading of the trope does less than justice to the complexity of Shakespeare's moral vision, and that like other systems of imagery in Shakespeare's plays this trope is fundamentally dialectical. If it suggests the illusoriness of life, it affirms by the same token its infinite meaningfulness and reality.

II

To illustrate the complex character of the stage-metaphors in Shakespeare's major drama, we can do no better than turn briefly to *Macbeth* and *Hamlet,* two plays which are often noted as particularly rich examples of this type of imagery. Mr. V. Y. Kantak begins his discussion of *Macbeth*[8] with the poor-player speech in Act V:

> Out, out, brief candle!
> Life's but a walking shadow; a poor player,
> That struts and frets his hour upon the stage,
> And then is heard no more: it is a tale
> Told by an idiot, full of sound and fury,
> Signifying nothing.   (V.v. 23–8)

Mr. Kantak rightly relates the image of the poor player to the 'borrowed robes' of Act I—'Why do you dress me in borrow'd robes?' (I.i. 108–9). Caroline Spurgeon had drawn attention to the frequent

---

[6] From the translation of Edward and Elizabeth Huberman in *Spanish Drama*, ed. Angel Flores (Baatam Classics. New York 1962), p. 225. A more schematic use of the theatre image to suggest the mingling of illusion and reality is found in the same dramatist's *El gran teatro del mundo*, though tnere the religious meaning of the trope is uppermost.

[7] Anne Righter, *op. cit.*, p. 169.

[8] 'An Approach to Shakespearean Tragedy: the "Actor" Image in *Macbeth*', *Shakespeare Survey*, XVI, pp. 42–52.

use of images of clothing, especially ill-fitting clothing in this play,[9] but its true significance is revealed in the light of the poor player speech. Macbeth is a poor player: therefore he is naturally dressed in borrowed robes.[10] Just as naturally he 'mocks the time with fairest show' (I.vii. 81), and just as naturally he remarks that he has strange things in his head

Which must be acted, ere they may be scanned. (III.iv. 139–40)

Similarly the painted faces of the grooms and the daggers 'unmannerly breached with gore' says Mr. Kantak 'have all a reference however dim to the mechanics of theatrical action'.[11] So far one may agree with both Mr. Kantak and Mrs. Righter who independently of one another had reached similar conclusions about the stage-metaphors as giving unity to the various strands of imagery in the play. The problem arises when one comes to evaluate the total function and meaning of this metaphor. Does it suggest simply, in reference to Macbeth, the 'automation of the stage-actor' as Mr. Kantak remarks —the hollowness of an illusory existence which has lost all its meaning? The comparison of the world to a theatre and of the people in it to actors had certainly served to 'stress the empty, ephemeral nature of life on earth' and certainly this represents the main direction of Macbeth's thinking in the fifth act. His 'way of life is fall'n into the sere, the yellow leaf': its permanent value has been lost, and therefore he speaks of himself as a poor player who struts and frets his hour upon the stage—performing a meaningless act surrounded by phantoms and clothed in borrowed costume.

From this point of view, Macbeth in his borrowed robes is like one of the characters in Jean Genet's horrifying play, *Le Balcon*, where the Bishop, the Judge, and the General also wear clothes that are too big for them! For Genet the world is a stage in which the actors are driven by a compulsive make-believe bordering on perversion. There is in such a world, nothing real, nothing permanent, nothing true. The Chief of Police who, it seems, has a *real* role in a *real* battle is ultimately shown as desiring nothing more than that his poses and gestures may be mimed in a world of fantasies. But such nihilism is far from the final meaning of *Macbeth*: Shakespeare is not 'our contemporary' to that extent, in spite of Jan Kott. If Macbeth sees himself as a poor player and thinks of his life as a tale signifying

[9] *Shakespeare's Imagery* (Cambridge, 1952), pp. 325–6.
[10] See also Anne Righter, *op. cit.*, p. 131.
[11] *op. cit.*, p. 50.

nothing—we surely do not come away from the play thinking that his act has been meaningless and insignificant. We are rather impressed with the fact that Macbeth is the actor in a drama which had the *maximum* of meaning—a drama of damnation. Is not the actor image essentially ambivalent? For whilst it implies on the one hand that life is a play of phantoms, a meaningless repeated cycle, in another sense surely it implies that life has the gripping significance of a dramatic plot, that it has design, intention, purpose. It may serve to introduce something not *less*, but *more* meaningful than the neutrality of a non-dramatic order of existence. The world of nature is without pattern; but the world of drama is full of pattern—a mighty maze but not without a plan. If we analyse carefully the origins of the *theatrum mundi* trope we shall see that it carries this dialectical possibility with it from the Christian middle ages and earlier. For St. Paul (I *Cor.* 4, 9) God appointed the apostles as a spectacle (theatron) for the world, angels and men; and Luther spoke of the drama of justification. He meant that the pattern of sin, grace, and election had the gripping and exciting quality of a dramatic plot. We wait with bated breath for the next scene of the drama. Life is given a new and miraculous significance by the awareness of a divine dramatist who has the business of our existence in hand. Such is the further meaning of the histrionic imagery in *Macbeth*, and this is confirmed by a more careful attention to what might be termed the dynamics of that imagery. Macbeth's question is, 'Why do you dress me in borrow'd robes?' This is different from Genet. He does not willingly undertake the role of actor: he feels that it is thrust upon him. He is a man who steps forward and suddenly finds himself on the boards of a theatre, before the lights, summoned to play a part for which, like Christopher Sly, he feels himself not quite fitted. We may note also the syntactical disposition of the play-image in the lines

> Strange things I have in head, that will to hand,
> Which must be acted, ere they may be scann'd.

I would wish to draw attention to the phrase 'which must be acted' —there is here a feeling of constraint. Macbeth is indeed called upon to play his part in what Luther called the drama of justification—or perhaps one should read in his case, 'the drama of reprobation'. For he is the man who, rather as in the Calvinist scheme, is elected for damnation. He may think his acting is a testimony to the meaningless futile quality of earthly existence, but we know better.

Harold Fisch

It is necessary to point out, though the point would seem obvious enough, that the *fons et origo* of the theatre metaphor is not in Macbeth himself: it is not the fruit of his introspection. It derives from the metaphysical order which surrounds him. To be quite precise, it originates from the witches. They are the stagiest of the figures that move about in the play, and Macbeth steps forward literally onto the stage that they have set for him to act on. This is born out by numerous verbal indications relating the witches to a stage play, even if it were not clear enough from their actual appearance and function. This feature deserves to be given weight. Banquo exclaims

> Are ye *fantastical*, or that indeed
> Which outwardly ye *show*? (I.ii. 53–4) (my italics)

Their histrionic character is made clear in the word 'fantastical'. It is they who later on produce for Macbeth the play within the play, namely the three apparitions and the show of eight kings. If not the actual authors of the plot in which Macbeth is acting, they have at least an important executive role. Theirs is the antic disposition from which Macbeth's own character as actor takes its rise.

> I'll charm the air to give a sound,
> While you perform your antic round (IV.i. 129–30)

—says Witch number one to her fellows. They too seem to have a hand in the final *tour de théatre*, the most theatrical moment of all— the marching of Birnam wood to Dunsinane, the final illusion which overthrows reality. Here is the histrionic frame for Macbeth's final act corresponding with the heath onto which he steps in Act I. In both cases Macbeth is the unwilling actor in a play not of his own devising. The player image in Act V thus takes on a certain dialectical character: it suggests a meaningless futile existence: but on the other hand, it also suggests an existence having the intensity of significance which we associate with a dramatic plot. This dialectic may be expressed differently. The stage-metaphor is Shakespeare's specific way of articulating the balance of free-will and determinism in Macbeth's life. To the extent that he steps forward unwillingly onto a stage which is prepared for him, he is the victim of a plot mounted by the metaphysical Spirits and Powers; but to the extent that he is an actor who deliberately chooses to play a part, to 'mock the time with fairest show' he is the author of his own tragedy. Shakespeare's characters here are not unlike the characters in the theatre of Pirandello. On the one hand they are controlled by a dramatic plot—on the other they are 'in search of an author'—strutting and fretting their hour in a scene of make-believe of their own devising. The duality of the theatre image is well conveyed by Macbeth's first reaction to his ennoblement as thane of Cawdor:

> Two truths are told,
> As happy prologue to the swelling act
> Of the imperial theme.   (I.iii. 127–8)

The 'swelling act' suggests that 'vaunting ambition' which prompts him to assume titles not his own and to create his own false theatrical world of pseudo-reality. But in another sense this is the happy prologue to the dramatic vision which the witches have revealed to him— that is the swelling act. They have supernaturally solicited him: they have drawn him into the charmed circle of a dramatic *schema* which both transcends and encloses the ordinary non-dramatic world of mere 'natural' existence.

This I think sufficiently demonstrates the moral depth of Shakespeare's use of the trope. The same dialectical pattern is revealed in *Hamlet*. Hamlet is acting throughout. So much so, that Mr. Maynard Mack has been prompted to suggest that the central question of *Hamlet* (which reaches its most crucial formulation in the second great soliloquy) is: 'When is an act not an act?,[12] Hamlet puts on an antic disposition: he also puts on a dramatic performance the object of which is to strip the world of illusion and falsehood and arrive at the unvarnished truth. The play is full of actors—there are the 'tragedians of the city': there is also Polonius who acted the part of Julius Caesar in his younger days: and there is Claudius who may smile and smile and be a villain—he is a player king, a king of shreds and patches. Hamlet undertakes to act a part in order to expose the false behaviour of the others and to reveal the truth which lurks behind and beneath the world of illusion. He is a kind of dramatist, inventing and acting out his own plot: but as long as he only thinks of it as his own plot, he cannot break through the net of illusion, of treachery, vanity, and absurdity which surrounds him. With all his desire to find a true mode of *action*, he continues until Act IV to perform the empty gestures of a mere 'actor' unpacking his heart with words. But again it is necessary to insist that Hamlet is, like Macbeth, involved in a larger drama, not one of his own invention,

[12] 'The World of Hamlet' in *Shakespeare: Modern Essays in Criticism*, ed. L. F. Dean (New York, 1961), p. 248.

and that it is the rhythm of this larger drama that finally directs his existence. As with Macbeth, so with Hamlet, the dramatic role given him comes from the world beyond: its source is to be located in the words and behaviour of the ghost. Horatio speaks of the ghost as a 'fantasy' and an 'illusion', and Hamlet likewise using the vocabulary of the theatre says, 'Thou comest in such a questionable shape That I will speak to thee'. This 'fellow in the cellarage' then functions like the witches in *Macbeth* (though in an opposite sense) as the manager of a supernatural stage play, and Hamlet's assumption of the theatrical metaphor is in keeping with the acceptance of the task imposed on him by this very theatrical visitor from beyond. Hamlet steps forward like Macbeth onto a stage already set for him, and becomes the unwilling actor in a drama the origin of which is to be sought in a supernatural soliciting. The theatrical imagery thus points finally to a providential plot or design in which Hamlet acts, a plot shaped by that same divinity which shapes our ends. As Dolly Winthrop says in *Silas Marner*, 'There's dealings?'

Hamlet's recognition of the larger design in which human destiny is contained finally comes to him—as critics have generally recognized—on the voyage to England. Still using the play-metaphor, he then seizes the opportunity which Providence (the word may carry its full theological load) has wonderfully afforded him:

> Ere I could make a prologue to my brains
> They had begun the play . . . (V.ii. 30–1)

And thus he sends his two friends to their death and sails back to Denmark to await the next Act of the drama which he senses is now in progress. He is acutely aware that every trivial circumstance is loaded with meaning: there is a providence in the fall of a sparrow: and all he has to do is wait attentively for his cue, for 'the readiness is all'. It arrives appropriately and incongruously enough with the entry of Osric (another antic-figure) and, in accepting the challenge of Laertes, he explicitly abjures his right to manage his own stage performance: he acknowledges himself to be an actor in a larger drama, a drama leading to death and salvation. This is the significance of the last act of the play. The duel is another stage performance, and he addresses the survivors as 'mutes and audience to this *act*'. This act is the final stage of the drama which had been initiated with the first summons of the ghost, and now that he has reached the end of his task, the trumpets sound for him on the other side—a moment well established for us in the closing words of Horatio: 'And flights of angels sing thee to thy rest.' There is no doubt that the 'act' here to which Hamlet refers no longer signifies an illusion or a fantasy: it rather suggests a scene fraught with destiny —truly an 'act' in the drama of salvation.

III

There is no doubt that in the seventeenth century development of this *topos* the second meaning is uppermost. Instead of reinforcing the idea of an illusory or meaningless form of existence, the world-theatre metaphor strongly suggests a providential pattern or plot. The history of man has an aim and meaning which the observer— like a good theatregoer—can observe. Thus Joseph Hall in 1605:

> The World is a stage; every man an actor, and plaies his part, here, either in a Comedie, or Tragedie. The good man is a Comedian; which (however he begins) ends merrily: but the wicked man acts a Tragedie; and therefore ends ever in horrour. Thou seest a wicked man vaunt himself on this stage: stay till the last act, and looke to his end (as *David* did) and see whether that be peace. Thou wouldest make strange Tragedies if thou wouldest have but one Act. Who sees an Oxe, grazing in a fat and ranke pasture, and thinkes not that he is neere to the slaughter? whereas the leane beast, that toiles under the yoke, is farre enough from the shambles. The best wicked man cannot be so envied in his first shewes, as he is pitiable in the conclusion.
>
> (*Meditations and Vowes*, Book II, sect. 30)

The wicked man 'vaunting himself on this stage' in the first act well fits the situation of Macbeth. Perhaps Shakespeare had even read this passage in Hall! The same thought with an even graver emphasis is found in the Preface to Sir Walter Ralegh's great *History of the World* (1614):

> For seeing God, who is the Author of all our Tragedies, hath written out for us, and appointed us all the Parts we are to Play, and hath not, in their distribution, been partial to the most mighty Princes of the World . . . why should other Men, who are but as the least worms, complain of wrongs?

These words could be read as a footnote to Calderon's morality play, *El gran teatro del mundo* of 1642. In the later seventeenth century the idea of a moral drama is enlarged and deepened to form a vision of universal history even more detailed in its reference to the theatre than that of Ralegh. Henry More in the second of his *Divine Dialogues* (1668) is concerned with God's providence as revealed in the world of

G 85

Nature. He believes it is a drama proceeding from the beginning of time to the millenium. Behind it, there is a divine dramatist: so that this drama is not a meaningless and repetitive cycle as in the speech of Jaques in *As You Like It:* but it is an unrepeatable performance, co-extensive with historical time. As a result, each event is important; it is full of meaning. Every flower is a symbol; every eclipse, an event loaded with dramatic weight. We are, he says, 'the spectators of this terrestrial stage play', and we are to observe 'the admirable windings of Providence in her Dramatick Plot which has been acting on this Stage of the Earth from the beginning of the World'. Nor do we ever see the whole plot. 'We cannot,' he says, 'judge the tendency of what is past or acting or present' but we are to attend patiently to what he calls 'the entrance of the last Act, which shall bring in righteousness in triumph'.

The quotation from Henry More shows us the full religious implication of this image. We are no longer concerned with the individual comedies and tragedies of human life, but with a grand universal pageant, in which God, Man, and Nature meaningfully collaborate. It becomes a metaphor for the covenant history of the world beginning with Creation, climaxed by Revelation, and culminating in the Salvation promised at the end of days.[13]

The metaphor of the stage, in fact, is fundamentally ambiguous. It has a biblical as well as a classical force. As a Greek metaphor—which is how it began—it suggests the cyclical, repetitive nature of time: it suggests the eternal sameness of things, their illusory quality, the emptiness of mere appearance. This is how Plato saw the world of phenomena. But as an adoptively Hebraic image—and in More it has been thoroughly Hebraized—it suggests the absolute and portentious quality of history itself as a covenant drama stretching from Adam to doomsday, a drama having room for both divine action and human freedom, promise and fulfilment.[14] As far as Shakespeare is concerned, it may be claimed that his plays, through such systems of imagery as the one before us, evoke both the Hebraic and Hellenic modes of existence. Nor does he show us the one mode conquering the other, but he rather suffers them to confront one another in an unmitigated dialectic. Only by recognizing this can we do justice to the complexity and richness of his imaginative statement.

[13] For further discussion, see, by the present author, *Jerusalem and Albion* (London, 1964), pp. 198–9.

[14] Cf. T. F. Driver, *The Sense of History in Greek and Shakespearean Drama* (New York, 1960), p. 129, and *passim.*

8

The Conclusion of *The Winter's Tale*

KENNETH MUIR

I

CHARLOTTE LENNOX in *Shakespeare Illustrated* (1753) spoke of the statue scene in *The Winter's Tale* as 'a mean and absurd contrivance':

for can it be imagined that Hermione, a virtuous and affectionate wife, would conceal herself during sixteen years in a solitary house, though she was sensible that her repentant husband was all that time consuming away with grief and remorse for her death: and what reason could she have for chusing to live in such a miserable confinement when she might have been happy in the possession of her husband's affection and have shared his throne? How ridiculous also in a great Queen, on so interesting an occasion, to submit to such buffoonery as standing on a pedestal, motionless, her eyes fixed, and at last to be conjured down by a magical command of Paulina.

Mrs. Lennox concludes that Greene's novel 'has nothing in it half so low and improbable as this contrivance of the statue', and that the play is 'greatly inferior to the old paltry story that furnished him with the subject of it'.

A German critic, Heinrich Bulthaupt (1889) makes a similar complaint. He finds it incredible that the Hermione of the first part of the play would consent to 'this farce of a statue' and he declares that every charm 'is put to flight by the every-recurring dense, rationalistic preparation of the scene';

Instead of using some means full of the miraculous, Shakespeare lets Paulina play Providence. Thus the scaffolding creaks in all its joints; human passion and grandeur are inconceivably mingled with the affectation of a comedian. Our tragic sympathy, our moral indignation has been quickened,—but she, whom we commiserated, trifles away our sympathy with a living statue which she represents, and the man, for whom we wished the heaviest punishment, garners the fairest harvest of indulgent fate. A plot which should have been treated only as a tragedy, is, without justification, conducted to a superficial end of reconciliation.

A number of critics have likewise complained of the penultimate scene of the play in which the discovery of Perdita's birth is reported in ornate prose instead of being displayed on the stage. Dr. Johnson remarked: 'It was, I suppose, only to spare his own labour that the poet put the whole scene into narrative'. Hartley Coleridge suggested that Shakespeare was in a hurry; that he could compose this sort of dialogue with the least aid from inspiration; and Gervinus said that Shakespeare wisely reported the recognition of Perdita, 'otherwise the play would have been too full of powerful scenes', to which Q retorted:

> If we really prefer this sort of thing, . . . then Heaven must be our aid. But if, using our own judgement, we read the play and put ourselves into the place of its first audience, I ask, are we not baulked? In proportion as we have paid tribute to the art of the story by letting our interest be intrigued, our emotion excited, are we not cheated when Shakespeare lets us down with this reported tale?

Lytton Strachey, it will be remembered, had declared that Shakespeare, while he was writing his last plays, was bored with both life and drama; and T. S. Eliot, putting it more positively, remarked that Shakespeare had ceased to be interested in character as such: he had gone 'beyond the dramatic'.

The two main complaints made by critics of the denouement of *The Winter's Tale* are that the reported recognition of Perdita is undramatic and lazy, and that the statue scene is both incredible in itself and false to the character of Hermione. Let us first consider the second complaint. It is significant that the complaints were made by readers rather than spectators. Spectators, even when they saw only eighteenth century adaptations, did not share the disapproval of many of the critics. Mrs. Inchbald, who foolishly included Garrick's adaptation in her collection of the *British Theatre*, admitted that when Mrs. Siddons played Hermione, the statue scene was 'far more grand in exhibition than the reader will possibly behold in idea'; and Thomas Campbell, the poet, replying to Mrs. Lennox remarked dryly: 'Mrs. Lennox says, that the statue scene is low and ridiculous.

The Conclusion of The Winter's Tale

I am sure Mrs. Siddons used to make it appear to us in a different light'. Campbell had the advantage of being Mrs. Siddons' biographer; and in describing her performance he said:

> Mrs. Siddons looked the statue, even to literal illusion; and, whilst the drapery hid her lower limbs, it showed a beauty of head, neck, shoulders and arms, that Praxitiles might have studied. This statue scene has hardly its parallel for enchantment even in Shakespeare's theatre. The star of his genius was at its zenith when he composed it; but it was only a Siddons that could do justice to its romantic perfection. The heart of everyone who saw her when she burst from the semblance of sculpture into motion, and embraced her daughter, Perdita, must throb and glow at the recollection.

There are more detailed accounts of performances of the statue scene by Macready and Helen Faucit in 1847. Helen Faucit herself gave a full account of the performance in her book *On Some of Shakespeare's Female Characters*[1] and there are long reviews in contemporary newspapers. Helen Faucit's performance was described as 'the finest combination of Grecian sculpture, Italian painting and British acting, that has in our day been seen on the stage'. Another reviewer said 'It was the most entrancing thing we ever remember to have seen—actually suspending the blood, and taking the breath away. It was something supernatural almost'. Hermione has a long period in which she does not speak, and in the space of 160 lines she had only one short speech, addressed not to Leontes but to Perdita. In Euripides' play, when Herakles brings back Alcestis from the grave, she remains completely silent for the rest of the play; and although there is no evidence that Shakespeare had read *Alcestis*, he seems to have shared Euripides' dramatic tact in this particular. But it is nevertheless difficult for the actress playing Hermione. It is a great strain on the nerves and muscles, as Helen Faucit observed, to stand motionless for so long, when even a movement of the eyelashes would destroy the illusion. Helen Faucit was helped by the fact that her arm was resting on a pedestal. But when music sounded, and she turned her head to let her eyes rest on Leontes, this had 'a startling, magnetic effect upon all'. She moved down the steps from the dais and paused at a short distance from Leontes. 'At first he stood speechless, as if turned to stone; his face with an awe-struck look upon it.' When Paulina says 'Nay, present your hand', Leontes advanced, hesitantly, and touched the hand held out to him. Then he cried, 'O, she's warm!' These words were deleted from many acting

---

[1] Helena Faucit, *On Some of Shakespeare's Female Characters* (1891, pp. 337–92).

versions, for fear they should raise a laugh, but the tone in which they were spoken impressed critics of both Macready and Gielgud. Helen Faucit had been warned, at one of the rehearsals, to be prepared for something extraordinary—but it was not until the first performance before an audience that she realized the point of the warning. Macready's joy at finding Hermione alive seemed uncontrollable. 'Now he was prostrate at her feet, then enfolding her in his arms.' The veil covering her head and neck fell off. Her hair came unbound and fell over her shoulders and Macready kissed and caressed it. The change in Macready was so sudden and overwhelming, that Helen Faucit cried out. Macready whispered to her 'Don't be frightened, my child! Don't be frightened! Control yourself'. As this went on, the audience were tumultuously applauding, with a sound like a storm of hail. When Perdita and Florizel knelt at her feet, Hermione looked, she was told, 'like Niobe, all tears'.

I have described this performance at some length to show that, however much the scene might be criticized in the study, it created a tremendous effect in the theatre; so much so, that at one performance, at Edinburgh, when Hermione descended from her pedestal, 'the audience simultaneously rose from their seats, as if drawn out of them by surprise and reverential awe at the presence of one who bore more of heaven than of earth about her'. As one Scottish critic said: 'When she descended from her pedestal, with a slow and gliding motion, and wearing the look of being consecrated by long years of prayer and sorrow and seclusion, it seemed to us as if we looked upon a being almost too pure to be gazed on with unveiled eyes'; and an Irish critic said 'We think not then of the symmetry of form, the perfection of outline, so far beyond the rarest achievements of art. For the spirit which breathes from the face, where grief has long grown calm, and suffering brightened into a heavenly pity, in the pure world of thought—the spirit which bears within it so much of heaven, with all that is best of earth, alone possesses our every faculty'.

These critics, in some ways typically Victorian, express themselves in a rather sentimental way; but they illustrate the impact of the scene on the spectators, and they show that Shakespeare had triumphantly overcome the improbabilities of his fable. The methods by which he achieved this triumph were well analysed in a preface written by Granville-Barker in 1912, but not included in his collected prefaces. He shows that Shakespeare prepares the audience:

through Paulina's steward, almost to the pitch of revelation, saving just so much surprise, and leaving so little, that when they see the statue they may think themselves more in doubt than they really are whether it is Hermione herself or no. He prepares Leontes, who feels that his wife's spirit might walk again: who is startled by the strange air of Hermione that the yet unknown Perdita breathes out; who, his egotism killed, has become simple of speech, simple-minded, receptive.

Barker goes on to speak of the way in which the previous scene postpones the revelation, and of the way in which, from the moment the statue is disclosed, 'every minor contrast of voice and mood that can give the scene modelling and beauty of form, is brought into easy use'. Music is used, as so often in the last plays, to create the appropriate atmosphere; and the alarm and scepticism of Camillo and Polixenes contrast with the rapture of Leontes. Above all, Shakespeare avoids what lesser dramatists would have indulged, any speeches of noble forgiveness. Robert Greene, for example, in *James IV*, makes his Dorothea forgive her erring husband in words which illustrate what Barker describes:

> Shame me not, Prince, companion to my bed.
> Youth has misled—tut! but a little fault.

The 'little fault' had consisted of attempted murder.

The actors taught the critics that the statue scene, far from being absurd, could be overwhelmingly effective on the stage; and no critic during the past hundred years has echoed Mrs. Lennox's complaints, with the sole exception of Robert Bridges. But, of course, a scene could be immensely effective on the stage without being satisfying to the reader, and without being great drama.

II

The first critic of *The Winter's Tale*, the astrologer, Dr. Simon Forman, who witnessed a performance at the Globe on 15th May, 1611, mentions the fact that Perdita is restored to her father after sixteen years and he gives a description of Autolycus,—from whom he deduced the moral that one should 'beware of trusting feigned beggars or fawning fellows'. But, oddly enough, he does not mention the statue scene or the restoration of Hermione. This has led some critics to suppose that in its original form Shakespeare's play was closer to its source, Greene's *Pandosto*, and though it is unlikely that he made Leontes fall in love with Perdita and commit suicide when he realized that she was his daughter, it is possible that Hermione was not restored to life. This receives some support from the fact that Hermione appears to Antigonus in a dream; this is not, of course, decisive, even though it leads the audience to assume that Hermione is dead. But if in the play, as Dr. Forman saw it, Hermione was not restored—and her restoration is not hinted at by the oracle—Shakespeare must have attempted to round off his tragi-comedy with the restoration of Perdita to her father, and the reconciliation of Leontes and Polixenes through the marriage of their children. The reconciliation would have been less satisfying than that in *Cymbeline* and *The Tempest*; and, on the whole, I think that the restoration of Hermione must have been part of Shakespeare's original plan.

By his jealousy Leontes has brought on himself a sixfold tragedy.[2] 1. He has lost his beloved wife. 2. He has lost his best friend. 3. He has lost his son and heir. 4. He has lost his new-born daughter. 5. He has lost his faithful councillor Camillo. 6. He has lost his faithful servant, Antigonus. At the end of the play he regains his wife, his friend, his daughter and his councillor; he obtains a son-in-law, who will rule in Sicilia instead of Mamillius; and only Antigonus, pursued by a bear, is not restored. The pattern of reconciliation fits in with that of the other Romances. In *Pericles*, the hero is reunited in the last act with his wife and daughter, and the daughter marries. In *Cymbeline* Posthumus is reunited to the wife he thought dead; Cymbeline recovers his lost daughter and her brothers. In *The Tempest*, Prospero is reconciled with his enemies, and the reconciliation is cemented by the marriage of Ferdinand and Miranda. In both *The Tempest* and *The Winter's Tale* the marriage of the children unites two thrones. But the denouement of *The Winter's Tale* differs from that of the other plays. In *Pericles* we have seen how Thaisa is restored to life by the medical skill of Cerimon, and we do not share Pericles' delusion that both Thaisa and Marina are dead. We know, therefore, that all may come right in the end. In *Cymbeline* we know that Pisanio has refused to obey his master's orders and that he has spared Imogen; and even when Fidele apparently dies, only a few minutes elapse between her funeral and her recovery from the drug. But in *The Winter's Tale* the audience is not let into the secret. News is brought by Paulina that Hermione is dead:

> O Lords,
> When I have said, cry woe: the Queen, the Queen,

[2] Cf. R. G. Moulton, *The Moral System of Shakespeare* (1903), p. 84.

The sweet'st, dear'st creature's dead: and vengeance for't
Not dropp'd down yet . . .
I say she's dead: I'll swear't. If word, nor oath
Prevail not, go and see: if you can bring
Tincture, or lustre in her lip, her eye
Heat outwardly, or breath within, I'll serve you
As I would do the Gods.   (III.ii. 200–8)

Leontes asks Paulina to take him to the dead bodies of Hermione
and Mamillius—'One grave shall be for both'. In the last scene
Leontes says of his wife:

I saw her
(As I thought) dead: and have (in vain) said many
A prayer upon her grave.   (V.iii. 139–41)

In between these passages there are many references to Hermione's
death. More significant is Antigonus' account of his vision of the
ghost of Hermione: he says to the babe on the coast of Bohemia:

thy Mother
Appear'd to me last night: for ne'er was dream
So like a waking. To me comes a creature,
Sometimes her head on one side, some another,
I never saw a vessel of like sorrow,
So filled, and so becoming: in pure white robes
Like very sanctity she did approach
My cabin where I lay: thrice bow'd before me
And (gasping to begin some speech) her eyes
Became two spouts; the fury spent, anon
Did this break from her. 'Good Antigonus,
Since Fate (against thy better disposition)
Hath made thy person for the thrower-out
Of my poor babe, according to thine oath,
Places remote enough are in Bohemia;
There weep, and leave it crying: and for the babe
Is counted lost for ever, Perdita
I prithee call't: For this ungentle business
Put on thee by my Lord, thou ne'er shalt see
Thy wife Paulina more'? And so, with shrieks,
She melted into air. Affrighted much,
I did in time collect myself, and thought
This was so, and no slumber. Dreams are toys,
Yet for this once, yea superstitiously,
I will be squar'd by this. I do believe
Hermione hath suffer'd death.   (III.iii. 17–42)

The vision behaves as a ghost, chooses a name for her daughter,

93

and prophesies Antigonus' death. I think there can be no doubt that even if Shakespeare did not intend Hermione to be dead at this point in the play, he intended us to think so. For this he has been taken to task by Professor B. Evans. Shakespeare does not normally deceive his audience. If he had written Jonson's *Silent Woman* he would have revealed early in the play that the supposed woman was a boy, as he lets us know, but not the characters on the stage, that Ganymede is Rosalind, that Fidele is Imogen, that Cesario is Viola, that Sebastian is not dead, that Marina is not dead, that the learned doctor is Portia, that the Friar in *Measure for Measure* is the Duke.

Why, then does Shakespeare in *The Winter's Tale* violate his normal principles of dramaturgy and leave us to suppose that Hermione is dead and buried? Some critics blame the influence of Beaumont and Fletcher, who put up a much higher value on surprise than Shakespeare ever did.

There is, of course, plenty of evidence that Beaumont and Fletcher were acquainted with Shakespeare's plays, and some slight evidence that Shakespeare knew Beaumont and Fletcher's. They wrote, after all, for the same company; and Fletcher and Shakespeare collaborated in *The Two Noble Kinsmen* and *Cardenio*, if not in *Henry VIII*. There are obvious resemblances between *Philaster* and *Cymbeline*; but as we don't know the exact dates of the plays, we don't know which dramatist was the imitator. If Shakespeare was imitating Beaumont and Fletcher, as Thorndike and others have argued, he transformed the material he borrowed. This can be seen from the fact that whereas in all the romances from *Pericles* to *The Tempest*, Shakespeare was concerned with reconciliation and reunion, and, in the three plays for which he was wholly responsible, with forgiveness, the tragi-comedies of Beaumont and Fletcher, though theatrically effective, have no such theme. The difference can be seen equally clearly, if one compares short passages which are clearly related to each other. A character in *Philaster*, for example, addresses a bank covered with wild flowers:

> Bear me, thou gentle bank,
> For ever, if thou wilt. You sweet ones all,
> Let me unworthy press you: I could wish
> I rather were a corse strewed o'er with you
> Than quick above you.   (IV.i)

In the fourth act of *The Winter's Tale*, Perdita ends her flower-catalogue with the words:

94

The Conclusion of The Winter's Tale

> O, these I lack
> To make you garlands of, and my sweet friend,
> To strew him o'er and o'er.   (IV.iv. 127–9)

Florizel asks 'What, like a corse?' and Perdita replies:

> No, like a bank for love to lie and play on;
> Not like a corse; or if, not to be buried,
> But quick and in mine arms.   (IV.iv. 130–2)

The character in *Philaster* would rather be dead than alive; and his death-wish is contrasted with Perdita's wish to have Florizel very much alive in her arms.

It would be wrong, then, to blame Beaumont and Fletcher for any characteristics of *The Winter's Tale*; for Beaumont and Fletcher used the tragi-comic form as an escape from the logic of tragedy; and Shakespeare, whatever else he was doing, was clearly not doing that.

A number of critics have argued that Shakespeare was writing a kind of immortality myth; and if the 'resurrection' of Hermione was to convey that kind of impression, it was necessary for the audience, as well as the characters, to suppose that she had actually died in Act III. Such critics can refer to Paulina's willingness to swear that Hermione was dead.

Professor J. A. Bryant (to take an extremist) argues that the play embodies 'something of the Christian view of the redemption of the human race' and that Shakespeare undertook to suggest 'the miraculous aspect of divine mercy that has always made Christian teaching about the subject seem "foolishness to the Greeks" '. To bring back Hermione after sixteen years was his own idea. Mr. Bryant goes on:[3]

Consequently many readers have regarded the play as a whimsical though lovely fairytale with serious overtones here and there. From the Christian point of view, however, *The Winter's Tale* makes the hardest possible sense . . . as having ended in the only possible way for a play designed to suggest not only man's utter folly and helplessness but also his only hope of salvation. Here in the end those who survive are 'precious winners all', as Paulina calls them; and they are that because the dead has miraculously come to life and they have been granted grace to see the resurrection.

Professor Wilson Knight, more cautiously, remarks that the resurrection of Hermione is 'the crucial and revealing event to which the whole action moves'.[4] To S. L. Bethell,

[3] J. A. Bryant, Jr., *Hippolyta's View* (1961), p. 222.
[4] G. Wilson Knight, *The Crown of Life* (1947), p. 76.

95

The restoration of Hermione, her coming back as from the dead, is a carefully prepared symbol of spiritual and actual resurrection, in which alone true reconciliation may be attained.

But, Bethell adds, 'Hermione's is not a genuine resurrection'.[5]

Professor Adrien Bonjour is surely right to point out[6] that Shakespeare calls attention to Hermione's wrinkles and to the fact that Paulina two or three times a day visited the house where Hermione was hidden. It is wrong to assert that Shakespeare does not explain the mystery in realistic terms. Bonjour quite convincingly suggests that

The reanimation of Hermione's statue may thus be considered as a symbol of the redeeming power of true repentance which may win again a long lost love and atone for the disastrous consequences of a past crime.

At this point we must turn to the penultimate scene of the play, which, as we have seen, has been criticized more frequently than the statue-scene.

III

If Shakespeare were merely saving himself trouble by reporting, instead of representing, the discovery of Perdita's birth, we could cheerfully throw him to the wolves. Nor can we seriously defend him on the grounds that the play would otherwise be too full of powerful scenes. But it may nevertheless be true that if he had dramatized the recognition of Perdita as powerfully as he did the restoration of Hermione, the emphasis of the play would be changed. Hermione has been absent from the stage for the best part of three acts, and another long scene with Perdita would have made it more difficult to restore Hermione, not merely to life, but as the central character of the play. A mere resurrection would be child's play compared with this feat of dramaturgy.

If we look at *Pericles* we see that Shakespeare was faced with a similar problem, but that he solved it differently. The reunion of Pericles and Marina is presented in a long scene of 265 lines; the reunion of Pericles and Thaisa and of Thaisa with Marina is presented in less than a third of the space. There were two good reasons for this. Shakespeare was probably not the author—and certainly not the original author—of the early scenes in which Thaisa appears

[5] S. L. Bethell, *The Winter's Tale: A Study* (1947), p. 103.
[6] A. Bonjour, 'The Final Scene of *The Winter's Tale*', *English Studies*, XXXIII (1952), pp. 15–16.

before the birth of Marina; and secondly his imagination was chiefly engaged by the story of Marina. He had shown the recovery of Thaisa by means of the skill of Cerimon and this, no doubt, was one of the reasons why he did not in *The Winter's Tale* show us another good physician restoring Hermione after her supposed death.

So again, when he wrote *The Winter's Tale* he did not wish to repeat himself too closely. He could not hope to surpass the great Marina-Pericles scene;—this is the climax of it:

> Tell thy story;
> If thine consider'd prove the thousandth part
> Of my endurance, thou art a man, and I
> Have suffered like a girl: yet thou dost look
> Like Patience gazing on king's graves, and smiling
> Extremity out of act. What were they friends?
> How lost thou them? Thy name, my most kind virgin?
> Recount, I do beseech thee: come, sit by me.
> *Mar.* My name is Marina.
> *Per.*   O, I am mock'd,
> And thou by some incensed god sent hither
> To make the world to laugh at me.
> *Mar.*   Patience, good sir,
> Or here I'll cease.
> *Per.*   Nay, I'll be patient.
> Thou little know'st how thou dost startle me,
> To call thyself Marina.
> *Mar.*   The name
> Was given me by one that had some power,
> My father, and a king.
> *Per.*   How! a king's daughter!
> And call'd Marina?
> *Mar.*   You said you would believe me:
> But not to be a troubler of your peace,
> I will end here.
> *Per.*   But are you flesh and blood?
> Have you a working pulse? and are no fairy?
> Motion? Well; speak on. Where were you born?
> And wherefore called Marina?
> *Mar.*   Called Marina,
> For I was born at sea. (V.i. 135–58)

I have said that Shakespeare always avoided too close a repetition of scenes he had written earlier. This can be seen by comparing scenes which might almost have been identical. For example, Julia in *The Two Gentlemen of Verona* is disguised as a page and sent by Proteus, whom she loves, to visit her rival, Silvia. In the same way Viola, disguised as Cesario is sent by Orsino, whom she loves, to plead his love with Olivia. The situation is superficially identical, but it is treated so differently in the two plays that no one watching *The Two Gentlemen* is likely to be disturbed by memories of *Twelfth Night*. Another example may be given. Sir Toby Belch extracts money from Sir Andrew Aguecheck, his dupe, by promising him the hand of Olivia, his niece. In the same way Iago extracts money from his dupe, Roderigo, by promising to further his suit with Desdemona. Sir Toby persuades Sir Andrew to fight with his supposed rival, Cesario; as Iago persuades Roderigo to fight with his supposed rival, Cassio. Once again, despite the similarity between the situations, no one is likely to feel that Shakespeare was merely repeating himself.

It will be recalled that when Keats abandoned *Hyperion* because he found it impossible to eliminate the influence of Milton, he said that he wished to devote himself to other sensations. This, I am sure, was the attitude of Shakespeare when he completed each play. Each new play had to be something different. That is why all attempts to define Shakespearian Tragedy have been unsuccessful. There is, indeed, no such thing as 'Shakespearian Tragedy'—there are only Shakespearian tragedies.

Shakespeare must have been aware of the similarity of theme of the four romances—all of them end with reunions, in three out of four voyages play a significant part, in three out of four the action covers two generations, in three out of four the climax is an act of forgiveness, and in two of them the parents are reconciled by the marriage of the children. Precisely because of these similarities, it was important to make the plays differ as much as possible in other ways. In two plays the wrong committed is caused by jealousy: but in one the jealousy is self-generated and in the other it is aroused by the cunning of a villain. In *The Winter's Tale* the central character is the jealous husband, the wife being banished from the stage during the central acts. In *Cymbeline* the central character is the wronged wife; and in *The Tempest* the wronged hero. In *Pericles* and *The Winter's Tale* there is a gap of sixteen years. *The Tempest* begins sixteen years after the commission of the crime which brought Prospero to the enchanted island.

Secondly, the assumption of literary critics that the scene is ineffective on the stage is quite unfounded. In every production I have seen, both professional and amateur, the scene has been very successful; and my experience has been confirmed by that of Professor

The Conclusion of The Winter's Tale

Nevill Coghill (in his article defending the stagecraft of the play in *Shakespeare Survey*).[7]

'In practice', says Coghill, 'this scene is among the most gripping and memorable of the entire play. Whoever saw the production of it by Peter Brook at the Phoenix Theatre in 1951–2 will remember the excitement it created. I know of at least two other productions of the play in which this scene had the same effect, and generated that mounting thrill of expectation needed to prepare us for the final scene.' As with the final scene, it looks as though the actors can sometimes teach the critics.

Coghill goes on to disagree with Bethell, who had suggested that in the penultimate scene Shakespeare was having his final fling at court jargon:

> There may be a case to be made against the Metaphysicals and their wit, but I do not believe that Shakespeare was here making it; we, if we admire Donne and Crashaw, should not gird at the conceits of the three gentlemen. Let us consider their situation; never in the memory of court-gossip has there been so joyful and so astounding a piece of news to spread; they are over the edge of tears in the happy excitement and feel a noble, indeed a partly miraculous joy, for the oracle has been fulfilled; so far as they can they temper their tears with their wit. What could be a more delightful mixture of drollery and tenderness, or more in the best 'Metaphysical' manner than

> > 'One of the prettiest touches of all and that which angled for mine eyes, caught the water though not the fish, was when, at the relation of the Queen's death, with the manner how she came to't gravely confessed and lamented by the King, how attentiveness wounded his daughter; till, from one sign of dolour to another, she did, with an "Alas", I would fain say, bleed tears, for I am sure my heart wept blood.'

> Could Donne [Coghill asks] have found a better hyperbole than 'wounded', or Crashaw a more felicitous conceit for eyes and tears?

Coghill, I believe, is partly right and partly wrong. He is right in his general account of the tone of the scene; but he is wrong to compare the conceits to those of the metaphysicals. Although a study remains to be written on the influence of the Metaphysicals on Jacobean Drama, and of the influence of the dramatists on the Metaphysicals, the style of this scene is purely Arcadian. Compare, for example, the passage in which Sidney describes his heroine wounding the cloth with her needle. It was appropriate that Shakespeare should use the Arcadian style in this play, for his main source,

---

[7] N. Coghill, 'Six Points of Stage-craft in *The Winter's Tale*', *Shakespeare Survey* XI (1958), p. 39.

Pandosto, was one of Greene's best 'Arcadian' novels; and it is significant that in the one play which used *Arcadia* as a source, *King Lear*, Shakespeare should write in the Arcadian style, when another anonymous gentleman describes the way in which Cordelia receives the news of her father:

> Patience and sorrow strove
> Who should express her goodliest. You have seen
> Sunshine and rain at once; her smiles and tears
> Were like, a better way; those happy smilets
> That played on her ripe lip seemed not to know
> What guests were in her eyes; which parted thence,
> As pearls from diamonds dropped. In brief,
> Sorrow would be a rarity most beloved,
> If all could so become it.   (IV.iii. 18–26)

There are two other observations I should like to make on this scene. First, beneath the artificial language, we can see careful preparation for the final scene and hints of the symbolical meaning of the play. When Leontes and Camillo, for example, are shown the proofs of Perdita's parentage, 'they looked as they had heard of a world ransomed, or one destroyed'. This links up with the language of redemption in the last scene.

The other point I want to make has been discussed by Leslie Bethell. The second gentlemen says that 'such a deal of wonder is broken out within this hour, that ballad-makers cannot be able to express it. . . . This news (which is called true) is so like an old tale, that the verity of it is in strong suspicion'. Later on the third gentleman says 'Like an old tale still'. Bethell thinks this is a deliberate attempt on Shakespeare's part to alienate the audience in a Brechtian sense:[8]

Such internal comments upon the nature of a story always remind us of its unreality, breaking through any illusion which may have been created. Thus they combine with the deliberately old-fashioned technique to insist that it is after all only a dramatic performance that the audience have before them.

I doubt whether this is true. When, after the murder of Caesar, Brutus says:

> How many ages hence
> Shall this our lofty scene be acted o'er . . .

I do not think the illusion of reality is destroyed so that the audience

[8] S. L. Bethell, *The Winter's Tale: A Study* (1947), p. 53.

are suddenly conscious that they are watching a play; and when Cleopatra is afraid that she will be represented on the stage, and that an actor will boy her greatness in the posture of a whore, Shakespeare risked this reminder of the stage because he knew that he had convinced his audience of Cleopatra's reality. In the same way, the continual references in *The Winter's Tale* to the incredible nature of the story have the paradoxical effect of undercutting the audience's scepticism.

IV

Our consideration of the last two scenes of *The Winter's Tale* should lead us to two main conclusions. In spite of the many crimes committed in Shakespeare's name during the past three hundred years by actors and producers, it is only fair to say that they sometimes demonstrate in performance that Shakespeare was wiser than his critics. The other conclusion I have not had time to develop. It is this: that Shakespeare, although he lived in the age of Spenser, never indulged in allegory as such; but nevertheless in many of his plays, and particularly in the last romances, there are allegorical undertones. It is impossible to believe that Shakespeare was writing these tragicomedies merely to emulate the successes of Beaumont and Fletcher and Heywood. He was concerned with such basic human questions as the necessity of forgiveness; and I think there is no doubt that in *The Winter's Tale* he was attempting, among other things, to reinterpret the story of Proserpine. Perdita refers herself to the Proserpine story; she is playing the role of the goddess Flora in the sheepshearing scene; she refers to Whitsun-pastorals; she is described by Leontes as a goddess, welcome as the Spring to the Earth.[9]

[9] Cf. K. Muir, *Last Periods of Shakespeare, Racine and Ibsen* (1961), pp. 39 ff.

9

A Yorkshire Tragedy and *Two Most Vnnaturall and Bloodie Murthers*

A. C. CAWLEY

The world in general, gentlemen, are very bloody-minded; and all they want in a murder is a copious effusion of blood.

THOMAS DE QUINCEY: 'On Murder Considered as One of the Fine Arts'

THE purpose of this essay is to make some comparison between *A Yorkshire Tragedy* and the pamphlet on which it was based,[1] in the hope of throwing some light on a Jacobean playwright's treatment of this kind of source-material.

There are at least three other domestic tragedies of the same period on subjects which were also dealt with in pamphlets: *A Warning for Fair Women* (1599), the lost play of *William Cartwright* (1602) and *The Witch of Edmonton* (written 1621, printed 1658).[2]

It is well known that *A Warning for Fair Women* was largely based

---

[1] Six copies have survived of the first quarto of *A Yorkshire Tragedy* (1608) and two copies of the pamphlet *Two most vnnaturall and bloodie Murthers* (1605). An old-spelling edition of the play is included in C. F. Tucker Brooke's *The Shakespeare Apocrypha* (Oxford, 1908), pp. 249–31. The pamphlet has been reprinted by T. D. Whitaker in *Loidis and Elmete* (Leeds, 1816), pp. 221–9, by J. P. Collier in *Illustrations of Early English Popular Literature* (London, 1863–4), I, item 11, and again by Collier in *The Plays and Poems of William Shakespeare* (London, 1878), VIII, pp. 33–51. The least inaccurate of these reprints is Collier's earlier transcription which preserves the original spelling.

[2] For the dependence of *The Witch of Edmonton* on Henry Goodcoale's pamphlet (1621) see *The Dramatic Works of Thomas Dekker*, ed. F. Bowers (Cambridge, 1958), III, p. 483.

on Arthur Golding's *A briefe discourse of the late murther of master George Saunders* (1573)[3] and *A Yorkshire Tragedy* on the pamphlet *Two most vnnaturall and bloodie Murthers*.[4] What has not been done for either of these plays is to make a detailed comparison between play and pamphlet, in order to discover what significant differences exist in structure, language, or characterization. Failure to do this has led some scholars to underrate the work of the playwrights concerned. For example, it has been said of *A Warning* that it is 'a (generally) very servile following of the contemporary accounts by Stow and others'.[5] In truth, a comparison with Stow and *A briefe discourse* shows that the dramatist has employed considerable inventiveness in shaping the structure of his play, in creating incident, and in deepening the motivation of his characters. Similarly, M. Friedlaender, writing about the relationship between *A Yorkshire Tragedy* and the pamphlet, claims that 'The closeness of the prose tract and the play in narrative and verbal characteristics is so striking that one must believe, either in identity of authorship, or else in slavish copying without the slightest inventiveness on the part of the playwright'.[6] In what follows an attempt will be made to show that the contrary opinion is nearer the truth: 'when we compare the pamphlet with the play, we recognize that dramatic instinct has transmuted the bald fact . . . The reporter's dry language is infused on every page with passionate intensity'.[7]

First of all it will be convenient to review briefly the evidence that *A Yorkshire Tragedy* was based on the pamphlet, and not the pamphlet on the play. Apart from the fact that the sequence of events is similar in both, there are many verbal parallels which point to a close connection between the two, although they do not in themselves establish the priority of the pamphlet. The following examples are representative:

Pamphlet	*Play*[8]
the three louely boyes you haue beene father vnto (p. 5)	Thinke on the state of these three louely boies You haue bin father to. (ii. 67)

[3] See R. Simpson, *The School of Shakespeare* (London, 1878), II, pp. 220 ff.
[4] B. Maxwell, *Studies in the Shakespeare Apocrypha* (New York, 1956), pp. 139 ff.
[5] Simpson, *op. cit.*, p. 210.
[6] 'Some Problems of *A Yorkshire Tragedy*', *Studies in Philology*, XXXV (1938), p. 242.
[7] S. L. Lee, 'The Topical Side of the Elizabethan Drama', New Shakespeare Society, *Transactions* (1887), pp. 33–4.
[8] Quotations from the play are taken from Tucker Brooke, *op. cit.*; quotations from the pamphlet are from the Bodleian copy.

Base strumpet (whom thogh I maried I neuer loued) (p. 5)	Ha done, thou harlot, Whome, though for fashion sake I married, I neuer could abide; (ii. 77)
Sir (answered she) in al this I will be a wife, what in all this the law will allow me to doe, you shall commaund (p. 6)	Sir, doe but turne a gentle eye on me, And what the law shall giue me leaue to do You shall command. (ii. 95)
Maister *Cauerley*, you are a Gentleman of an antient house, there hath beene much good expected from you, deceyue not mens hopes, you haue a vertuous wife . . . (p. 9)	Y'are of a vertuous house, . . . Much good has bin expected in your life, Cancell not all mens hopes: you haue a wife . . . (ii. 188)

The *external* evidence for the priority of the pamphlet is that it was entered for publication on June 12th, 1605, only seven weeks after the murders had been committed by Walter Calverley on April 23rd, and was published in the same year. The play, however, was not printed until three years later (entered on May 2nd, 1608, and published in the same year); it is therefore unlikely to have been written as early as the pamphlet.

The *internal* evidence confirms that the play was indeed written later than the pamphlet (perhaps a year or more later), and was undoubtedly influenced by it:

(1) *The oaths in the play.* The Act of Abuses (May 27th, 1606) provided that actors in a stage play should not, on pain of a fine of ten pounds, 'jestingly or prophanely speake or use the name of God or of Jesus Christ, or of the Holy Ghoste or of the Trinitie, which are not to be spoken but with feare and reverence'.[9] A comparison of play with pamphlet shows that the playwright has far fewer references to God and heaven than are to be found in the pamphlet. The playwright's economy in the matter of oaths may sometimes have had a dramatic purpose, especially as it has the appropriate effect of reducing God's share in the Husband's thought and language. But, equally, the playwright may have exercised greater restraint than the writer of the pamphlet because he had the censor in mind, It is also noticeable that *A Yorkshire Tragedy*, by virtue of its restraint in the

[9] E. K. Chambers, *The Elizabethan Stage* (Oxford, 1923), IV, pp. 338–9.

use of oaths, stands in contrast to *The Miseries of Inforst Mariage* (printed 1607 but probably written before May 1606).[10] As the Act of Abuses applied only to the spoken word, the use or non-use of oaths in a printed play does not provide reliable evidence for a date of composition earlier or later than May 1606. Still, the use of religious oaths in the *Tragedy* is sparing enough to suggest a date of composition later than May 1606 rather than earlier.[11] It could perhaps be argued that the oaths in the *Tragedy* were originally more numerous and varied but were pruned by the book-keeper for theatrical presentation; however, this argument would be difficult to maintain since there are no other indications that the copy-text of the first quarto of 1608 was a prompt copy prepared for the stage.

(2) *Factual details in the pamphlet but not in the play*. The pamphlet has certain factual details which are not in the play, such as the information that Calverley's eldest son was 'a childe of foure yeeres' (p. 13) and that his youngest child was 'an infant of halfe a yeare old at nurse some twelue mile off' (p. 16). These details, and others like them, indicate that the pamphlet could not have been derived from the play, unless an additional source of information was available to the writer of the pamphlet. At the same time, there is nothing in the play which could not have been borrowed or elaborated from the story as told in the pamphlet.

(3) *Couplets in the play*. There are at least 50 couplets in the play (of 798 lines, according to Brooke's numbering), and these occur in every scene except i and vi. Not a single one of these couplets is found in the pamphlet. If the pamphlet had been based on the play, it is improbable that every one of the couplets would have been removed.[12]

Once it is accepted that the pamphlet is the main source of *A*

[10] See Maxwell, *op. cit.*, p. 177.

[11] Maxwell, *ib.*, conjectures that *A Yorkshire Tragedy* was written 'in the later part of 1605'. But the kind of evidence he uses to support this dating—e.g. the ending of the play with the Husband's arrest, suggesting that 'the dramatist may have been writing before Calverley's execution [August 5th, 1605], or at least in ignorance of it'—is most unreliable. The obvious explanation of the ending of the *Tragedy* is that it was based, here as elsewhere, on the pamphlet, which also ends with Calverley's arrest and imprisonment. The proposition that the *Tragedy* was written after May 1606 and the *Miseries* before this date would not be easily tenable if it could be shown that the *Tragedy* has influenced the *Miseries;* but a comparison of the two plays shows few signs of either play influencing the other, and what slight evidence there is may suggest that the influence worked from *Miseries* to *Tragedy*.

[12] Cf. Wilkins' novel *The Painfull Aduentures of Pericles*, which contains several of the blank-verse lines of the play *Pericles*, used by Wilkins as one of his main sources. See K. Muir, *Shakespeare as Collaborator* (London, 1960), pp. 59–62.

Yorkshire Tragedy, the way is clear to examining some of the changes made by the playwright, and to considering what kind of play results from them.

Place and Time. The *Tragedy* is shorter than the pamphlet, which takes 18 quarto pages (35 lines to a page) to tell the story of Calverley's violation of his vow of betrothal to a 'vertuous Gentlewoman' in Yorkshire, and of the unhappy marriage and brutal murders that lead to his arrest and imprisonment. The play, divided into ten scenes by Malone,[13] is concerned with the same incidents and characters as the pamphlet, except for the first scene which owes very little to the pamphlet apart from the allusion to 'my yong Mistrisse', who is waiting for 'our young maister' (presumably the Husband) to return from London and marry her.[14]

In the pamphlet the action begins 'within the Countie of Yorke, not farre from Wakefield', moves to London with Calverley's departure and subsequent marriage to his guardian's niece, and returns at some unspecified time to Yorkshire, where it stays except for Mistress Calverley's visit to her uncle in London. The playwright, however, localizes all the action in Yorkshire, in the Husband's house or its vicinity. This he manages in Scene iii by making the Wife report the meeting with her uncle in London after her return; and there is a resulting change of sequence in two events of the play. In the pamphlet the meeting between Mistress Calverley and her uncle in London precedes the episode of the fight between Calverley and a Gentleman, which takes place while she is away. But in the play the episode of the fight, since it takes place during the Wife's absence, has to be moved so that it comes before, not after, the Wife's report of her meeting in London.

The playwright deals with time, no less than place, in a more concentrated fashion than the writer of the pamphlet. In common with *The Miseries of Inforst Mariage* the pamphlet covers a period of about five years, beginning while Calverley is still a ward and lasting until he is twenty-two or twenty-three, when his eldest son is four years old. The main narrative of the pamphlet—the story of the

---

[13] Malone's *Supplement to . . . Shakespeare's Plays* (London, 1780), II, pp. 629–79.
[14] The problem of Scene i of *A Yorkshire Tragedy* lies outside the scope of this essay. Unlike Scenes ii–x it makes no verbal borrowings from the pamphlet, and this may suggest either (*a*) that the beginning of the pamphlet was not used by the playwright or (*b*) that Scene i was written by someone who used his source-material differently from the playwright (or playwrights) responsible for Scenes ii–x. The problem of whether one or more playwrights wrote Scenes ii–x is also, happily, outside the pale of the present essay.

events immediately leading to Calverley's murder of his children—
leaves the passing of time indefinite, although it gives the impression
that these events took place within a fairly short period. The playwright responsible for Scene i of the *Tragedy* sums up the preceding
five years by telling us that the marriage has already produced 'two
or three children'. While it makes nonsense that the 'yong Mistrisse'
should have been waiting four or five years for her lover to return
without hearing about his marriage and offspring, at least this first
scene does nothing to dilute the concentrated essence of time in
the rest of the play. From Scene ii onwards the speed of events never
slackens: the scenes all follow hard on one another, and even the
Wife's visit to her uncle, by being reported, is not allowed to slow
down the action. We are swept along at such a rate that we may easily
overlook the fact that an indefinite period has elapsed between the
Wife's departure and her return, i.e. between the end of Scene ii and
the beginning of Scene iii. This telescoping of events is unrealistic,
but the effect of it is to give speed and urgency to the action.

Themes. The dramatist establishes at the outset that his play is to
be something more than a simple dramatization of prodigal behaviour
and brutal murder. At the beginning of Scene ii the Wife soliloquizes
on two of the main themes of the play: the Husband's dissolute
behaviour which is rapidly reducing the house of Calverley to beggary
and ruining the 'auncient honor' of its name; and the impenitent
state of his mind, for he

> Walks heauyly, as if his soule were earth:
> Not penitent for those his sinnes are past,
> But vext his mony cannot make them last:—
> A fearefull melancholie, vngodly sorrow. (ii. 18)

After the Husband's brief and stormy appearance on stage, the Wife
takes up again the theme of the soul's abasement:

> Bad, turnd to worse! both beggery of the soule,
> As of the bodie. And so much vnlike
> Him selfe at first, as if some vexed spirit
> Had got his form vpon him. (ii. 36)

Here is the dominant theme—the Husband's spiritual consumption,
which is serious enough to suggest to the Wife the possibility of
demonic possession. The pamphlet has all the other themes of the
play—the Husband's squandering of his money and his good name,
his groundless suspicion and brutal treatment of his wife, the beggar-

ing of his children, his unnatural conduct towards his brother, his overwhelming sense of guilt—but the theme of spiritual beggary and demonic possession represents the playwright's own attempt to explore the mentality of a murderer.

Abbreviation and Amplification. The playwright both abbreviates and amplifies his source-material. The most striking examples of abbreviation are provided by the euphuistic passages in the pamphlet which the playwright regularly does not use. Passages like the following, typically cast in the form of fanciful metaphors or similes, are rejected by the dramatist:

there was so pittifull lamentation betweene them, that had flint had eares, it would haue melted into water. (pp. 17–18)

nor was he distracted with the sight [of his dead children], but all like a pillar of salt, and the remembrance of their liuely shape, reflected such a natural heate vpon him, that he was melted into water, and had not power to take any farewell of them, but onely in teares. (p. 18)

The playwright, no less than the pamphleteer, is intent on raising his play above the level of a sordid murder story; but he has other ways of doing it.

Equally important is the omission from the play of the pamphlet's explicit references to God's providence controlling events. In particular, the suggestion in the pamphlet (p. 4) that Calverley's misfortunes were visited on him by God as a punishment for having jilted his betrothed—this is completely given up by the playwright, who sees the devil playing a more important part than God in the unhappy story of Calverley's prodigality, domestic unhappiness and murder of his children. Again, when Calverley's horse stumbles and throws him as he is riding off to murder his third child, the pamphleteer indulges in pious musings on the subject of God's intervention in human affairs:

But God that ordereth the life of a Wren, hath then a care of his reasonable creatures. . . . So for Maister *Cauerley*, though God permitted the Sunne to blush at his vnnaturall acts, yet he suffered him not to escape without his reuenge: (p. 16)

The dramatist has the good sense to reject all this; God's intervention is probably implied, but the Husband (whose thoughts are far from God at this moment) is made to curse his bad luck—

Hart of chance!
To Throw me now within a flight oth Towne, (viii. 4)
108

The playwright's amplifications of his source are no less interesting than his abbreviations. The parts of the play for which there is nothing corresponding in the pamphlet include many lines in Scenes ii-ix and most of Scene x. These lines, which are written in blank verse and couplets as well as in prose, are the most vitally worded parts of the play. In general they serve to heighten the pathos and terror of the action. Thus the following words of the young son to his father have no exact parallel in the pamphlet; the pathos of the child's unsuspecting innocence is reminiscent of the medieval dramatization of the story of Abraham and Isaac:

Pamphlet	*Play*
his eldest son being a childe of foure yeeres olde, came into the gallery, to scourge his toppe, and seeing his father stand in a study, looked prettily vppe to him, saying, Howe doe you father? (p. 13)	*Enters his little sonne with a top and a scourge.* What, aile you father? are you not well? I cannot scourge my top as long as you stand so: you take vp all the roome with your wide legs. Puh, you cannot make mee afeard with this; I feare no vizards, nor bugbeares. (iv. 111)

Again, the brief narrative in the pamphlet of the second child's murder gains in terror when it is translated into the rapid action and dialogue of the play:

she caught vp the youngest . . . her husband comming backe, met her, and came to struggle with her for the childe which shee sought to preserue with words, teares, and all what a mother could do from so tragicall an end; and when he saw he could not get it from her, he most remorcelesse stabbed at it . . . (p. 14)	*[catches vp the yongest.* *Hus.* Strumpet, let go the boy, let go the beggar. *Wi.* Oh my sweet husband! *Hus.* Filth, harlot. *Wi.* Oh what will you doe, deare husband? *Hus.* Giue me the bastard. *Wi.* Your owne sweet boy! *Hus.* There are too many beggars. *Wi.* Good my husband— *Hus.* Doest preuent me still? *Wi.* Oh god! *Hus.* Haue at his hart! *[Stabs at the child in hir armes.* (v. 18)

This is a violent situation which the medieval dramatist had long before mastered; the Jacobean dramatist may well have drawn on his memories of plays on the Massacre of the Innocents.

Above all, the additions to the play have the effect of strengthening the characterization of the Wife and the Husband and of developing the playwright's own theme of diabolic possession (and dispossession).

The Wife. The Wife, like the Husband, belongs to a dramatic tradition: she is the 'faithful wife' who so often gets burdened with a 'prodigal husband'. The dramatist's problem with the Wife, no less than Chaucer's problem with Griselda, was to make her extra-ordinary behaviour credible. This he tries to do in a number of ways. Mistress Calverley of the pamphlet is wordy, pious, and submissive; she speaks in long rhetorically balanced sentences, appeals to God continually, and promises to perfect her wifely love for His sake. The Wife of the play is, by comparison, endowed with much more sense and spirit than some critics are willing to give her credit for.[15] Her first soliloquy in Scene ii, in which she makes a severe analysis of her husband's condition, shows the playwright working inde-pendently of the pamphlet. Of particular interest, as we have seen, is her intuition—unparalleled in the pamphlet—that her husband may be possessed by a devil (ii. 36–9). She again displays some spirit in a later scene, after her visit to her uncle in London, when she tells a servant that her husband's deserts

> Are in forme vglier then an vnshapte Bear, (iii. 18)

—a detail which is not derived from the pamphlet. Up to the time of the murder of her children the Wife's behaviour is recognizably human. Her sharp criticism of her husband, her craving to be loved by him, her frantic efforts to save her children: all these things we can understand and admire. But her behaviour goes beyond the bounds of credibility in the last scene, when she only once mentions her children: this is her cry of anguish—

> Oh, our two bleeding boyes
> Laid forth vpon the thresholde. (x. 35)

It is the Husband who mourns for them; the Wife's thoughts are dominated by her husband, who seems to monopolize her sorrow and her love. We must either accept the Wife's behaviour as a miracle of forgiveness or psychologically suppose that she con-centrates all her feelings on her husband in order to suppress her unbearable sorrow for her dead children. But neither the miraculous nor the psychological explanation is really convincing.

[15] H. Tyrrell, *The Doubtful Plays of Shakespeare* (London and New York, 1851), p. 83, has not a good word to say for the Wife: she 'is all tears, morality, and crouching submission. She is not an interesting, but a painful character'.

The Husband: the language of violence. The imagery of the *Tragedy* is engrossed by decay, disease and death, by violence, blood and murder. The language of the Husband, in particular, is loaded with the imagery of physical violence, in which the body and its members figure prominently: flesh, skin, head, neck, face, cheeks, tongue, tooth, hand, nails, joint, heart, breast and blood—

> It is thy quarrel that thus rips my flesh,
> And makes my brest spit blood. (ii. 201)

> Why, he can haue no more on's then our skins,
> And some of em want but fleaing. (viii. 25)

> I thought it the charitablest deed I could doe
> to cussen beggery and knock my house oth head. (ix. 18)

> Ile breake your clamor with your neck: (v. 11)

> My childrens bloud
> Shall spin into your faces, (iv. 134)

> And both your murthers shoote vpon my cheekes; (x. 41)

> The surest waie to charme a womans tongue
> Is break hir neck: (v. 13)

> Has the dogg left me, then,
> After his tooth hath left me? (ii. 197)

> I did my murthers roughly, out of hand, (x. 16)

> now glides the deuill from mee,
> Departes at euery ioynt, heaues vp my nailes. (x. 19)

> oh, my hart
> Would faine leape after him. (ii. 198)

The Husband, who has a monopoly of violent language, reinforces physical imagery with an emphatic repetition of words:

> A vengeance strip thee naked! thou art cause,
> Effect, quality, property, thou, thou, thou! (ii. 34)

Even his non-violent language is a debased coinage. *Angels* for him are coins to gamble with (ii. 26); to be damned in this world is to have no money (ii. 29); a 'charitablest deed' is one of brutal murder (ix. 19); the heart, far from being the seat of noble or tender emotions, is in himself a hell's kitchen of torment and revenge (ii. 198, iv. 105), and in others a vital organ to be destroyed—

> Haue at his hart! (v. 29)

111

Moreover, the Husband has his favourite words which are either not used at all by the other characters or used only with reference to him —such words as *hell, devil, damned, damnation, tricks, dust, slave, bawd, bastard, cuckold, harlot, strumpet, whore.*[16] On the other hand, words like *heaven, soul, grace,* and *honour* have little or no place in his vocabulary before the final scene of contrition and demonic dispossession. It is not until the final scene that the man and his language return to normal: in this scene he uses *angels* in a religious sense for the first time, *heaven,*[17] *soul*[18] and *grace* exist for him again, *heart* regains a compassionate meaning, and the *eyes* (not mentioned by the Husband before) are now referred to no fewer than three times to symbolize the illumination which follows his release from the devil's power. And yet even the repentant Husband is unable to give up his violent language all at once; he cannot help thinking of his restoration to humanity in terms of the wounding and killing of his old self. He says to his wife:

> but thou hast deuiz'd
> A fine way now to kill me, thou hast giuen mine eies
> Seauen woonds a peece;   (x. 17)

The Husband's language is, then, a reflex of the man himself—of his violence and spiritual blindness and, later, of his illumination.[19]

Demonic possession. Some of the best passages in the play, for which there is no source in the pamphlet, describe the Husband in his several roles as husband, father and brother, as man and monster. He is a sinful man, guilty of most of the deadly sins, with pride at their head:

> Shall I that Dedicated my selfe to pleasure, be nowe confind in seruice to crouch and stand like an old man ith hams, my hat off? I that neuer could abide to vncouer my head ith Church?   (iii. 57)

The playwright makes no attempt to account for the Husband's dedication to pleasure, his violence and unreasonable jealousy, his

---

[16] *Harlot, strumpet* and *whore* are in ascending order of opprobrium; *whore* is not used by the Husband until Scene iii.

[17] *Heaven* occurs only once in a speech by the Husband before Scene x, where he uses it three times.

[18] Before Scene x *soul* is mentioned once by the Husband (iv. 107, where he refers to it as something that can be mortgaged); in Scene x he uses it four times (once as a term of endearment to his wife).

[19] The other characters are also given their characteristic words: the Wife frequently appeals to *heaven*; the Gentlemen make repeated use of *honour, honours, honourably*; the Master of the College uses the language of theology—*soul, heaven, judgment, repentance, amends.*

passion for gambling; or to explain his falling away from the promise of his youth, to which both the Wife and Gentleman refer (ii. 6, 151). We have to accept him as he is: there is no suggestion (as in the pamphlet) that God is avenging a broken troth-plight or (as in *The Miseries of Inforst Mariage*) that the Husband is taking refuge from a loveless marriage and a bad conscience. The author of the *Tragedy* is writing as the heir to a long tradition of 'prodigal' plays;[20] he has no need to justify such natural sinful behaviour. He is much more interested in trying to explain how a prodigal husband can become an unnatural monster who stabs his wife and murders two of his children.

The writer of the pamphlet makes it clear that Calverley commits his monstrous crime in a fit of madness; his sense of sin is so strong that it creates 'a seuerall distraction in him' (p. 13), and he is 'ouer-whelmed by the violence of his passion' (p. 13). But to the playwright the Husband is suffering from a disease worse than madness; the Gentleman says to the Husband:

> Those whom men call mad
> Endanger others; but hee's more then mad
> That wounds himselfe, whose owne wordes do proclaym
> Scandalls vniust, to soile his better name: (ii. 113)

The Husband's malady is first identified by his wife as 'beggery of the soule' (ii. 36), and it is she who first observes that her husband behaves 'as if some vexed spirit Had got his form vpon him' (ii. 38). After this the idea of diabolic possession grows in strength until the end of the play, and is repeated in one form or another by the Gentleman (to the Husband):

> in thy change,
> This voice into all places wil be hurld:
> Thou and the deuill has deceaued the world. (ii. 155)

by the Servant (to the Wife):

> If he should not now be kinde to you and loue you, and cherish you vp,
> I should thinke the deuill himselfe kept open house in him. (iii. 24)

by the Servant (to the Husband):

> Were you the Deuil, I would hold you, sir. (v. 40)

> Nay, then, the Deuil wrastles, I am th[r]owne. (v. 48)

[20] For the prodigal tradition in drama see M. C. Bradbrook, *Themes and Conventions of Elizabethan Tragedy* (Cambridge, 1937), pp. 57 ff.

by the Servant (soliloquizing):

> Ha's so bruizd me with his diuelish waight,
> And torne my flesh with his bloud-hasty spurre.
> A man before of easie constitution
> Till now hells power supplied, to his soules wrong.
> Oh, how damnation can make weake men strong.[21] (vii. 2)

by the Servant (to the Wife):

> We strugled, but a fowler strength then his
> Ore threw me with his armes; (vii. 28)

by the Knight:

> The serpent of his house![22] (ix. 9)

and by the Husband himself:

> Oh, twas the enemy my eyes so bleard. (x. 48)

It will be noticed from the above quotations that it is not until Scene v. 48—after the Husband has murdered two of his children—that any of the other characters positively identifies his malady. The devil presumably begins to take possession of the Husband sometime after Scene ii. Up to the end of this scene he still has his normal strength: wounded and brought to the ground by the Gentleman, he is mad to be revenged on his wife, whom he blames for his humiliation and his lack of money. It may be his crazy desire for revenge on a completely innocent person—for there are apparently no grounds for the accusation of adultery he makes against his wife—which gives the devil his first real chance of entry. Certain it is, according to King James, that the devil seduces his victims by exploiting 'passiones that are within our selues . . . thrist of revenge, for some tortes deeply apprehended: or greedie appetite of geare, caused through great pouerty'.[23] The process of possession probably becomes complete in Scene iv, just after the meeting between the Husband and the Master of the College, and just before the murders are committed. The Husband has been physically humiliated by the Gentleman, who

[21] Abnormal strength was considered to be one of the surest signs of demonic possession; e.g. King James, *Daemonologie* (1957), ed. G. B. Harrison (London 1924), p. 70: 'the incredible strength of the possessed creature, which will farre exceede the strength of six of the wightest and wodest of any other men that are not so troubled'.

[22] Cf. Reginald Scot's *The Discoverie of Witchcraft* (1584), ed. B. Nicholson (London, 1886) ,p. 452: '*Moses*, under the person of the poisoning serpent or snake, describeth the divell that poisoned *Eve* with his deceiptfull words, and venomous assault. Whence cometh it else, that the divell is called so often, The viper, The serpent, &c'.

[23] *Daemonologie*, p. 8.

spares his life but makes him listen—at the sword's point—to a homily on his sins; he has been spiritually humiliated by the Master, whose solemn diatribe on his shameful treatment of his brother fills him with self-loathing. He is now at his lowest ebb, physically and spiritually, and is ripe for possession. The devil has been on his lips before (e.g. ii. 55, ii. 77); but now, for the first time, he is willing to 'take vp mony vpon his soule, Pawn his saluation' (iv. 107). By his willingness to let hell and eternal damnation take care of themselves if he can live in plenty in this world, he is in effect pawning his soul to the devil. The murders immediately follow, and the Husband displays a new and monstrous strength that only the devil can have given him.

In the final scene the Husband becomes aware of the devil's presence at the moment when the devil takes agonizing leave of him:

> now glides the deuill from mee,
> Departes at euery ioynt, heaues vp my nailes.[24] (x. 19)

The Husband—and the playwright—both feel that such a violent and unnatural crime cannot satisfactorily be explained in human terms alone. After the murders the distracted Wife asks—

> What is it has beguild him of all grace
> And stole awaie humanity from his brest?
> To slaie his children, purpose to kill his wife,
> And spoile his saruants. (vii. 33)

The Husband indirectly gives two different answers to this question. When the Gentleman asks him what made him 'shew such monstrous crueltie', he replies:

In a worde, Sir, I haue consumd all, plaid awaie long acre, and I thought it the charitablest deed I could doe to cussen beggery and knock my house oth head. (ix. 17)

This is the explanation in human terms: the Husband has brought himself to a pass where he cannot live with himself or with the family he has ruined, and he is determined to wipe out the consequences of his criminal prodigality by destroying those who will suffer most because of it. But, after his dispossession, when his eyes have been opened to his spiritual malady, he gives quite another explanation to his wife:

[24] For the signs of dispossession see John Darrell, 'A True Narration of the Strange and Grevous Vexation by the Devil of seven Persons in Lancashire, and William Somers of Nottingham' (1600); repr. in *The Somers Collection of Tracts*, ed. Walter Scott (London, 1810), III, p. 210.

A. C. Cawley

> Let him [the devil] not rise
> To make men act vnnaturall tragedies,
> To spred into a father, and in furie,
> Make him his childrens executioners:
> Murder his wife, his seruants, and who not?
> For that man's darke, where heauen is quite forgot. (x. 23)

This is the explanation in terms of the devil. Both explanations—the human and the diabolic—are valid, for one complements the other: 'The power of divels is in the hearts of men, as to harden the heart, to blind the eyes of the mind'.[25]

It is doubtful whether a psychiatrist could produce a much more convincing explanation of the Husband's unnatural murders. Even Shakespeare has recourse to agents of evil with the supernatural power to encourage Macbeth's ambitious dreams; and Lady Macbeth adjures the powers of darkness to take possession of her (*Macbeth* I.v. 41 ff.).

The final scene of A Yorkshire Tragedy. In Scene x the play goes well beyond the pamphlet. This final scene describes the Husband's physical dispossession, his spiritual illumination, and his return to humanity. In doing so, it heightens the pathos of the last meeting between husband and wife. There is little or no suggestion for any of this in the pamphlet. Furthermore, the pamphlet gives no hint of the Husband's hopelessness and boundless despair. It is not simply that his position is hopeless in this world—his children dead, his wife lost to him, execution awaiting him. The Husband's despair stretches out from this world to the next; he is guilty of the deadly sin of despairing of God's grace. When he sees his dead children, he cries:

> Oh, were it lawfull that your prettie soules
> Might looke from heauen into your fathers eyes,
> Then should you see the penitent glasses melt,
> And both your murthers shoote vpon my cheekes;
> But you are playing in the Angells lappes,
> And will not looke on me . . .

> Oh, would you could pray heauen me to forgiue,
> That will vnto my end repentant liue . . .

> My soull is bloudied, . . .
> Farewell, ye bloudie ashes of my boyes!
> My punishments are their eternall ioyes. (x. 38)

[25] George Gifford, *A Dialogue concerning Witches and Witchcraft* (1603); quoted by Kenneth Muir in the Arden Shakespeare edition of *Macbeth* (London, 1951), p. lxiii.

116

It is clear from these lines that the Husband has no hope of escaping eternal punishment for his crime: his repentance, although it includes acknowledgment of sin and contrition for it, still excludes the trust in God's mercy that is needed to make repentance complete. Like Faustus he believes himself to be damned, and sees no loophole through which his soul can escape to salvation. He is freed from diabolic influence, but his spiritual defeat remains.

By emphasizing the Husband's acceptance of eternal damnation as his lot, the *Tragedy* departs radically not only from the pamphlet but from the tradition of the murder plays. The theological pattern of the typical murder play is inherited from the 'full-scope' morality which 'begins with a period of innocence terminating in a fall, reaches its climax at a reversal whereby the central character is saved or re-born, and ends with reconciliation and hope'.[26] This is the pattern of domestic murder plays like *Arden of Feversham* (1592), *A Warning for Fair Women* (1599), and Robert Yarrington's *Two Lamentable Tragedies* (1601); all of these end with scaffold speeches of repentance in which the murderers, before paying the extreme worldly penalty for their crime, express their trust in divine mercy.[27] Such plays are basically moral plays in outlook and teach that 'no sin, even avarice or murder, is so black as to be beyond the hope of divine grace. . . . By paying for a sin with suffering, the wrongdoer learns to turn with repentance to God and so to escape everlasting damnation'.[28] Like the moral plays they are essentially Christian penitential plays stressing the efficacy of full and sincere repentance. Plays of this kind cannot be tragedies, unless the term 'tragedy' be applied to any play that ends in death for the protagonist; for they offer 'clear and obvious solutions to the problems of man's relation to God'[29] and show the way to escape the ultimate Christian tragedy of the soul's damnation. *A Yorkshire Tragedy*, on the other hand, is precisely this kind of Christian tragedy: the devil supplants God in the Husband's soul and body; the Husband lives for a time in a world of violent words and actions; but from him is exacted in the end the double penalty of the body's death and the soul's death. Superficially, the *Tragedy* may seem to have the conventional morality pattern of sin—repentance—sin

[26] O. B. Hardison, *Christian Rite and Christian Drama in the Middle Ages* (Baltimore, 1965), p. 289.

[27] It should, however, be pointed out that in *Arden of Feversham*, while Alice and Susan make formal speeches of repentance, Mosbie and Michael do not.

[28] H. H. Adams, *English Domestic or Homiletic Tragedy* (Columbia University Press, 1943), p. 111.

[29] *ib.*, p. 184.

I   117

intensified—final repentance. In fact, there is nothing resembling true or perfect repentance in the *Tragedy*. In one sense it is a grim burlesque of the morality play, for it shows what happens in real life, as distinct from what is made to happen in the carefully composed picture of life presented by the moral dramatist.[30]

In conclusion, *A Yorkshire Tragedy* is based on a pamphlet that tells a jog-trot tale of murder, bolstered up with a few Latin tags, warnings of God's vengeance, and euphuistic similes. The play transforms this tale into a swift and violent tragedy which, like *Macbeth*, is about damnation and tries 'to get inside the skin of a murderer'.[31] Although it has been influenced by the prodigal husband-faithful wife motif and by the conventional theology of the morality play, it goes beyond both of these. It is prevented from being high tragedy by its failure to create any real tension between good and evil: its colours are black and white, and the Husband's black is more than a match for the Wife's dazzling white. Nevertheless, on a humble domestic level, it is an excellent documentary play, a remarkable miniature of evil which portrays the devil incarnate with insight and linguistic vitality.

---

[30] I fail to understand why there must of necessity be a conflict between Christianity and the tragic vision, as Clifford Leech, Robert Ornstein and others have argued. A distinction can be made between a penitential type of play, in which the sinner's punishment is terrestrial and finite and a play such as *A Yorkshire Tragedy*—untypical though it may be as a domestic tragedy—in which the sinner's destruction is made devastatingly complete in this world and the next. The first is a call to repentance for any kind of sin; the second warns that there are sins too monstrous for repentance. *A Yorkshire Tragedy*, no less than *Faustus* and *Macbeth*, is concerned to show how a man, if his sins are heinous enough, can bring himself to damnation despite the existence of a personal and kindly God.

[31] Muir, *op. cit.*, p. l.

10

The Fourth Stage

(Through the Mysteries of Ogun[1] to the Origin of Yoruba Tragedy)

WOLE SOYINKA

THE persistent search for the meaning of tragedy, for a re-definition in terms of cultural or private experience is, at least, a recognition by man of certain areas of depth experience which are not satisfactorily explained by general aesthetic theories: and of all the subjective unease that is aroused by man's creative insights, that wrench within the human psyche which we vaguely define as tragedy is the most insistent voice that bids us return to our own sources. There, illusively, hovers the key to the human paradox, to man's experience of being and non-being, his dubiousness as essence and matter, intimations of transience and eternity and the harrowing drives between uniqueness and Oneness.

Our course to the heart of the Yoruba Mysteries leads by its own ironic truths through the light of Nietzsche[2] and the Phrygian deity; but there are the inevitable, key departures. 'Blessed Greeks!' sings our mad votary in his recessional rapture, 'how great must be your Dionysos, if the Delic god thinks such enchantments necessary to cure you of your Dithyrambic madness.' Such is Apollo's resemblance to the serene art of Obatala[3] the pure unsullied one, to the 'essence' idiom of his rituals, that it is tempting to place him at the end of a creative axis to Ogun in a parallel evolutionary relationship to

---

[1] Ogun: God of creativity, guardian of the road, god of the metallic lore and artistry. Explorer, hunter, god of war, Custodian of the sacred oath.

[2] Nietzsche: *The Birth of Tragedy*.

[3] Obatala: God of creation (by syncretist tradition with Orisa-nla), Essence of the serene arts.

119

Nietzsche's Dionysos-Apollo brotherhood. But Obatala the sculptural god is not the artist of Apollonian illusion but of inner essence. The idealist bronze and terra-cotta of Ife died at some forgotten period, evidence only of the universal surface culture of courts and never again to be resurrected, testifying to its alienhood to the Obatala spirit of Yoruba 'essential' art. The idiom of the plastic god Obatala is not however, Nietzsche's Apollonian 'mirror of enchantment' but a statement of world resolution. The mutual tempering of illusion and will, necessary to an understanding of the Hellenic spirit, would mislead us, confronted in Yoruba art by a similarity in the aesthetic serenity of the plastic arts to the Hellenic. But this art is not ideational but 'essential'. As for Ogun, he is best understood in Hellenic values as a totality of the Dionysian, Apollonian and Promethean virtues. Nor is this all. Transcending, even today, the distorted myths of his terrorist reputation, traditional poetry records him as 'protector of orphans', 'roof over the homeless', 'terrible guardian of the sacred oath'; Ogun stands in fact for a transcendental, humane but rigidly restorative justice. The first artist and technician of the forge, he, like Nietzsche's Apollonian spirit, creates a 'massive impact of image, concept, ethical doctrine and sympathy' Obatala is the placid essence of creation, Ogun the creative urge and instinct.

> Rich-laden is his home, yet decked in palm fronds
> He ventures forth, refuge of the down-trodden,
> To rescue slaves he unleashed the judgment of war
> Because of the blind, plunged into forests
> Of curative herbs, Bountiful One
> Who stands bulwark to offsprings of the dead of heaven
> Salutations, O lone being, who swims in rivers of blood.

Such virtues place Ogun apart from the distorted dances which Nietzsche's Dionysiac frenzy led him in his search for a selective 'Aryan' soul, yet do not detract from Ogun's revolutionary grandeur. Ironically it is the depth illumination of Nietzsche's intuition into basic universal impulses which negates his exclusivist conclusions on the nature of art and tragedy. In our journey to the heart of Yoruba tragic art which indeed begins in the Mysteries of Ogun and the choric ecstasy of revellers we will not find that the Yoruba, like the Greek, ever 'built for his chorus the scaffolding of a fictive chthonic realm and placed thereon fictive nature spirits . . .' on which foundation, claims Nietzsche, Greek tragedy developed. Yoruba tragedy plunges straight into the 'chthonic realm', the seething cauldron of

120

the dark world will and psyche, the transitional yet inchoate matrix of death and being. Into this universal womb plunged and emerged Ogun, first actor, disintegrating within the abyss, nor has his spiritual re-assemblage needed even a 'copying of actuality' in the ritual re-enactment of his devotees. (Equally true is this of plastic representation in the art of Obatala.) The actors of the Ogun Mysteries are the communicant chorus who contain within their collective will the essence of that transitional abyss. But only as essence, held, contained and mystically expressed. Within the mystic summons of the chasm the actor (every god-suffused choric individual) resists, as Ogun before him, the final step towards complete annihilation. From this alone is found the eternal actor of the tragic rites, first as the unresisting mouthpiece of the god, uttering visions symbolic of the transitional gulf, interpreting the dread power within whose essence he is immersed as one of the choric will. Only later, in the evenness of release from the tragic climax, does the serene Obatala self-awareness reassert its creative control. He, the actor, emerges still as the mediant voice of the god, but stands now as it were beside himself, observant, understanding, creating. At this stage is known to him the sublime *aesthetic* joy, not within Nietzsche's heart of original oneness but in the distanced celebration of the cosmic struggle. This resolved aesthetic serenity is the link in Ogun tragic art with Obatala plastic beauty. The unblemished god, Obatala, is the serene womb of world memory, a passive strength awaiting and celebrating each act of vicarious restoration to his primordial being. (We shall come later to the story of that first severance.) His beauty is enigmatic, expressive only of the resolution of plastic healing through the wisdom of acceptance. Obatala's patient suffering is the well-known aesthetics of the saint.

For the Yoruba, the gods are the final measure of eternity, and humans of earthly transience. To think, because of this, that the Yoruba mind reaches intuitively towards absorption in godly essence is to misunderstand the principle of religious rites and to misread, as many have done, the significance of religious possession. The past, the present and the future, being so pertinently conceived and woven into the Yoruba world view, the element of eternity which is the gods' prerogative does not have the same quality of remoteness or exclusiveness which it has in Christian or Bhuddist culture. The belief of the Yoruba in the contemporaneous existence within his daily experience of these aspects of time has been long recognized but again misinterpreted. It is no abstraction. The Yoruba is not, like European man, concerned with the purely conceptual aspects of time—they are too concretely realized in his own life, religion, sensitivity to be mere tags for explaining the metaphysical order of his world. If we may put the same thing in fleshed-out cognitions, life, present life, contains within it manifestations of ancestor, the living and the unborn. All are vitally within the intimations and affectiveness of life, beyond mere abstract comprehension.

And yet the Yoruba does not, for that reason, fail to distinguish between himself and the deities, himself and the ancestors, between the unborn and his reality, or discard his awareness of the immense gulf which lies between one area of existence and another. This gulf is what must be constantly diminished by the sacrifices, the rituals, the ceremonies of appeasement to the cosmic powers which lie guardian to this gulf. Spiritually, the primordial fear of the Yoruba mind may be seen as the existence somewhere in the collective memory of the primal severance in transitional ether, whose first effective defiance is symbolized in the myth of the gods' descent to earth and the battle with immense chaotic growth which had sealed off reunion with man. For they were coming down, not simply to be acknowledged but to be re-united with human essence, to reassume that portion of re-creative transient awareness which the first deity Orisa-nla possessed and expressed through his continuous moulding of man images—brief reflections of divine facets—just as man is grieved by a consciousness of the loss of the eternal essence of his entity and must indulge in symbolic settlements to recover his total being.

Tragedy, in Yoruba traditional drama, is the anguish of this severance, the fragmentation of essence from self, of essence from itself. Its music is the stricken cry of man's blind soul as he flounders in weightless void and crashes through a deep abyss of a-spirituality and cosmic rejection. Tragic music is an echo from that void; the celebrant speaks, sings and dances in authentic archetypal images from within the abyss. All understand and respond, for it is the language of the world.

It is necessary to emphasize that the gods were coming down to be reunited with man, for this tragedy could not *be*, the anguish of severance could not attain such tragic proportions if the gods' position on earth (i.e. in man) was to be one of divine remoteness. This is again testified to both by the form of worship, which is marked by camaraderie and irreverence just as departure to ancestor-hood is marked by bawdiness in the midst of grief. The anthropo-morphic origin of uncountable deities is one more leveller of divine class-consciousness but, finally, it is the innate *humanity* of the gods themselves, their bond with man through communal animist essence with nature and phenomena. Continuity for the Yoruba operates through the animist interfusion of all matter and consciousness.

The first actor therefore was Ogun, first suffering deity, first creative energy, the first darer and conqueror of transition. And the first art was the tragic art, for the drama of the syncretic successor to Orisa-nla, Obatala's 'Passion' play, is only the plastic resolution of Ogun's tragic engagement. The Yoruba metaphysics of accom-modation and resolution could only come *after* the passage of the gods through the transitional gulf, and the demonic test of the self-will of the explorer god in the creative cauldron of cosmic powers. Only after such testing could the Yoruba harmonious world be born, a harmonious will which accommodates every material or abstract phenomenon within its infinitely stressed spirituality. The artifact of Ogun's conquest of separation, the 'fetish', was iron ore, symbol of earth's womb energies, cleaver and welder of life. Ogun in his redemptive action became the first symbol of the union of con-tradictions when from earth itself he extracted elements for the subjugation of chthonic chaos. In tragic consciousness the votary's psyche reaches out beyond the realm of nothingness, potentially destructive of human awareness, into areas of terror and blind energies because it was the gods, the eternal presences, who first became aware of their own incompletion. Anguish is therefore primal transmission of the god's despair, vast, numinous, always incom-prehensible. In vain we seek to capture it in words, there is only the certainty of the existence of this abyss—the tragic victim plunges into it in spite of ritualistic earthing and is redeemed only by action. Without acting, and yet in spite of it he is forever lost in the maul of tragic tyranny.

And acting is therefore a contradiction of the tragic spirit, yet it is also its natural complement. To act, the Promethean instinct of rebellion, channels anguish into creative purpose which releases man from a totally destructive despair, releasing from within him the most energic, deeply combative inventions which, without usurping the territory of the infernal gulf, bridge them with visionary hopes. Only the battle of the will is thus primally creative, from its spiritual stress springs the soul's despairing cry which proves its own solace, which alone reverberating within the cosmic vaults usurps (at least, and however briefly) the powers of the abyss. At the charged climactic moments of the tragic rites we understand how music came to *contain*, the sole art form which does contain, tragic reality. The votary can be led by no other guide into the pristine heart of tragedy. Music as the embodiment of the tragic spirit has been more than perceptively exhausted in the philosophy of Europe; there is little to add, much to qualify. And the function and nature of music in Yoruba tragedy is peculiarly revealing of the shortcomings of long accepted conclusions of European intuition.

The European concept of music does not fully illuminate the relationship of music to ritual and drama among the Yoruba. We are inhibited even by recognition of a universality of concepts or the European intuitive grasp of the emotions of the will. First, it is 'unmusical' to separate Yoruba musical form from myth and poetry. The nature of Yoruba music is intensively the nature of its language and poetry, highly charged, symbolic, myth-embryonic. We acknowledge quite readily the technical lip-service paid to the correspondence of African music to the tonal patterns (meaning and allusion) of the language, but the aesthetic and emotional significance of this relationship has not been truly absorbed. For this goes deeper than a mere technical relationship, it is a clue to the conceptual unity of poetry and melody among the Yoruba, one which springs from the primal simultaneity of art forms in a culture of total awareness and phenomenal involvement. Language therefore is not a barrier to the profound universality of music but a cohesive dimension and clarification of that wilfully independent art form which we label music. Language reverts in religious rites to its pristine existence eschewing the sterile limits of particularization. In cult funerals, the circle of initiate mourners, an ageless swaying grove of dark pines, raise a chant around a mortar of fire, and words are taken back to their roots, to their original poetic sources when fusion was total and the movement of words is the very passage of music and the dance of images. Language still is the embryo of thought and music where myth is daily companion, constantly mythopoeic. Language in Yoruba tragic music has therefore undergone transformation through myth into a secret masonic correspondence with the symbolism of tragedy, a symbolic language from spiritual emotions within the heart of the choric union and beyond to the tragic source whence springs the weird disruptive melodies. This masonic union of signs and melody, the true tragic music, unearths, like certain questioning rain phases, cosmic uncertainties which pervade human existence, reveal the magnitude and power of creation, but above all, create a harrowing sense of omnidirectional vastness where resides this force and prompts the soul to futile exploration. The senses do not at such moments interpret myth in their particular concretions, rather are we left only with the emotional and spiritual values and experience of those truths (which are symbolically not rationally triggered off in memory and shared as a communal experience). The forms of music are not correspondences at such moments to the physical world, not at this nor at any other moment. The singer is a mouthpiece of the chthonic forces of the matrix and his somnabulist 'improvisations', a simultaneity of musical and poetic forms, are not representations of the ancestor, living or unborn recognitions, but of the no-man's-land of transition between and around these temporal definitions of experience. The past is the ancestor's, the present the living, and the future the unborn. In a parallel relationship, that is, the relationship of what is directly attainable and what is not, the deities stand in the same situation to the living as do the ancestors and the unborn, obeying the same laws, suffering the same agonies and uncertainties, employing the same masonic intelligence of rituals for the perilous plunge into the fourth area of experience, the immeasurable gulf of transition. Its dialogue in liturgy, its music takes form from man's incomprehensible knowledge of this area of existence, buried wholly from rational recognition. The source of the possessed lyricist, chanting hitherto unknown mythopoeic strains whose antiphonal refrain is however immediately recognized and thrust with all its terror and awesomeness into the night by swaying votaries, this source is residual in the numinous area of transition.

This is the fourth stage, the vortex of archetypes and home of the tragic spirit.

It is necessary to recall again that the past is not a mystery and although the future (the unborn) is yet unknown, it is not a mystery to the Yoruba but co-existent in present consciousness. Tragic terror exists therefore neither in the evocation of the past nor of the future. The stage of transition is however the metaphysical abyss both of god and man, and if we agree that, in the European sense, music is the 'direct copy or the direct expression of the will', it is only because nothing rescues man (ancestral, living, unborn) from loss of self within this abyss but a titanic resolution of the will whose summons, response and involuntary expression is the strange alien sound to which we give the name of music. And yet the gulf must be perpetually crossed and recrossed. On the arena of the living when man is stripped of excrescences, when disasters and conflicts (the material of drama) have crushed and robbed him of self-consciousness and pretensions, he stands in present reality at the spiritual edge of this gulf, he has nothing left in physical existence which successfully impresses upon his spiritual or psychic perception—it is at such moments that transitional memory takes over and intimations rack him of that intense parallel of his progress through the gulf of transition, of the dissolution of his self and his struggle and triumph over subsumation through the agency of will. It is this experience that the modern tragic dramatist recreates through the medium of physical contemporary action, reflecting emotions of the first active battle of the will through the abyss of dissolution. Ogun is the first actor in that battle, and Yoruba tragic drama is the re-enactment of the cosmic conflict.

To recognize why Ogun was elected for his role (and the penalty of horror which he had to pay for his dare) is to penetrate the symbolism of Ogun both as essence of suffering and as combative will within the cosmic embrace of the transitional gulf. We have said that nothing but the will—for that alone is left untouched—rescues being from annihilation within the abyss. Ogun is embodiment of Will and the Will is the paradoxical truth of destructiveness and creativeness in acting man. Only one who has himself undergone the experience of disintegration, whose spirit has been tested and psychic resources laid under stress by the most inimical forces to individual assertion, only he can understand and *be* the force of fusion between the two contradictions. The resulting sensitivity is also the sensitivity of the artist and he is a profound artist only to the degree to which he comprehends and expresses the principle of destruction and re-creation. Nor can we lose sight of the fact that Ogun is the artistic spirit, and not in the sentimental sense in which rhapsodists of negritude would have us conceive the negro as pure artistic intuition. The significant creative truth of Ogun is affirmation of the re-creative will, irreconcilable with naive intuition. The symbolic artifact of his victory is metallic ore, at once a *technical* medium as it is symbolic of deep earth energies, a fusion of elemental energies, a kernel of the binding force between disparate bodies and properties. Ogun, tragic actor, primordial voice of creative man is also, without a contradiction of essences, the forerunner and ancestor of paleotechnic man. The principle of creativity when limited to pastoral idyllism as negritude has attempted to limit it, shuts us off from the deeper, fundamental resolutions of experience and cognition. The tragic actor for the future age (already the present for Europe) is that neotechnic ancestor Sango,[4] god of electricity, whose tragedy stems equally from the principle of a preliminary self-destruction represented (as in a later penalty of Ogun) in the blind ignorant destruction of his own flesh and blood. What, for Ogun, was a destructive penalty leading to a drama of 'Passion' was in Sango the very core of his tragedy. The historic process of dilution in tragic dare is manifest in the relationship of these two myths. Sango, anthropomorphic deity, his action revolved around petty tyranny, his self-destruction was the violent, central explosion from ego inflation and where Ogun's terrestrial excision was the tail-piece error, an exaction for victory over the transitional guardians of the gulf, Sango's was a wild vengeful slaughter upon menials who had dared defy his strength. But the 'terror and pity' is undeniable, only it is the 'terror and pity' of human disavowals of a new disciple standing on the abyss of that sublimation within which Ogun the first actor had fought the first battle of Will against disintegration. We will not find the roots of tragedy in the Mysteries of Sango.

Yoruba myth is a recurrent exercise in the experience of disintegration, and this is significant to the isolation of Will among a people whose mores, culture and metaphysics are based on seeming resignation and acceptance but are, experienced in depth, a statement of man's penetrating insight into the final resolution of things and the constant evidence of harmony. What impulse for instance do we discover in the drama of Obatala, representative though it is of the first disintegration experienced by godhead? We are further back to the origin, not now engaged in the transitional battle of Ogun, but in the fragmentation of Orisa-nla, the primal deity, from whom the entire Yoruba pantheon was born. Myth informs us that a jealous slave rolled a stone down the back of the first and only deity and shattered him in a thousand and sixty-four fragments. From this first act of revolution was born the Yoruba pantheon.

The drama which stems from this is not the drama of acting man

---

[4] Sango: God of lightning and electricity. A tyrant of Oyo, he was forced to commit suicide by factions and his own overreaching. His followers thereupon deified him and he assumed the agency of lightning.

but that of suffering spirit, the drama of Obatala. Yoruba myth equates Obatala, god of purity, god also of creation (but not of creativity!) with the first deity Orisa-nla. And the ritual of Obatala is a play of form, a moving celebration whose nearest equivalent in the European idiom is the Passion play. The drama is all essence—captivity, suffering and redemption; Obatala is symbolically captured, confined and ransomed. At every stage he is the embodiment of the suffering spirit of man, uncomplaining, agonised, full of the redemptive qualities of the spirit of endurance and martyrdom. The music that accompanies the rites of Obatala is all clear tone and winnowed lyric, of order and harmony, stately and saintly. Significantly, the motif is white for transparency of heart and mind; there is a rejection of mystery, tones of vesture and music combine to banish mystery and terror; the poetry of the song is litanic, the dramatic idiom is the processional or ceremonial. It is a drama in which the values of conflict or of the revolutionary spirit are excluded, attesting in their place the adequacy and inevitable aftermath of harmonious resolution which belongs in time and human faith. It is antithetical to the tragic dare of Ogun in man.

Proportion in tragedy is related to an element of the unknown in the forces of opposition or by a miscalculation by the tragic victim of such powers. The drama of Obatala dispenses with the effect of the unknown and his agony is an evocation of the loneliness of the first deity, for this drama is, as we have stated, all essence. And the essence is the emotional prelude to the creation of man, the limited, serene aesthetics of creating man, not to be compared to the cosmic eruption intuitive to the recreation of the self. The sentimental but moving, sympathetic need to be redeemed by evidence of love and human contact, by extension of the self into recognizable entities and other units of consciousness, this is the province of Obatala, the delicate shell of the original fullness. The profounder aspect of self-recreation, the anguish of the Will, is the portion of original restoration which has been left to the peculiar talents of Ogun—and the statement of Yoruba tragic rites is the complement of Will to the essence of anguish. The latter by itself is crystallised in the Passion play. The drama of Obatala is prelude, aftermath, symbolic firstly of the god's unbearable loneliness and next of the lurking memory within his incomplete godhead of a missing essence. And so with the other gods who did not avail themselves, as did Ogun, of the chance for a redemptive combat each to recreate each by submission to a distintegrating process within the matrix of cosmic essence, whence the will performs the final reassemblage. The weightiest burden of severance is that of each from self, not of godhead from mankind, and the most perilous aspect of their journey is that in which the deity must truly undergo the experience of transition. It is a look into the very heart of phenomenon. To fashion a bridge across it was not only Ogun's task but his very nature, and he had first to experience, to surrender his individuation once again (the first time, as a part of the original Orisa-nla Oneness) to the fragmenting process, to be resorbed within universal Oneness, the Unconscious, the deep black whirlpool of mythopoeic forces, to immerse himself thoroughly within it, understand its nature and yet by the combative value of the will to rescue and re-assemble himself and emerge wiser, powerful from the draught of cosmic secrets, organizing the mystic and the technical forces of earth and cosmos to forge a bridge for his companions to follow.

It is true that to understand, to understand profoundly, is to be unnerved of the will to act. For is not human reality dwarfed by the awe and wonder, the *inevitability* of this comic gulf? It must be remembered that within this abyss are the activities of birth, death and divine phenomena (for the abyss is the transition between the various stages of existence), and life, the true mirror of enchantment, the paltry reflection of the forces of the matrix, becomes suddenly inadequate, patronizing and undignified when the source of creative and destructive energies is glimpsed, Suffering cancels the opaque pleasures of human existence; suffering, the truly overwhelming suffering of Sango, of Lear, of Oedipus, this suffering hones the psyche to a finely self-annihilating perceptiveness and renders further action futile and above all, lacking dignity. And what has been the struggle of the tragic hero after all but an effort to maintain that innate concept of dignity which impels to action only to that degree in which the hero possesses a true nobility of spirit. At such moments he is close to the acceptance and wisdom of Obatala in which faith is rested, not on the self, but on a universal selfhood to which individual contributions are truly meaningless. It is the faith of 'knowing', the enigmatic wisdom of spiritual serenity. It is this which is often misinterpreted as the philosophy of the African, but philosophies are the result of primal growth and formative experience, and the oracular wisdom of a race based and continually acted upon by the collective experience of the past, present and unborn existences of the community and the intuitive glimpse and memory of the heart of transitional being. Yoruba art is an expression of the Obatala resolution and humane beneficence, utterly devoid, on the surface, of conflict and disruption. The masks alone occasionally suggest a correspondence to the chthonic realm and hint of the archetypes of transition, yet even the majority of them flee the full power of cosmic vision, take refuge in deliberately grotesque and comic attitudes. Such distortions are easily recognized as the technique of evasion from the fullness of numinous powers. Terror is both contained by art in tragic form and released by art through comic presentation and sexual ambience. The tragic mask however also functions from the same source as its music—from archetypal essences whose language derives not from the plane of physical reality or ancestral memory (the ancestor is no more than agent or medium), but from the numinous territory of transition into which the artist obtains fleeting glimpses by ritual, sacrifices and a patient submission of rational awareness to the moment when his fingers and voice relate the symbolic language of the cosmos. The deft, luminous peace of Yoruba religious art blinds us therefore to the darker powers of the tragic art into which only the participant can truly enter. The grotesquerie of the terror cults misleads the unwary into equating fabricated fears with the exploration of the Yoruba mind into the mystery of his individual will and the intimations of divine suffering to which the artistic man is prone. Ifa's cycle of masonic poetry, curative, prognostic, aesthetic and omniscient expresses a philosophy of optimism by its oracular adaptiveness and unassailable resolution of all phenomena; the gods are accommodating and embrace within their eternal presences manifestations which are seemingly foreign or contradictory: it is no wonder therefore that the overt optimistic nature of the total culture is in the quality attributed to the Yoruba himself, one which has in fact begun to affect his accommodativeness towards the modern world, a spiritual complacency with which he encounters threats to his human and unique validation. Alas, in spite of himself, from time to time, the raw urgent question beats the blood against his temples demanding, what is the will of Ogun? For the hammering of the Yoruba will was done at Ogun's forge and any threat of disjunction is, as with the gods, a memory code for the resurrection of the tragic myth.

Yoruba morality has also contributed to the mistaken exclusion of tragic myth from present consciousness; for, as always, the placid surface of the processes of healing for spiritual rupture is mistaken also for a non-existence of the principles of psychic experience that went into the restoration. Morality for the Yoruba is that which creates harmony in the cosmos, and reparation for disjunction within the individual psyche cannot be seen as compensation for the individual accident to that personality. Thus it is that good and evil are not measured in terms of offences against the individual or even the physical community, for there is a knowledge from within the corpus of Ifa wisdoms that rupture is often one visage of the Ogun destructive-creative unity, that offences even against nature may in fact be part of the exaction by deeper nature from humanity of acts which alone can open up the deeper springs of man and bring about a constant rejuvenation of the human spirit. Nature in turn benefits by such broken taboos, just as the cosmos by the demand made upon its will by man's cosmic affronts. Such acts of hubris compel the cosmos to delve deeper into its essence to meet the human challenge. Penance and retribution are not therefore aspects of punishment for crime but the first acts of a resumed awareness, an invocation of the principle of cosmic adjustment. Tragic fate is the repetitive cycle of the taboo in nature, the karmic act of hubris, witting or unwitting, into which the demonic will within man constantly compels him. Powerful tragic drama follows upon the act of hubris, and myth exacts this attendant penalty from the hero where he has actually emerged victor of a conflict. Olurombi[5] emerged unscathed from his quest for possession of psychic strength but fulfilled the self-destructive destiny in the sacrifice of his son. Sango's taboo is based on a more elementary form of hubris. Overreaching even beyond the generous toleration due to a monarch, he fell victim to a compulsion for petty intriguing which finally led to his downfall. A final, desperate invocation of unnatural strength gave him temporary ascendancy and he routed his disloyal men. Then came the desecration of nature in which he spilt the blood of kin. Ogun not only dared to look into transitional essence but triumphantly bridged it with knowledge, with art, with vision and the mystic creativity of science—a total and profound hubristic assertiveness that is beyond any parallel in Yoruba experience. The penalty came later when, as a reward and acknowledgement of his leadership of the divinities, gods and humans joined to offer him a crown. The first he declined but later he consented to the throne of Ire. At the first battle the same

[5] Olurombi: A mytho-historical figure.

demonic energies were aroused but this was no world womb, no chthonic lair, no playground of cosmic monsters, nor could the divisions between man and man, between I and you, friend and foe, be perceived by the erstwhile hero of the transitional abyss. Enemy and subjects fell alike until Ogun alone was left, sole survivor of the narrowness of human separation. The battle is symbolic of tragic hindsight common alike to god and man. In the Ogun Mysteries the drama is 'Passion' of a different kind, released into quietist wisdom, a ritual exorcism of demonic energies. There is no elation, not even at the end of purgation, nothing like the beatified elation of Obatala after his redemption, only a world weariness on the rockshelf of Promethean shoulders, a profound sorrow in the chanting of the god's recessional.

Once we recognize, to revert to his Hellenic equation, the Dionysian-Apollonian-Promethean essence of Ogun, the element of hubris is seen as innate to his tragic being, requiring definition in Yoruba terms, taking it to its cyclic resolution of man's metaphysical situation. Of the profound anguish of Dionysos, the mythic disintegration of his origin is the now familiar cause, and the process of the will, no less, is what rescues the ecstatic god from being, literally, scattered to the cosmic winds. The will of Zeus is as conceptually identifiable with that of Dionysos as the elemental fragmentation of Orisa-nla can be recognized as the recurrent consciousness within Ogun (and other gods) of this kernel of terror of a previous rendering. Ripped in pieces at the hands of the titans for the unwilled (by him) act of hubris, a divine birth, Dionysos-Zagreus commences divine existence by this experience of the destruction of the self, the transitional horror. For it is an act of hubris not only to dare the gulf of transition but to mingle essences for extra measure. We approach, it seems, the ultimate pessimism of existence as pronounced by Nietzsche's sage Silenus—it is an act of hubris to be born. It is a challenge to the jealous chthonic powers, to *be*. The answer of the Yoruba to this is just as clear—it is no less an act of hubris to *die* as to be born. And the whirlpool of transition requires both hubristic complements as catalyst to its continuous regeneration. This is the serene wisdom and essential art of Obatala. All acts are lesser to these ultimates of the human condition and creative will. To dare transition is the ultimate test of the human spirit, and Ogun is the first protagonist of the abyss.

The Phrygian god and his twinhood with Ogun exercise irresistible fascination. His thyrsus is physically and functionally parallelled by the *opa Ogun* borne by the male devotees of Ogun. But the thyrsus of Dionysos is brighter, it is all light and running wine, Ogun's stave is more symbolic of the labours of Ogun through the night of transition. A long willowy pole, it is topped by a frond-bound lump of ore which strains the pole in wilful curves and keeps it vibrant. The bearers, who can only be men, are compelled to move about among the revellers as the effort to keep the ore-head from weighting over keeps them perpetually on the move. Through town and village, up the mountain to the grove of Ogun this dance of the straining phallus-heads pocks the air above men and women revellers who are decked in palm fronds and bear palm branches in their hands. A dog is slaughtered in sacrifice, and the mock-struggle of the head priest and his acolytes for the carcass, during which it is literally torn limb from limb, inevitably brings to mind the dismemberment of Zagreus son of Zeus. Most significant of all is the brotherhood of the palm and the ivy. The mystery of the wine of palm, bled straight from the tree and potent without further ministration, is a miracle of nature acquiring symbolic significance in the Mysteries of Ogun. For it was instrumental to the tragic error of the god and his sequent Passion. Like Obatala also, the gods commit their error after an excess of the potent draught. Ogun was full of wine before his battle at the head of the Ire army. After his dark deed, the wine fog slowly lifted and he was left with nothing but dread truth. Obatala, moulder of lives, fell also to the fumes of wine; his craftsman's fingers lost their contro and he moulded cripples, albinos, the blind and other deformities. Obatala the eternal penitent therefore forbids wine to his worshippers in or out of his seasonal rites while Ogun, in proud acceptance of the need to create a challenge for the constant exercise of will and control, enjoins the liberal joy of wine. The palm fronds are a symbol of his wilful, ecstatic being.

And how else may the inhibitive bonds of man be dissolved when he goes to meet his god, how else may he quickly enter into the god's creative being or his inner ear and eye respond to the fleeting presences which guard the abode of gods, how else partake in the psychic revelry of the world when it celebrates a crossing of the abyss of non-being. The sculpted rites of the worship of Obatala are rapturous also, but lacking in ecstasy. It is a dance of amelioration to tyrannic powers, not a celebration of the infinite will of the Promethean spirit. The one is withdrawal, the other an explosion of the forces of darkness and joy, explosion of the sun's kernel, an eruption of fire which is the wombfruit of pristine mountains, for no less, no different were the energies within Ogun whose ordering and control by the will brought him safely through the tragic gulf. Even through the medium of this ecstasy, a glimpse is obtained of the vastness of the abyss; the true devotee knows, understands and penetrates the god's anguish. In the centre of the swaying, milling, ecstatic horde where his individuation is routed and he submits to a union of joy, the inner being encounters the precipice. Poised on the heights of the physical mountain home of Ogun he experiences a yawning gulf within him, a menacing maul of chthonic strength yawning ever wider to annihilate his being; he is saved only by channelling the dark torrent into the plastic light of poetry and dance, not however, as a reflection or illusion of reality, but as the celebrative aspect of the resolved crisis of his god.

11

G. Wilson Knight: Stage and Study

FRANCIS BERRY

THE poetic imagination is prophetic—if that is not an exact
quotation from G. Wilson Knight, it might well appear to be
so.[1] Some of us might feel that if a single statement could sum
his gospel, this would be it.

The poetic imagination is prophetic both in a local and exact or
in a wide and general application. In an exact and local sense it has
been illustrated by Knight in his interpretation of Richard II's
speech beginning 'I have been studying how I may compare . . .',
where Shakespeare, in the person of Richard, prophesies his own
later poetic and dramatic development.[2] Cranmer[3] prophesies over
the infant Elizabeth,[4] although Shakespeare is then writing from a
vantage point in time when the events the archbishop forsees had
already happened. But Pope is prophetic, in a more general sense, as
Knight shows in his discussion of *Windsor Forest* where the poet's
feeling for the growing oaks is related to a perception that the trees
will become the walls of Britain's navy.[5] In a yet wider sense however,
because remote human destinies are now envisioned, the poetic
imagination is prophetic. The books in which Knight most fully
investigates the prophetic nature of major poets are *The Christian*

---

[1] But cp. 'The poet is the prophet. We must henceforth see great poetry as prophetic,
so that Shelley's words may be fulfilled in all their splendour.' (*The Christian Renaissance*, enlarged ed., 1962, p. 265).

[2] 'The Prophetic Soul' in *The Imperial Theme*, (1951 ed.), pp. 351 ff.

[3] *Henry VIII*, V.v.

[4] *The Crown of Life* (1947 ed.), pp. 331 ff.

[5] *Laureate of Peace* (1954 ed.), p. 21.

Renaissance[6] and *Christ and Nietzsche* (1948), especially in the section in the latter devoted to Goethe.[7]

No wonder that Wilson Knight has shown that the major poets are prophetic. Most of his readers and listeners would agree that he himself looks to the future with a love and so can engage these poets, who though dead are operating powers, in a kind of mutuality of sympathy and understanding. Knight is positive; he believes in the subjects of his interpretations; he trusts the adventure of life. Confronted by their writings, of how many other recent eminent English men of letters could one say this?

And how, granted this endowment, would Wilson Knight have Shakespeare produced on the stage? What measure of agreement is there between his interpretative studies and his ideals of stage representation as set out in *Shakespearian Production*[8]—perhaps his most soberly entitled book, yet concerned with what is his deepest passion of all? The answer to the last question is that there is a full agreement—that in the theatre he would 'body forth' what he has perceived in his literary studies. This at once dismisses the jibe (callous and shallow) that the scholar who neglects 'character' in his studies of the texts makes much of 'character', in a rhetorical Edwardian mode, as a man of the theatre. It is justly dismissed because the premise, apparent to any scrupulous reader of *The Wheel of Fire*, is false. Instead, it would be wiser to face up to, if only to challenge, this complaint: that on the stage, Wilson Knight would not have Shakespeare as our contemporary; that he would present him as a very late Victorian or Edwardian Romantic dramatist. Such objectors might point out that *Shakespearian Production* is dedicated to 'the memory of the late Herbert Beerbohm Tree' and 'of his disciple in the art of acting Leslie Harris'.

If to make Shakespeare *our* contemporary, it is necessary to believe that the poet conceived Othello not as a 'noble' Moor (except in his own self-estimation) but throughout as a vain, self-regarding, rhetorical fool, that he aimed so to present him on the stage that this would be the audience's sustained view of him; or that it is necessary to believe that Troilus' talk of 'honour'[9] is submitted to the audience

---

[6] 1962 ed. p. 265.

[7] pp. 105–16.

[8] Enlarged ed., 1964. Originally published in 1937 as *Principles of Shakespearian Production*. Besides setting out his own principles, the book has great interest as a record of the author's responses to productions of others, extending in time from those of Tree to the very recent (including those on the 'open stage').

[9] *Troilus and Cressida*, II. ii.

for ironic appraisal—then Knight makes Shakespeare no contemporary of ours on or off the stage. And rightly: for, in such a view, Shakespeare is changed into a Jonson—one who habitually worked the vein of irony. Shakespeare's art includes, of course, satire and irony. Thersites, Lucio, Iago exercise these highly-rated skills, but their function is destructive; and no one has analysed this 'destructive wit' in the problem plays and tragedies, its force, so thoroughly or so well as has Knight. But to treat the component as the circumscribing whole, and to present it on the stage as such, is an error, a 'slanting' or crookedness. This I would myself say, I hope, without ever having read Wilson Knight's exposure of the error. What Knight would, and does, aver is that Othello and Antony *are* noble—though the one comes to see himself as a 'fool' and the other as 'betrayed'. And the Macbeth of Act V, 'though likely to be damned from a Christian viewpoint' (as Knight says in correspondence), has grandeur. Irony is there, possibly judgment, but the circumscribing —and animating—power is sympathy, imagination passionate and compassionate. The contemporary fear of acknowledging or betraying this power propels many post-1930 critics and theatrical producers, British, American or European, to canvass a Shakespeare as oblique in utterance as early Eliot or late Henry James. A trust in this power issues from a trust in life and a conviction that the poetic imagination is prophetic.

Nor is Wilson Knight as Shakespearian producer 'contemporary' to the point of being unhistorical: as was Komisarjevsky when, at Stratford before the last war, he arranged a *Macbeth* where Macbeth started at projections on a cinematographic screen, seeing no ghosts or witches' apparitions but merely his own projected fears; or as when a New York production in modern costume of *Julius Caesar*, of the same period, high-lighted, built up so that it became dominant, the tearing of Cinna the poet to illustrate the irrational ferocity of fascist mobs. Nor is he unhistorical as Kott, in *Shakespeare Our Contemporary*, is unhistorical when he sees *A Midsummer Night's Dream* as a bloody and anguished piece of the Theatre of Cruelty, though Knight had himself pointed the fearsome elements in this Romantic Comedy in *The Shakespearian Tempest*. Knight, as producer, does not attempt to present a Shakespeare tilted to gratify our own decade's special, and passing, preoccupations. No less has he refused to countenance stage-tricks to startle. He would never, simply for the sake of an irrelevant effect, depart from a grouping or movement authorized by Shakespeare. He is innocent of trying to make the central peripheral or the peripheral central merely for the sake of submitting the play to a novel angle (the producer's, not Shakespeare's) from fear of a time-hallowed, yet obviously right, mounting.

Wilson Knight offers us no 'contemporary' Shakespeare in any of these senses. Neither does he offer a Shakespeare confined to Shakespeare's own theatrical period. For myself, I have much sympathy with the pioneer efforts of William Poel and Nugent Monck; and many of us, I suppose, would give much to see a *King Lear* or *Winter's Tale* in conditions reproducing the 1606 Globe or the 1611 Blackfriars conditions. But this is impossible. No two scholars are exactly agreed as to those conditions, Burbage is dead, and we—no Jacobean audience—would be *voyeurs* at an archaeological display of doubtful authenticity. Better such attempts with *The Spanish Tragedy* or *The Maid's Tragedy*, plays whose great interest is at least partly historical and contingent on Shakespeare.

Shakespeare was 'not of an age, but for all time', and, if he did not transcend his conditions during his life, though Jonson said he did, he does so now. Of course this is *the* result of his greatness; it is also, less obviously, the result of three hundred years of continuous Shakespearian production—that theatrical tradition has itself become part of Shakespeare which cannot be ignored. Wilson Knight knows as much history as he needs but his imagination is future-directed. His nature answers to the sovereign and the sovereignty of Shakespeare. He will not shrink Shakespeare and, if he can not actually enlarge him, has disclosed in his studies what is an authentic enlargement. Add to this, his early experiences of Shakespeare in the theatre were of Beerbohm Tree's productions at His Majesty's in all their ceremonial grandeur. And Tree's productions were the culmination of a tradition of grandeur—'Charles Kean—Henry Irving—Beerbohm Tree': a tradition which was dedicated to the revealing of Shakespeare's colourful abundance. On the other hand, for Granville Barker's Savoy productions, Knight has expressed always a respectful, but somewhat reserved, admiration—while the *Prefaces* leave him cold.

Colourful. Shakespeare's abundance, besides its terrors from which Knight has never flinched, is colourful. 'Colourful' and 'rich' are Knight's favourite words of approbation. He delights in colours and the colourful. Now when we agree that Shakespeare is colourful, as Chaucer is colourful, while Wordsworth is not, what exactly do we mean?

G. Wilson Knight: Stage and Study

When a word is used so that it is at once understood both literally and metaphorically there is a traffic between letter and spirit. Such words are the language of poetry and drama—but they are also used to describe the reader's impressions.

Shakespeare is colourful in that his work contains a profusion of direct colour adjectives ('scarlet sin', 'twixt the green sea and azur'd vault', 'the sere, the yellow leaf', 'now purple with love's wound', 'as black as Acheron', 'a green and guilded snake', 'the red pestilence' are random examples where the adjective is literal, metaphorical or both). Or he is colourful when reader or listener knows the colour of an object well enough to react to the adjective denoting simply the shade (e.g. 'pale primroses') or the object well enough to react to the adjective derived from the noun (e.g. 'sooty bosom'). Or Shakespeare employs words like 'blazon', noun ('with loyal blazon'), or 'blazon', verb ('blazoning our injustice'), where the modern reader, with his scant knowledge of heraldry and heraldic terms, derives a sharp, if confused, sense of colour. Or Shakespeare's apprehension of something is so complete and intense that its colour and shade, though unexpressed, is part of the reader's or audience's apprehension of the thing, as in 'Now does he feel His secret murthers sticking on his hands'. Here mention of colour could only have weakened. It is the verb, the word 'sticking', which gives the exact shade of the blood, half-way to coagulation. By these linguistic means, and by other linguistic means, Shakespeare ceaselessly activates in his reader's mind impressions of colour.

But Shakespeare the poet is Shakespeare the dramatist and so, besides the verbal creation of colour, there is a physically visible exposure on the stage of the colours—of properties, of hangings, etc. These can be explicitly demanded by the text. Thus, for instance, *The Merchant of Venice* contains a direction for the actor of the Prince of Morocco's make-up, 'Mislike me not for my complexion, The shadow'd livery of the burnish'd sun', and for the appearance, in three scenes, of three caskets, of 'gold, silver and base lead'. And where the directions are not so explicit as this, Shakespeare still implicitly prescribes. It would be sheer lunacy or wicked perversity to clothe Bassanio in sombre garments when he ventures his luck at Belmont or Shylock in gay or garish garments at the trial scene. Yet some contemporary producers come near to committing such lunacies or perversities.

But not Wilson Knight who responds to the Shakespearian colouration as a mirror unflawed and unclouded. This faithful and eager response might be attributed to his youthful enjoyments (too slight a word) at His Majesty's: 'for at His Majesty's you attended always something beyond entertainment, of noble if extravagant artistry'.[10] For this tradition still commands his loving, if not unreserved, admiration: 'we have scrapped one great tradition without creating another'. Even more certainly it can be attributed to his own colourful nature answering Shakespeare's. And how important it is that it should be answered! Since in Shakespeare, as we have suggested, its colour is an essential constituent of an object's identity. (But it does not follow that the objects of Wordsworth's grey world are dead.)

We suppose it is the ample recognition of this, as well as a constitutional delight in colour, that induces Knight to write so well and so fully of the colours within particular plays. Refer to *The Wheel of Fire*, *The Imperial Theme* or *The Crown of Life* and observe how, in his handling of tragedy, sombre or Roman, or of a final play, he reacts to and makes clear the individual colour-pattern of the play; he apprehends the weight, density or rondure of Shakespeare's verbal images as part of his realization of their colour. It is the same when the focus is not on the verbal but on the pattern of a scene. Thus, and it is in one of the earliest essays:

Alone in the gay glitter of the court, silhouetted against brilliance, robustness, health and happiness, is the pale, black-robed Hamlet, mourning.[11]

where very nearly every word in the sentence defines the colour constitution of a scene. It swiftly expresses the impact of *Hamlet* I.ii on the raising of the curtain.

This in itself refutes those who allege that there is a discordance between Knight's 'literary studies' and his 'theatrical practice'. Rather, when writing of Shakespeare's poetry, he is acutely aware—while seeing all in terms of the play as a whole—of the dramatic persons uttering that poetry, their relations to each other, and their theatrical setting: language and spectacle, the audible and the visible, are sensed as one. It gives Knight, at once literary interpreter and producer for the theatre, his authority. Note then: it is not a 'romantic' indulgence that he reflects or asserts in his handling of colour of either language or spectacle; the latter cannot be avoided except on monochrome film. But note also that, though nurtured on

[10] *Shakespearian Production*, enlarged ed. 1964, p. 21.
[11] *The Wheel of Fire*, 1947 ed., p. 17.

the Edwardian magnificence, he realizes that modern economic conditions, limiting expenditure, brings its consolations. He is an exponent of the uninterrupted flow of action and is not friendly toward lavish irrelevance. The stage- and hand-properties, the costumes, the *décor*, the sound-effects must be those demanded by Shakespeare; and being demanded, they must be noticeable, and so positive. Naturally, since a production is a collaborative effort, the ideal as it exists in the imagination cannot always be attained, but it can be approached.

As to practice: the present writer saw Wilson Knight's early Benvolio, saw his early productions of *A Midsummer Night's Dream* and *Twelfth Night*, acted in his pre-war London *Hamlet*, has seen—to limit oneself to Shakespeare—his Leeds production of *Timon of Athens* and his performances of Othello, King Lear and Shylock. From all these I received not only a stronger impression of Knight's vision of Shakespeare but a stronger vision of Shakespeare and conclude that the visions are of one and the same reality; that the productions and performances bodied out in space and time the perceptions that have animated his literary Interpretations. Nevertheless, if I am to concentrate on a single performance it would be on that of Shylock, and if on a single prospectus for an 'Ideal Production', it would be that for *The Merchant of Venice* (which is in fact a subject of 'The Ideal Production' chapter of *Shakespearian Production*) and do because, although this comedy is the subject of some beautiful pages in *The Shakespearian Tempest*,[12] it, like the other Romantic Comedies, has received less extended study from Knight in his Interpretations than have the later plays.

In the literary interpretation he had stressed how the imagery of previous plays—the venture over dangerous seas in the quest for riches or the riches of love; gold; jewels; music—is becoming, in *The Merchant of Venice*, 'the very plot itself'; and therefore 'in no play of this period is there so clear and significant a contrast between the tempests of tragedy and the music of romance'. This contrast is presented scenically: 'Venice is the scene of tragedy, Belmont of love'. From his Interpretations we could deduce that Knight would find this comedy especially attractive for stage-production.

Turning to the appropriate section of *Shakespearian Production*, we find that he asserts that 'our permanent set must help to mark out these contrasted worlds'. There should be a difference of level, stage

[12] pp. 127–37.

R (remembering the second syllable of Belmont) should be higher than stage L: then, 'Venetian scenes will concentrate on the lower, Belmont on the higher, level'. What is structurally essential in an imaginative reading must be physically and visibly projected on the stage. From this all follows. The one world is grasping, squalid, precarious, urban, and the other a world of boundless but seemingly carelessly regarded riches, of romance and prized love; and from this world Portia will stoop down to Venice to conquer. The three caskets must be 'solid and dominating'[13] or 'large and solid-looking';[14] for to make them small, light-weight or of *papier-maché* is to make the choosing-scenes, Belmont, its opposition Venice, and the whole play unserious and cheap. It will also be apparent that the human embodiments of the two worlds will be Portia and Shylock. All this is clearly true when said; Wilson Knight said it, but how many producers care to make the obviously true their top priority?

Though Wilson Knight has sought order and significance in Shakespeare, in literature, in life, he has not simplified and he has not made *The Merchant of Venice* schematic. If ever he had been tempted to do so, his playing of Shylock would have prevented that. However wrong the bloody vindictiveness of Shylock and 'right' the radiant justice of Portia, there are occasions when a sensitive reader or spectator feels that he is more sensitive than the victoriously just (or justly victorious) Portia and her fellow-Christians and lovers. The degradation and stripping of Shylock have gone too far. His own recent acting of Shylock impelled Knight to return to the play in the other role of commentator. His commentaries have long been valued for the wisdom and compassion which they enforce, and in such sayings as the following the experiences of literary scholar, producer, actor, thinker, human sufferer all play their part:

What we find here is a maximum of external humiliation supervening on our sympathy and our clear sense of a richness in Shylock's personality beyond anything apparent in his dramatic associates. . . . Such disasters (as Shylock's in IV.i.) in real life will often enough be accompanied by condemnation and humiliation, but we should seldom allow ourselves to feel that such an outcome covers the human problem.

'Ethic and society' have their rights,

but it is just because those rights so violently and even crudely assert themselves against our tragic sympathies that the end of the Trial scene

[13] p. 129.
[14] p. 128.

appears so deeply shocking. The shock, made of the crushing together of two seemingly incompatible and yet unavoidable truths, should leave the reader disturbed.[15]

'*Should* leave the reader disturbed.' The passage is one of many where the commentator concentrating on a specific Shakespearian situation, offers us his wisdom as a help in our own lives. And we learn that Shakespeare was also disturbed; for Shylock's 'inward soul-worth' promoted the growth that lead to the series of great tragedies: 'the problems posed by Falstaff and Shylock forced Shakespeare on to his more metaphysically patterned dramas'.[16]

Wilson Knight has said that what has driven him has been 'the instinct less of a scholar or even of a producer than, despite a host of deficiencies, as an actor'. He undoubtedly has a vision wherein each part of the bodily life is expressive of the spiritual, and perhaps *vice-versa*. Be that as it may, many—including some who care little essentially for Shakespeare, for poetry, for the theatre—have come to realize that he is a friend to our lives and a help in our problems. He has been companionable to Shakespeare's prophetic imagination in its course through tragedy to the Final Plays and this is an evidence in itself that he perceives a harmony beyond suffering.

[15] pp. 196–7.
[16] p. 197.

12

Notes on a Production of Wilson Knight's 'Ideal *Macbeth*'

LINDEN HUDDLESTONE

T
HERE has been a tendency to regard critics of Shakespearian poetic drama as split into two opposing factions, the Dramatic and the Poetic, and to place G. Wilson Knight exclusively with the latter. Of the situation in the 1930s Alan S. Downer writes: 'on the one side is the Shakespeare-as-a-dramatist brigade commanded by Granville Barker and J. Isaacs; on the other, Shakespeare-as-a-poet, better equipped and manned, and officered by Spurgeon and Murry and G. Wilson Knight';[1] and D. J. Palmer in the 1960s sums up Wilson Knight's method as 'not, of course, the natural way to respond to a play in performance, but it is an attempt to explain how our more fragmentary responses cohere at a level beyond the judicial and ethical concern with character and plot'.[2] While this may be true of an eclectic work like *The Shakespearian Tempest*, a corrective is supplied by the record of Wilson Knight's stage practice and theory, first published in 1936 and reissued in 1947 as *Principles of Shakespearian Production*, and reissued in revised form with major additions and minor subtractions[3] as *Shakespearian Production* in 1964, when it took its place in a revival of scholar-producer writing in the Granville Barker tradition.[4]

[1] 'The Life of Our Design': *The Hudson Review*, II, 2 (Summer 1949), p. 242.
[2] 'G. Wilson Knight': *The Critical Survey*, II, 2 (Summer 1965), p. 82.
[3] One loss to be regretted was the section now reprinted as 'The Making of *Macbeth*', Ch. VIII of *Shakespeare and Religion* (1967).
[4] As a teacher-producer, I have found most help from the regular extended reviews in *Shakespeare Survey*, the work of Ronald Watkins (*Moonlight at the Globe, On*

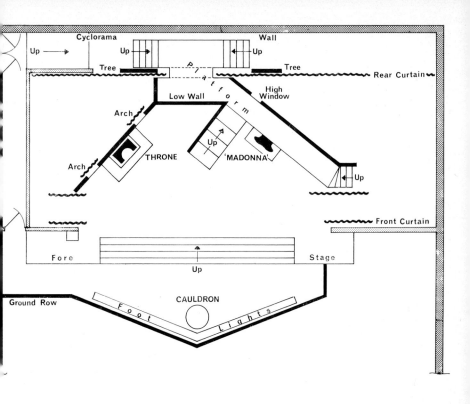

FIG I

Plan of set for Macbeth: Ecclesfield, 1958

FIG II

The three key features: throne, 'Duncan's room', 'Madonna and child'

Notes on a Production of Wilson Knight's 'Ideal Macbeth'

In 1958 I found myself with an opportunity of putting Wilson Knight's 'ideal *Macbeth*' to proof on the stage with a promising group of school actors at Ecclesfield in Yorkshire. We had productions of *The Knight of the Burning Pestle* and *The Tempest* behind us, and wanted to attempt a Shakespeare tragedy. *Macbeth* suggested itself, and I began to think about what I wanted to do, remembering two productions which gave me negative starting-points: one shattered to fragments by the use of curtains and houselights between scenes, and one aggressively and distractingly Ancient Briton in dress and decor. Our *Macbeth* must have continuity and must be Elizabethan, two points which are made in the course of Granville Barker's early 'Preface' to *The Tragedie of Macbeth* in The Players' Shakespeare: 'no swifter movement [towards the murder of Duncan] is well possible than that which the Elizabethan stage provides'; and 'in *Macbeth*, too, archaeology will insensibly undo us'.[5] However, the run of Granville Barker's 'Preface' advocating some astonishing textual cuts and strange character readings was disappointing. For *The Tempest* I had used the complete text of the Penguin edition with its Folio-based pointing, and had found with my actors that what Flatter and Watkins say about it as an acting score was proved in practice. I had also been strongly drawn to the 'interpretations' of *Macbeth* by Wilson Knight in *The Wheel of Fire* and *The Imperial Theme*,[6] so that when I came upon the then current Penguin edition of *Principles of Shakespearian Production* I was fascinated to discover a blueprint of an 'ideal *Macbeth*' which would be technically possible within the comparatively limited resources of my stage. I wrote to him asking permission to use his plan and found that, although he had incorporated a few details in his wartime production at Stowe school, the whole design had never been tried out. He was enthusiastic

---

Producing Shakespeare, and the 'Harrow' edition of *Macbeth*), Richard Flatter's *Shakespeare's Producing Hand*, and the work of J. Russell Brown: *Shakespeare's Plays in Performance* and the eloquent plea at the 1964 International Conference at Stratford (*Sh.Sur.* 18, pp. 58–69). To these I would add the all-too-thinly documented work of Nevill Coghill at Oxford, and that of George Rylands with the Marlowe Society, both at Cambridge and for the British Council/Argo gramophone recordings.

[5] *Op. cit.* (1923), xxxiii (Footnote) and xxxvi. This 'Preface' was not revised for publication with the main series of *Prefaces*. Cf. Robert Speaight: *William Poel and the Elizabethan Revival* (1954), p. 184: 'None of Shakespeare's Tragedies is more Elizabethan in feeling than this one: the bloodguiltiness of Holyrood and Fotheringay darkens the corridors of Dunsinane . . . There is barbarism in *Macbeth*, to be sure, but it is the barbarism of Bothwell not of Boadicea.'

[6] 'Macbeth and the Metaphysic of Evil' (154–74) and 'The Milk of Concord' (125–53) respectively.

145

about the experiment and urged that his essay was 'to be used with elastic and experimental freedom'.

The purpose and outline of Wilson Knight's version are worth looking up at this point,[7] for in practice we followed his main suggestions closely, and the notes below are concerned with particular points rather than overall effect. Briefly, Wilson Knight's version aims to use a permanent set; to 'solidify' imagery and symbolism through the action; to project the supernatural adequately; and to emphasize the play as great literature rather than rhetorical melodrama.

Staging

Wilson Knight's staging owes something, I think, both to Craig's early settings of richly coloured curtains and to Granville Barker's three descending levels in the 1912–14 Savoy productions.[8] It provides important effects of descent for entries and ascent for exits important in this play, as well as a quickly adaptable means of suggesting internal or external location. Our own adaptation of it, as shown in the plan facing p. 144, brought the lower level forward of the inevitable proscenium arch right into the auditorium, where just behind the vee of masked footlights the cauldron was placed. A combination of painted scenery and curtains is out of fashion in the professional theatre now, but it does enable significant changes in the set to be made without loss of continuity and distracting swirls of stage-hands and scenery.[9] We did, in fact, abandon one of Wilson Knight's ideas at an early stage of planning, the alternating green and red carpet, because the changeover would have involved otherwise unnecessary closing of the front curtains.[10] The idea was, however, incorporated in the throne, which had a green cushion for Duncan and a red one for Macbeth.

The throne and the 'Madonna-figure and child' are the most striking and most controversial features of the set. Time and again modern criticism has drawn attention to double images, equivocation, and the tug of opposites in *Macbeth*, and here is an attempt to focus this aspect of the play through the action. Used crudely, these objects

[7] *Op. cit.* (1936), pp. 193–211; (1947), pp. 140–55; (1964), pp. 131–44.

[8] W. A. Armstrong: 'The Art of Shakespearian Production in the Twentieth Century', *Essays and Studies*, XV (1962), pp. 74–87.

[9] Cf. *Shakespearian Production*, p. 59.

[10] Cf. also *Op. cit.*, p. 72: 'Supposing central steps are made to look too like palace stairs: an actor standing on them no longer commands the universe; he is half way between his bedroom and the front door.'

could turn the play into a kind of tennis-match of good and evil, but in fact, with the interplay of grouping and the emphases of tactful lighting, they can be accepted both as what they are and as what they stand for, especially as both are present from beginning to end. The throne, which in our production carried by itself both the gold tints Wilson Knight suggests might streak the black drapes and the red patterning also, is significant for Duncan's kingship, the Weird Sisters' prophecies, and Banquo's 'sovereignty of nature' in life and death, as well as for Macbeth's ambition and uneasy kingship. For the third act the back of the throne was arranged so that it could be raised several inches, emphasizing together with Macbeth's posture Wilson Knight's point: 'Macbeth in his throne looks lost. It is so big. An all but ludicrous effect is wanted.'[11] This is what Alan S. Downer has called 'the "language of props", the realization of the verbal image in dramatic terms', which he illustrates from *Macbeth* by showing the significance of Macbeth's changes of costume: armour in the first and last acts contrasting with the 'borrowed robes' of deceit, the 'nightgown' and regalia, when 'old robes sit easier than . . . new'.[12] In the 'naked frailties that suffer in exposure' (II.iii), costume—or rather lack of it—has also a strong dramatic function, a piece of visual grotesque to go with the verbal grotesque of the Porter.

The 'Madonna' is a much more difficult problem, and Wilson Knight was uneasy about it, in that it 'points rather dangerously to a rigid orthodoxy' (1947), although he later refers to some of his early reservations as 'pusillanimous' (1964). With my set-designer I found certain problems in its construction, positioning and use. First: it must be a Madonna *and child* if it is to reinforce the 'naked new-born babe' symbolism sufficiently. Consequently it is extremely difficult to make it recognizable and non-realistic at once ('slabbed out in rough modernistic fashion . . . denied a too assertive particularity . . . taken under certain lights for rocks'). Its size in relation to the throne is critical: it must not be too insignificant nor too massive. Wilson Knight felt it was too low in our production: 'I think you may have wished it not to dominate too much, to appear to be half-submerged

---

[11] Cf. Terence Gray's treatment of Wolsey in *Henry VIII* at the Festival Theatre, Cambridge: 'Until the end of the play Wolsey wore stilt-like *cothurnoi* beneath his robes which made him tower above the other characters . . . but when his fall from power came, he no longer wore the *cothurnoi* and literally seemed to wither in stature.' Norman Marshall: *The Other Theatre* (1947), p. 66.

[12] *Op. cit.* in Note 1. Cf. 'If we consider the beginning and ending, we find a very clear rhythm of courage, fear, and courage.' *The Imperial Theme*, p. 125.

in the surrounding hostilities; and that, in itself, may have been good, provided that it was seen.' It had to be stressed or hidden by grouping and lighting, and Wilson Knight gave me some shrewd practical advice about this during rehearsals:

> My hope would be that you could by grouping *unobtrusively* draw attention to, cut out and define the figure in scenes where she is important; and tend to obscure her in others, by figures on the stage. You must remember that once an object is there permanently the audience don't in fact *think* of it all the time. A very little—one person—will serve to blot it out, indeed, if it is not in some way forced on their attention, they will hardly stop following the story to *think* of it.
>
> The most awkward occasion is the Cauldron chant. Can the Madonna be seen here? Is it possible to have a small drape just enough to kill the *line* of the figure, which can be removed before the show of kings?
>
> At 'Show his eyes and grieve his heart' the lights can all dim and the moving witches can easily slip it off. Then the lights can come up. This is the effect you want:—the audience are to *think* that at the start it is just blurred—they *know* it is there of course, but they see it's not *effectively* there, and are satisfied; when the lights come up on it they *think* it has all been done by lights, and this seems a good and acceptable way to them; they never know a drape did part of the job.
>
> You see, one half of the audience's mind is *absolutely rational* and knows what is actually there; the other half is *willingly* and *consciously* deceived. The worst fault is to play unfair tricks with their two halves, trying to deceive them unnecessarily and failing. If they are left saying: 'the M[adonna] was not there just now—now it is—how was that done?' this would be a bad effect. I suggest that my plan might work.
>
> Above all, remember that nothing should seem obtrusive. Any of my remarks such as, 'in saying this he looks at . . .' need not be followed if the effect is in any way striking enough without any such underlining.

Similar principles of unobtrusiveness—what Richard David has called 'genuine producer's sleight of hand, worth all the flying ballet apparatus in the theatre workshop'[13]—must also apply to treatment of the Weird Sisters and the ghost of Banquo. Wilson Knight specifies very carefully the effects and means of achieving them at these points, and we followed them equally carefully. However, influenced to some extent by 'The Hecate Scenes in *Macbeth*', (Appendix B of *The Shakespearian Tempest*), we included the Hecate scenes, and in the Cauldron scene it was the still and at first obscure figure of Hecate that hid the Madonna, until she led the Weird Sisters up the stair away from Macbeth at 'seek to know no more', when the lights brought out the Madonna for the show of kings.

---

[13] 'The Tragic Curve', *Sh.Sur.* 9, p. 128.

Notes on a Production of Wilson Knight's 'Ideal Macbeth'

Like the throne, and in conjunction with it, the Madonna served as a significant acting focus, particularly in the soliloquies of Macbeth and Lady Macbeth; and at one point it was actually used as part of a scene link when, at the end of III.i Macbeth knelt before it for 'Banquo, thy soul's flight, If it find heaven, must find it out tonight' and remained there during Lady Macbeth's entry (III.ii) and soliloquy ('Nought's had, all's spent . . .') until she spied him and addressed him. Macduff dedicated his sword before it on entry into Dunsinane, as suggested by Wilson Knight; and it was the place of concealment of the 'armed head' become 'the usurper's cursed head', the body of Macbeth falling before it (Stage Direction *Exeunt fighting* omitted). Wilson Knight writes: 'The body lies on the steps before it, sacrificed': well, it lay there: that was right and effective, dramatically and theatrically; but 'sacrificed' is quirky theologically, and impossible, surely, to convey to an audience in the absence of textual warrant.

Continuity and Music

Wilson Knight's outline does not mention intervals as such but divides the play into three acts after II.iv and after IV.i. This accords with the Duncan/Banquo/Macduff structure, but it seemed a pity to release the tension twice in so short a play. We placed our interval between III.v and vi, using what J. Russell Brown calls 'this carefully constructed verbal "fix" ',[14] (III.vi) as a kind of Chorus recapitulating the events of the first half. III.v with its two important couplets:

> He shall spurn fate, scorn death, and bear
> His hopes 'bove wisdom, grace, and fear:
> And you all know, security
> Is mortals' chiefest enemy

made, with the added song from Middleton, a point of rest, and a release of tension in the perhaps rather incongruous so-called 'Locke' Act Music. Wilson Knight's suggestion that III.vi should be performed among the disordered remains of the banquet (III.iv)— 'Free from our feasts, and banquets bloody knives'—is attractive, but causes the stage clearance necessary before IV.i to collide with the opening of the Cauldron scene, though this could be done in mid-scene.

Elsewhere in the play continuity is important, and music and sound are integrated and integrating elements. The Folio stage-directions seem carefully judged, the opening *'Thunder'* mingling with *'Alarums'*, and modulating to the *'Flourishes'* which open and close

---

[14] *Studies in English Literature: Macbeth* (1963), p. 54.

the scene of King Duncan's proclamation (I.iv). *'Hoboyes'* accompany
Duncan's progress into Macbeth's castle, and the feasting. We used
a recorder-consort playing Orlando Gibbons's 'The Earl of Salisbury's Pavane' and its Galliard-en-suite for the *'Enter a sewer'* link,
and added between I.vii and II.i further music for Wilson Knight's
suggested 'ceremonious procession' of Duncan and his train to bed.
The music chosen here was 'The Irish Ho-Hoan', a lament for a dead
chieftain, and therefore a piece of musical irony equivalent in sound
to Wilson Knight's 'red door'.

Equivocation and irony extend to the sound-effects, too, in the
following scene:

> Go bid thy mistress, when my drink is ready,
> She strike upon the bell . . . (II.i. 31–2)
>
>   . . . the bell invites me.
> Hear it not, Duncan, for it is a knell
> That summons thee to Heaven, or to Hell. (II.i. 62–4)

This bell, domestic yet ominous, connected with drugged possets,
and dutch courage, bedtime drinks on a night that will 'murder
sleep', rings at the climax of the terrible dagger speech: the timing,
tone, and rhythm of the off-stage sound need very careful judgment if
the double effect is to be gained, and need to be carefully differentiated
from the clamouring toll that will arouse the household to 'the great
Doom's image' in the next scene and add a defiant note to the
alarums of the final battle. It must cut into the 'infinities of horror'
where Macbeth's mind is: its effect is almost the chastisement 'with
the valour of [her] tongue' of Lady Macbeth herself.

The middle part of the play is without music, apart from the
'Sennet' for the Macbeths' entry as King and Queen. Possibly this
substitute for a Flourish is a musical indication of the reduced status
of the pair: we used a shorter piece for fewer trumpets. There is no
music at the second banquet.[15] In the Cauldron scene the *'Thunder/
Hoboyes'* contrast again underlines the difference between the death-
bringing Apparitions and the life-line of the show of kings; the
dance of the Weird Sisters is an obscene parody of courtly homage.
The music reverts to orderly trumpet calls overlaying confused
Alarums during the final battle, and the last scene contains no fewer
than three *Flourishes* for the new king, Malcolm.[16]

---

[15] Ronald Watkins is surely wrong to suggest music here for such a trivial reason
as the removal of the banquet. (*On Producing Shakespeare*, p. 295).
[16] For Duncan we used the flourish in E. W. Naylor's *Shakespeare and Music*, Ex. 27

Notes on a Production of Wilson Knight's 'Ideal Macbeth'

One of the reasons for writing these notes on the Staging and on the Continuity and Music has been to emphasize the point that the scholar can select and juxtapose, but the producer has a total non-stop commitment to everything heard and seen, in its sequence during a performance, including such obvious and less obvious things as the transitions from scene to scene, the music and the noises-off, the costumes, the positioning and movement of the actors, the choice of variant readings, the pointing of the lines, the duration of pauses, who the Third Murderer is, and how many servants had Lady Macbeth.[17] Much could be learned from documents similar to that used as source material for these notes: fully annotated prompt-copies, with photographs, costume-designs, lighting plot, etc.; the high cost of reproducing some of these would be justified by their usefulness to Shakespeare studies which take the stage into account.[18]

It now remains to consider how far the Ecclesfield production succeeded in realizing Wilson Knight's four aims.[19] The advantage of the single set for continuity has been noted, but perhaps the most important effect was the way it enabled 'the grouping and the action continually [to] reflect, not the passing incident only, but its relation to the whole'.[20] Lady Macbeth invoked the 'spirits that tend on mortal thoughts', reproducing in her location at the foot of the stairs and in her widdershins movement the Weird Sisters' circlings in the previous scene; earlier in the same speech she looked down the forestage steps to where the 'fatal entrance of Duncan' was to be made in the following scene and he came between her and the throne; there was similar visual recall in the sleepwalking scene. Banquo's relationships with the throne are described in detail by Wilson

---

(*a*), p. 200; for Malcolm that in his *Shakespeare Music*, p. 28; for the Macbeths' sennet his *Shakespeare and Music*, Ex. 27 (*d*), p. 202.

　In spite of the collections of Naylor, F. W. Sternfeld, and others, it is still difficult for a producer to assemble all the Elizabethan music necessary for any single play. As John Stevens has pointed out, 'The contemporary Elizabethan music edited by Thurston Dart for the complete recorded Shakespeare sponsored by The British Council (Argo Record Company) provides a splendid guide *in sound*' (*Shakespeare in Music* (1964), n. 1, p. 29), but finding printed sources is not easy.

[17] It should be emphasised that Wilson Knight's omission of details described above as added by us was a calculated one.

[18] The nearest approaches to anything like this are the accounts of part of *Julius Caesar* and of *Macbeth* in Ronald Watkins's *On Producing Shakespeare*, and his 'Harrow' *Macbeth*; some single pages in W. Moelwyn Merchant's *Shakespeare and the Artist*; Rosamund Gilder's *John Gielgud's Hamlet: A Record of a Performance* (1937); and C. Stanislavsky *Stanislavsky Produces 'Othello'* (1948).

[19] See Note 7 ante.

[20] This (45) and subsequent bracketed references in the text are from *Shakespearian Production*.

Knight (139). Notable, too, was the darkly glowing arch formed by the almost closed rear curtains which swallowed Macbeth after he had silently climbed 'from the visible world into infinities of horror' (74). The quick exterior-interior changes made possible by closing the rear- and arch-curtains were particularly effective at the end of the Cauldron scene where 'the sky-strips are again red-curtained doors, the wild nightmare crags are the corridors of his own palace. He stands dazed in sudden daylight' (139). For the spectator, place was at once familiar and ambiguous. The photograph shows the set at an early stage of painting: the details of stonework were considerably toned down before the performances to avoid too obvious a realism, and to blend with the curtains in a variety of light settings.[21]

The 'rich production' Wilson Knight envisages 'to bring out and solidify *with the help of the action* layers in the play's imagery and symbolism' (131) is partly provided by the setting and its use, but a prime consideration is what Granville Barker called his 'golden rule': 'Gain Shakespeare's effects by Shakespeare's means when you can',[22] avoiding what Wilson Knight calls 'elaborations that do not properly relate to the play' (47)—he instances bringing on the Weird Sisters at the end of the play. There is much to be said for working as closely as possible to the Folio text and stage-directions, particularly in the Banquet and Cauldron scenes. Wilson Knight writes of the latter:

'The three Apparitions form a precise miniature of the whole play's dramatic conflict. Appropriately, they rise from the cauldron to thunder. They are followed shortly by the line of kings. These, being creative and harmonious visions hostile to the evil, the Weird Sisters are loth to show. Macbeth insists. The cauldron vanishes and the kings, who do not rise from the cauldron, pass to the music of hautboys, like the hautboys of the mystic music in *Antony and Cleopatra*. Modern productions hardly ever leave us clear as to what is happening in this scene.' (56)

The position of the cauldron, the evil presidency of Hecate, the solidity of the Apparitions, the use of the voices of Malcolm and Macduff for the Child and the Head, the advancing of the kings from concealment behind the footlight ground-row up the forestage steps towards a Macbeth whose reactions were clearly visible to the audience, and the appearance of Banquo in the throne, all helped to make this scene meaningful as well as solemn.

[21] Wilson Knight has a particularly good section on Costume, Lighting, and Scenery (pp. 60–1 and p. 292).
[22] *Prefaces to Shakespeare* (1963), p. 25.

Notes on a Production of Wilson Knight's 'Ideal Macbeth'

The problem of 'giving the element of supernature an adequate projection' (131) is not, of course, merely that of the Weird Sisters; there is much else: Lady Macbeth's 'spirits that tend on mortal thoughts' and her sleepwalking have already been mentioned; there are also Macbeth's 'wither'd Murther' and 'Night's black agents', the horses 'wild in Nature', and so on—all of which find their prime expression in the actors' words and the off-stage sounds, and in what Wilson Knight calls the 'hushed tensity' of the words alone at certain moments. Unexpected moments like this were revealed when the actor found his tune and pace; notable were Macbeth's interview with the two Murderers, and the linked[23] scene following, with its slow build-up to that couplet clotted with evil:

> 'Good things of Day begin to droop and drowse,
> Whiles Night's black agents to their preys do rouse'

and the final 'strong . . . by ill' half-line when Lady Macbeth, panic-stricken, scurried to Macbeth's side at the window over-looking the place where 'Light thicken[ed]' round the doomed Banquo.

The Weird Sisters present an almost insuperable problem today; it is not, as Nevill Coghill recently pointed out in an unpublished lecture, merely a problem of suspending disbelief, but also a problem of the modern technologically-minded audience who will look for the means rather than receive the effect, so that any attempt to play tricks with them is likely to be disastrous. Coghill suggested present-ing the Weird Sisters in the opening scene of the play as looting camp-followers on the battlefield, tearing rings from the fingers of corpses, until one corpse screams, and is the bloody Sergeant, and we are in Scene 2: they would thus begin closer to human than to supernatural evil, whatever they might become later. We presented them, not in Wilson Knight's suggested front-scene, but on the fore-stage steps, apparently suspended in darkness; they were in the full set, but without spatial reference to it until they named Macbeth, when the throne was dimly picked out. The eerie cries of the familiars stirred them into movement (74–5), and the rhythm of their final couplet was taken up by a drum, which changed to a crisper military rhythm as the lights silhouetted the arches, suggesting a ruined hovel used as a command post, and there arrived, to the call of a trumpet, Duncan's guards, the royal party, and the bloody Sergeant. The drum

[23] See page 149, ante.

rhythm was used again for the transition between I.ii and I.iii, with rhythms imitating the spoken cadences of the closing and opening sentences, and distant thunder. Very careful attention was given to the speaking of the Weird Sisters' trochaic rhythms and to such calculated dislocations (often smoothed by editors) as 'I'll drain him dry as hay'. An incisive, hard tone was adopted, rather than the wailing one suggested by Wilson Knight or the traditional raucously conversational gossips' cackle. Their costumes were black and dark green with hoods, and cut to emphasize their almost beaked faces and their arm movements, for their utterances are predominantly outgoing, to others and to each other. Hecate was treated as an altogether superior being in the hierarchy of evil, with slower, more powerful movements and speech; her costume design (based on Michael Ayrton's design for Night in the 1947 Covent Garden production of Purcell's *The Fairy Queen*, and deriving in turn from Inigo Jones) was midnight blue and black with silver details and a sinister crown of hooked twigs; her make-up was based on Coleridge's description of Life-in-Death in 'The Rime of the Ancient Mariner'. Her part in the masque-like conclusion of the first half of the play leading into the interval has been mentioned: the whole conception perhaps helped the audience to accept the element of evil somewhat in terms of the more familiar nineteenth-century convention of the 'Romantic Agony'.

If the impression given by these notes has been one of '*Macbeth* without the Thane of Glamis', this will have been because my aim has been to show the importance of detail in the whole design, and because I have not wished to suggest that my schoolboy Macbeth, good as he was, could convey everything that Wilson Knight sees in the character. The physical stature necessary for the opening scenes, and to some extent for the final ones was obviously impossible of realization, although this did not seem to matter so much as the play proceeded, and even the first entry was made impressive by the dominating platform. There was no question, as there too often is in the professional theatre, of 'star' billing, and if anything justified the production it was the extent to which Wilson Knight's plan helped to realize what Richard David has prescribed for the successful modern production:

A Shakespeare play, like any other work of art, has one overall shape, style, pattern, essence which any translation into modern terms must preserve; and . . . within this overall pattern there are contrasts and balances of tone, temper, and even of convention, that must be carefully observed if the structure is to stand.[24]

Degeneration into 'rhetorical melodrama', a mere sequence of lurid language and bloody deeds, is prevented by the preservation of the pattern; and Wilson Knight's plan by its faithfulness to the dramatist's intentions embodied in the text, the significances of his permanent setting, and its web of detail, every strand vibrant to every other, was a rewarding experience for players and audience alike in 1958, and remains a challenge to the professional theatre.[25]

[24] 'Actors and Scholars', in *Sh.Sur.* 12, p. 85.

[25] I am grateful to the President and Fellows of St. John's College, Oxford for the term's Schoolmaster Studentship which enabled me to prepare these notes; and to Derek Alliban for the photograph.

13

Milton's Austerity and Moral Disdain

D. W. JEFFERSON

THE following paragraph from the survey of the false gods in Book I of *Paradise Lost* is a splendid example of a special kind of virtuosity that distinguishes Milton:

> For those the Race of *Israel* oft forsook
> Their living strength, and unfrequented left
> His righteous Altar, bowing lowly down
> To bestial Gods; for which their heads as low
> Bow'd down in Battel, sunk before the Spear
> Of despicable foes. With these in troop
> Came *Astoreth*, whom the *Phoenicians* call'd
> *Astarte*, Queen of Heav'n, with crescent Horns;
> To whose bright image nightly by the Moon
> *Sidonian* Virgins paid their Vows and Songs,
> In *Sion* also not unsung, where stood
> Her Temple on th'offensive Mountain, built
> By that uxorious King, whose heart though large,
> Beguil'd by fair Idolatresses, fell
> To Idols foul. *Thammuz* came next behind,
> Whose annual wound in *Lebanon* allur'd
> The *Syrian* Damsels to lament his fate
> In amorous dittyes all a Summers day,
> While smooth *Adonis* from his native Rock
> Ran purple to the Sea, suppos'd with blood
> Of *Thammuz* yearly wounded: the Love-tale
> Infected *Sion's* daughters with like heat,
> Whose wanton passions in the sacred Porch
> *Ezekiel* saw, when by the Vision led
> His eye survay'd the dark Idolatries
> Of alienated Judah.   (I. 432–57)

156

The sombre and condemnatory parts of the passage are so satisfying rhetorically and sensuously, that it is as if righteousness and purity of life were demonstrating their superiority by the beauty of the words alone. All Milton's humanistic equipment is present in this statement of what we should otherwise refer to, in commonplace terms, as 'Old Testament severity' or 'puritanical rigour'. The poetry compels us to seek different terms, if we are to do justice to our pleasure in the extraordinary refinement that he gives to these attitudes. For example, in the lines about the 'uxorious King', the verbal effect of the stages of descent from 'heart though large' through 'fair Idolatresses' down to 'Idols foul', aided by piquant alliterations and vowel sequences, is most felicitous; and the closing cadence of the passage conveys impressively the fine denunciatory gaze of the prophet. If austerity delights us here more than sexuality this does not mean that the poet has no awareness of the wanton appeal of the pagan rites. There is no lack of sexual suggestion in the lines about the wound and the blood. The story excites real lust in 'Sion's daughters' and, superbly distant though the poet's moral position is from all this infamy, the words convey the atmosphere of voluptuousness. 'In amorous dittyes all a Summers day', the one lightweight line in the whole passage, has the effect of bringing into contempt, through its very thinness as poetry (though it would pass muster elsewhere) and through its presence in such a context, a convention of erotic lyricism in which such slightness is the norm. Milton in this passage establishes an ascendency, moral and poetic, of the most august order; and a reader not of his party can submit to it wholly. The ascendancy is personal. Though not one of the personal passages of *Paradise Lost*, it has a tone in keeping with them.

A somewhat hostile view of Milton as a man has been widely accepted in our century. T. S. Eliot said that he is 'antipathetic', that 'judged by the ordinary standards of likeableness in human beings, Milton is unsatisfactory.'[1] A full discussion of such statements would involve a good deal of weighing up of what we know about his life, and it may be questioned whether the evidence assembled, for example, in the *Early Lives of Milton* edited by Helen Darbishire, warrants anything like so much animus. Some of it points to a much more sympathetic view. But we are concerned here with the Milton whose attitudes and emotions reach us through the poetry, and with the aspect of himself that he so feelingly presents here. And when

[1] *On Poetry and Poets* (1957), p. 138.

we try to describe the great personal passages of *Paradise Lost* we realize that they cannot be discussed in terms of personal qualities such as would be made manifest in relationships with the man himself. The voice in these passages is not that of a man speaking to men about himself. The epic medium—and this is sacred epic—permits him to project a lofty fiction, to represent himself in relation to a uniquely exalted function rhetorically conceived. This places him beyond the accusation of ordinary spiritual pride or egoism. Any attack would have to be against the fiction itself and its treatment, and the uniquely elevated quality of the poetry forestalls this. Milton is equal to the representation of himself in this sublime role. But, paradoxically, his achievement has immense *personal* appeal; with the authority of his art Milton imposes himself supremely.

His manner of introducing himself into the epic situation has an audacity which succeeds by not being noticed as such. It was surely an extraordinary audacity to halt the action of the poem at heaven's threshold (Book III) to dwell at length on himself, his blindness and his sublime confidence in the divine inspirer of his colossal under-taking. To use the theme of Light to bring this about was resourceful: he did not live in an age of poetic ingenuity for nothing. The transi-tion from the poet in his august function as epic narrator ('Thee I revisit now with bolder wing . . .') to the poet as a man, addressing light from the standpoint of his loss ('but thou Revisit'st not these eyes . . .') is masterly. When Milton dwells upon his personal situation in the passage that comes after, it is in language of the greatest poignancy. The perfection of the note of religious and poetic vocation already established gives a special beauty and pathos to the lines where the thoughts relate to self, albeit a self in harmony with the vocation:

> . . . nor sometimes forget
> Those other two equal'd with me in Fate,
> So were I equal'd with them in renown,
> Blind *Thamyris* and blind Maeonides . . .

and

> . . . Thus with the year
> Seasons return, but not to me returns
> Day, or the sweet return of Ev'n or Morn.

Perfect as the tone is we are still left with the fact that Milton has been able to divert his epic for so long a space into a personal channel, an exquisite indulgence.

This personal poetry belongs to his greatest period. The moral and spiritual idealism of his earlier years does not find expression in anything so satisfying. The work especially devoted to the theme of chastity, the Ludlow *Mask*, lacks an appropriate moral focus, in spite of the fine eloquence of its key speeches. To quote the Lady's own words, Comus uses 'lickerish baits fit to ensnare a brute'. The tempter, with his 'rabble' and the 'oughly-headed monsters', and the form of the temptation (the cup), have nothing that could possibly appeal to her. Spenser's exponent of chastity, Britomart, confronts situations involving love and passion. It is in the previous book of the *Faerie Queene* that the hero, Guyon, represents the plodding virtue of mere abstinence; and this would seem to be the theme of Milton's little drama, though A. S. P. Woodhouse, by very careful scanning of parts of the text not obviously relevant to the central debate, found much more. There have been many conflicting interpretations of the *Mask* in recent years, some so elaborately abstract as to deflect attention almost entirely from what, to an uninstructed reader, looks like a very straight scene of attempted seduction. It has been argued, reasonably, that the work was intended primarily as an entertainment, an occasion for spectacle, with actors not only young but also the offspring of the noble house that commissioned it, and that moral tension should not be too much stressed. Virtue undismayed and nobly eloquent, scorning vice with its fine speeches: this, in all its simplicity, one might claim, is as much as we should look for. Certainly we need something to mitigate the effect of the Lady's robust invulnerability:

> Foole do not boast
> Thou canst not touch the freedom of my minde . . .

If these approaches do not come to our aid we are liable to find Milton tactless in exposing the Lady to such crude allurements.

C. L. Barber, in an essay on the *Mask*,[2] describes chastity in beautiful terms: 'For preserving chastity involves keeping a relation with what is not present: the chaste person is internally related to what is to be loved, even in its absence.' But in spite of his reference to the Epilogue ('The end of Chastity is love fulfilled, "Two blissful twins

---

[2] '*A Mask Presented at Ludlow Castle:* The Masque as a Masque' in *The Lyric and Dramatic Milton. Selected papers from the English Institute* ed. Joseph H. Summers (1965), pp. 50, 62.

. . . Youth and Joy" ') the implication that Milton's *Mask* is about any such thing seems to be contrary to its tone and atmosphere. It announces only a simple moral disdain of sensuality (seen in brutish and degrading terms) and a chastity characterized by little more than conscious dignity and pride in its power to resist. And this attitude, with all its limitations as an attitude, does not come to us, through the poetry of the *Mask*, with sufficient human impact. If we cannot quite believe in the Lady's predicament, it does not help very much if we treat the affirmation as relating to Milton himself.

A much more personal note is present in a moving passage of *Lycidas* ('Alas! What boots it with incessant care . . .'), where thoughts of an early death and of the strain and deprivation in a life of chastity and disciplined effort produce a crisis of emotion. 'To sport with Amaryllis in the shade' is not nothing; and the 'blind Fury with th'abhorred shears' conveys a real terror. The word of reassurance comes to 'trembling ears'.

One of the advantages of Milton's mature style, and, in particular, of the exalted role that he succeeds in filling as the poet of *Paradise Lost*, is (as we have already noted) that ordinary human qualities which in themselves might be jarring become transformed into something of rare purity and power, so that ordinary moral criticism does not touch them. The language of the *Mask* contains elements, here and there, uncomfortably suggestive of a haughty, rather unlovely antipathy to sexual pleasures. The dreadful word 'priggish' could almost be used for these touches of harshness in the feeling. But the moral elevation of the personal passages of *Paradise Lost* is something to which we might respond as we would to Michelangelo's face of the prophet Daniel in the Sistine Chapel.

As for the fine disdain in the passage quoted on the first page the question of what place moral disdain has or should have in our outlook need not arise, or not directly. The Milton of *Paradise Lost*, whatever conjectures we may hazard about the man, is a figure who impresses us and moves us by qualities that seem not those of common clay. In this age not to seem to be of common clay may be no recommendation; but to the reader who can respond to Milton there is a special joy in the encounter with a mind and spirit so superior. (One regrets that the word 'superior' has now become impossible.) The superiority may express itself in great tenderness and refinement of sensibility—for example, in the treatment of Eden and of Eve—or it can make itself felt in an incredible strength, buoyancy and control in passages like the following:

> . . . through many a dark and drearie Vaile
> They pass'd, and many a Region dolorous,
> O'er many a Frozen, many a Fierie Alpe,
> Rocks, Caves, Lakes, Fens, Bogs, Dens and shades of death,
> A Universe of death, which God by curse
> Created evil, for evil only good,
> Where all life dies, death lives, and nature breeds,
> Perverse, all monstrous, all prodigious things,
> Abominable, inutterable, and worse
> Then Fables yet have feign'd, or fear conceiv'd,
> *Gorgons* and *Hydras*, and *Chimeras* dire.   (II. 618–28.)

To produce the avalanche of the great monosyllabic line, and not make it the ending of the paragraph, was in itself an heroic gesture. Milton keeps up the pressure for seven more lines; and the two lines that follow the avalanche are, in their totally contrasting way, just as shattering. This kind of poetic impact is the expression of an unusually untrammelled energy. We need not enter here into the question of the nature of Milton's Hell, of the relation between his epic fictions and whatever metaphysical coherence the description did or did not call for. The important thing about the effect is its magnitude, the sheer art with which so much force is brought to bear. Some modern critics have referred to Milton's heroic energy as a quality less valuable than other qualities in poets. But it may be noted that energy of this order does not often manifest itself in poetry.

We may refer to it as moral energy. The theme of the tremendous passage is the fact of a world under God's curse, its denizens swept across unimaginable spaces of desolation; the poetry is a statement of wrath and judgment. But it is not more moral than personal. Milton's ability to discharge this kind of epic function with the maximum effect maintains the immensity of his subject and also of his work, establishing him ever more irresistibly in his role and reducing his reader to willing subjection.

The opening of Book VII has something in common with the opening of Book III, but with significant differences. It has, in the last line, what appears to link it with our main theme: that is, a note of repudiation, in the dismissal of the pagan muse as an 'empty dream'. As in Book III an epic invocation at an important turning point in the action provides the poet with an opportunity for personal self-expression. He begins with the address to Urania, 'by that name if rightly thou art call'd'. It is 'the meaning not the Name' that he calls; and here, as in the earlier passage, we are in an atmosphere especially Miltonic: one of clear, serene religious faith that turns for inspiration to the divine source. Urania is not one of the nine muses; she is to be contrasted later with the fiction that he dismisses;[3] but nevertheless, under cover of these opening words or in spite of them, we have been persuaded to accept a fiction. At least Urania is a 'she', and if Orpheus' feminine guardian failed him in his hour of terror this poet can turn to another feminine being for succour. In the personal part of the passage the tone at first has an elevated calm; but then, with the extraordinary account of the fate of Orpheus, he creates an image of vulnerability which, applied to himself, gives the poetry a daring and wonderful pathos:

> Standing on Earth, not rapt above the Pole,
> More safe I Sing with mortal voice, unchang'd
> To hoarce or mute, though fall'n on evil dayes,
> On evil dayes though fall'n, and evil Tongues;
> In darkness, and with dangers compast round,
> And solitude; not yet alone, while thou
> Visit'st my slumbers Nightly, or when Morn
> Purples the East: still govern thou my Song,
> *Urania*, and fit audience find, though few.
> But drive farr off the barbarous dissonance
> Of *Bacchus* and his Revellers, the Race
> Of that wilde Rout that tore the *Thracian* Bard
> In *Rhodope*, where Woods and Rocks had Eares
> To rapture, till the savage clamor dround
> Both Harp and Voice; nor could the Muse defend
> Her Son. So fail not thou, who thee implores:
> For thou art Heav'nlie, shee an empty dreame.

To come so near to the thought of horrible danger to himself might have looked like a falling off had the note of dependence not been given special appeal through the feminine character of the succourer. There is the suggestion of a need for the maternal, an indulgence of weakness. A simple invocation of the Deity would hardly have accommodated this effect. The repudiation of the 'empty dream', within the same line and a half that contains this moving appeal, completes the subterfuge. It is difficult to say briefly why this is such a master stroke. It has the partial air of restoring austerity, of

---

[3] E. R. Curtius has pointed out that the rejection of the Muses became a *topos* in Christian poetry from the fourth century onwards (*European Literature and the Latin Middle Ages*, trans. Willard B. Trask, 1953, pp. 235–44).

cutting pathos short by the scornful dismissal of heathen delusions; but he has committed himself so deeply in the Orpheus passage that the dismissal means less than its decisive note suggests. He says that the pagan muse could not help Orpheus, that she is an empty dream; but Orpheus belongs himself to the world over which the muse presides. What has been repudiated if Milton's imagination still enjoys its freedom with the things of the classical world? The very expression 'heavenly muse' looks like a concession to this graceful tradition.

Paradise Regained contains a passage in which this repudiation of the classical world actually takes place. In this work we have a situation with limitations similar to those of the *Mask*. The tempter is as ineffective, his temptations just as irrelevant; and we are left again with the impression of calm, unshakeable virtue scorning all encroachments. The Jesus of Milton's epic has never known uncertainty, and the debate with Satan entirely lacks dialectical tension. But something near to poignancy may be found in the passage in question if we misread it a little:

> Where on the *Aegean* shore a City stands
> Built nobly, pure the air, and light the soil,
> *Athens* the eye of Greece, Mother of Arts . . . (IV.ii. 238 ff.)

As a speech delivered by Satan to Jesus it is meaningless, and Jesus's response to it has no moral interest. But if we take the debate as going on within the life of Milton: if the first speaker represents the side of him that greatly loved Greek literature and that could refract its beauties so exquisitely in his own poetry; and the second speaker the side of him that craved, for his declining years, a strict, unequivocal attachment to the divine message and to '*Sion's* songs, to all true tastes excelling', this section of the poem is moving and of great personal interest. The fact that the repudiation of Greece is harsh and uncompromising, which some readers have found so offensive, may be regarded simply as part of the price to be paid for a decisive farewell; and it helps if we can feel that the other side, after all, has been heard. Unfortunately, as the poem stands, the spokesman is Satan. If the passage as a whole were viewed in this way one could say that here two worlds are presented with a spacious fullness, two rival cultures spanned, that Milton gives epic breadth to his statement—the theme has large implications for civilization—and speaks with an authority that ranges over the entire field of reference. It would not be the only case where something like misreading seems to give the best results with a passage of Milton.

More than one critic of Milton has stressed that his essential subject-matter and intention are not quite the same as he declared them to be. Through the transforming effect of his language, and in some places through the felicitous management of allusions and transitions, he could, as we have seen, diversify his role as the poet of *Paradise Lost* in a number of ways that make for sympathetic appeal or personal ascendancy, without compromising its supreme decorum. His role called for a note of unblemished righteousness, a magnificent severity, and Milton's poetry achieved it. But the achievement gives enormous pleasure that has little to do with austerity.

14

The Waking Dream:
Coleridge and the Drama

PATRICIA M. BALL

URING December 1803 Coleridge resolved in his notebook:
'I must devote some one or more days exclusively to the
Meditation on *Dreams*. Days? Say rather Weeks!' (1.1726).[1]
While it is unlikely that he ever meditated 'exclusively' on anything,
and least of all when engaged with such a comprehensive topic as
dreams, Coleridge in the course of his life certainly devoted a great
deal more than weeks to this subject. In a sense it was never far from
his attention, being one aspect of his whole concern with 'these
experiences of the world within us', as he phrases it in *The Friend*;
and his own dreaming was so vivid—often so terrible—a part of his
life that fresh material for research was constantly forced upon him.
His notebooks illustrate this, with their frequent entries recording
not only recent dream-experiences but his speculations and deduc-
tions arising out of them. For example, in October 1802, noting
down what he recalls of the previous night, he observes, 'my Dreams
uncommonly illustrative of the non-existence of Surprize in sleep
. . .' (1.1250).

He is certain that there is a significant relationship between the
dream and the waking life; this is the incentive to his vigilance in
scrutinizing the world released in sleep. However bizarre the fantasies, he recognizes that they reveal a consistent logic in terms of the
whole personality and history of the dreamer: 'O it was a wild dream,

[1] The numbers after notebook quotations refer to the entries in K. Coburn's edition,
Notebooks Vols. 1 and 2 (1957–62).

yet a deal of true psychological Feeling at the bottom of it' (1.1824: January 1804). And more particularly he is interested in memory's part in dreams, the interplay of past and present, emotion aroused by the appearance of people absent or lost from present life. His dreams involving Sara Hutchinson on the voyage to Malta show this to a tormented degree. Equally, he is fascinated by the curious mixed state between sleep and waking where dream events succeed in weaving into their own fabric voices or ticking clocks, the half-conscious mind registering the sounds but unable to identify them as extraneous occurrences. The influences of bodily position, or ailments, the pressure of blankets and all such mundane detail he frequently connects with his more 'hag-ridden' dreams, finding in the terrors of nightmare abundant evidence for the mind's ability to demoralize itself by creating fiends and ogres out of the merest hints provided by physical sensations. He notices too that 'in a distempered dream, things and forms in themselves common and harmless inflict a terror of anguish' (1.205:1796–97), and again in this state, the phenomenon of double consciousness recurs, the phantoms and the bed-post both being accepted together in one universe of fear.

Coleridge's observations on these various aspects of dream-experience feed his thinking on the mind's powers in general, and on the 'varying degrees of consciousness' (2. editor's note to 2543). He applies his researches to the development of other related theories. His views on the primarily psychological origins of ghosts, for example, as elaborated in *The Friend* where he explains Luther's apparitions, spring from his study of the way in which the actual and the 'unreal' may be superimposed upon each other in some states of consciousness, with no critical distinction being made. And his contention that there is nothing 'absurd and nonsensical' in dreams leads him to argue for the strong probability of the mind's being able to exercise powers of presentiment. This he maintained at least as late as 1823, for according to *Table Talk* he made the point in conversation on 1 May that year, and at least as early as 1804, when in April he jotted down a verse about dreams, describing them as 'So faithful to the Past, or so prophetic' (2.2018). Memory likewise is apostrophized in 1807 in these terms: 'Great Guide of Things to come, Sole Presence of Things Past' (2.3089), and in the first Lay Sermon also he suggests the close links between the mental feats of memory as an aspect of imagination and the perception of the future:

The Waking Dream: Coleridge and the Drama

... who shall decide how far a perfect reminiscence of past experiences ... who shall determine to what extent this reproductive imagination ... may or may not be concentred and sublimed into foresight and presentiment?[2]

With such intimate connections implied between the creative capacities of the mind and its functioning in dreams, it is not surprising that his ideas on dreaming should directly impinge upon and affect Coleridge's literary theory. Lecturing on Spenser in 1818, he draws an obvious comparison between our experience in reading *The Faerie Queene* and our dream lives:

... it is truly in land of Faery, that is, of mental space. The poet has placed you in a dream, a charmed sleep, and you neither wish, nor have the power, to inquire where you are, or how you got there.[3]

But this idea of a distinctive state of mind brought about by poetry is applicable beyond the specialized enchantment of Faery-land, as Coleridge's reminiscent remarks of the *Lyrical Ballads* experiment in Chapter XIV of the *Biographia Literaria* show. Here he speaks of 'poetic faith' and defines this as 'that willing suspension of disbelief for the moment'. In other words, the reader's experience of poetry is one of assent to the conditions of a world existing in its own right. The poem is a territory which the reader agrees to enter and accept on its terms, provided that he is persuaded to do so. In this contract Coleridge exemplifies the links and the differences between this situation and that of the dreamer. The latter 'suspends his disbelief': he submits to what happens without surprise, he is involved in an uncritical spirit with whatever occurs and he is affected by it as one living the scene. But the reader of the poem suspends his disbelief by an act of will: he takes a voluntary part in this experience and hence he submits to its laws because he is converted to such participation. If the poet fails to convince, disbelief is not suspended, the work is exposed to adverse criticism.

What Coleridge here propounds as poetic faith is strikingly close to his theory of dramatic faith. In his statements on this he makes extensive and fundamental use of the psychological connections with the dreaming mind. But first of all we can see this connection established in reverse, because several times he speaks of the 'dramatic' quality of dreams. Thus on the Malta voyage in May 1804 he notes 'One remarkably affecting Dream in which I saw Sara, and the whole

---

[2] Quoted by H. N. Coleridge, note to *Table Talk* entry, 1 May 1823.
[3] *Coleridge's Miscellaneous Criticism*, ed. T. M. Raysor (1936), p. 36.

perfectly dramatic . . .' (2.2078); and some months after this, he remarks on his active role in dreams: '. . . one is much less . . . a spectator only—one seems always about to do, or suffering, or thinking, or talking . . .' (2.2302). While in 1810, he is ready to claim not only an actor's part in the dream but that of the dramatist also: in *The Friend* he expresses a long-standing wish to explain 'the mode in which our thoughts, in states of morbid slumber, become at times perfectly dramatic (for in certain sorts of dreams the dullest wight becomes a Shakespeare) . . .'[4]

The 'dullest wight' has other opportunities to become a Shake-speare too, and that is by co-operating in the theatrical experience. Coleridge's theory insists that this be regarded as a psychological event for the audience, one in which they are as intimately and actively involved as in dreaming, but again with the difference that this is a chosen condition and only attainable if all are equal to its creation: dramatist, actors, and audience. The aim of stage per-formance is to produce 'a sort of temporary half-faith',[5] he says in a fragment of criticism probably written about 1808, and in the more formulated exposition in his lecture on *The Tempest* ten years later, he calls the theatrical state one of 'willing illusion'. His purpose here is to cut a fresh route for dramatic theory, one which avoids the two opposed camps of the literal school: on the one side, the French upholders of the view that the theatre should offer a 'perfect delusion' of reality, and on the other, Dr. Johnson's rejection of this on the grounds that any delusion is impossible since we know we are only in a theatre. This argument centres on the necessity or otherwise of the unities—the French maintaining that complete fidelity is essential, Dr. Johnson that any pretence of conformity to actual time or location is pointless. Neither party allows for the crucial fact as Coleridge sees it, that our state of mind in the theatre is one of a particular 'inward excitement', a heightened and receptive condition where imaginative expectation supersedes our ordinary judgments. We enter this world, we do not demand that the action should either conform to or ignore an external set of rules, any more than we do in dreams. Dreaming is the highest degree of such illusion, Coleridge says, and in sleep we pass no judgment on the reality of events; they simply happen and we concur. So it is in the theatre, save for the

---

[4] Bohn's Standard Library edition (1883), p. 89.
[5] *Coleridge's Shakespearian Criticism*, ed. T. M. Raysor, Everyman edition (1960), Vol. 1, p. 178.

difference that here quality counts and there must be the voluntary confederation of several parties if this assent is to be achieved:

... in an interesting play ... we are brought up to this point ... gradually, by the art of the poet and the actors; and with the consent and positive aidance of our own will. We *choose* to be deceived.

And again:

... all the ... excellencies of the drama ... as far as they tend to increase the inward excitement, are all means to this chief end, that of producing and supporting this willing illusion.[6]

A summary of the lecture brings out the implications of this 'illusion' from a more negative point of view:

... as in a dream, the judgment is neither beguiled, nor conscious of the fraud, but remains passive. Whatever disturbs this repose of the judgment by its harshness, abruptness, and improbability, offends against dramatic propriety.[7]

We can see here how Coleridge makes a critical tool out of his psychological material, and how he provides himself with a standard for dramatic composition which is allied to his central poetic theory of organic form and the nature of imaginative logic. This relationship is emphasized in a passage of the critique on *Bertram*, first published in the *Courier* in 1816, then added to the *Biographia* as Chapter XXIII. Here he argues that if a dramatist once establishes an inner coherence in his work, we are ready to go with him, however strange the journey:

... a specific *dramatic* probability may be raised by a true poet, if the whole of his work be in harmony: a *dramatic* probability, sufficient for dramatic pleasure, even when the component characters and incidents border on impossibility. The poet does not require us to be awake and believe; he solicits us only to yield ourselves to a dream; and this too with our eyes open, and with our judgment *perdue* behind the curtain, ready to awaken us at the first motion of our will: and meantime, only, not to *dis*believe.

The violation of our rapt state of mind means artistic failure, the breakdown of the creative process in the dramatist. All parts of the drama, in short, should be 'compatible with a sound sense of logic in the mind of the poet himself'.[8] Both creator and spectator must be

[6] *ib.* pp. 115–17.
[7] *ib.* Vol. II, p. 258.
[8] *ib.* Vol. I, p. 183.

able to live within the world of the play, sharing in and trusting the imaginative experience, the waking dream. In this lies the essential unity of the work, as distinct from the artifice of unities.

These statements I have quoted show that Coleridge was actively concerned with dramatic theory for many years, while his interest in dream phenomena spans his whole career. The stimulus that brought the two things together in his mind may well have been his experience as a practising playwright. At all events, this is the third point on the triangle, and the plays *Remorse* and *Zapolya* belong as integrally to Coleridge's thinking on these issues as any of his notebook meditations or his public discourses. The plays offer creative exploration of what is elsewhere critical surmise.

As the first version of *Remorse*, called *Osorio*, was written in 1797, a period when Wordsworth also was active as a dramatist, it seems highly probable that this was influential in shaping the talk which led to the *Lyrical Ballads*. The theories concerning the reader's engagement with a poem and the poet's sustaining an homogeneous universe could certainly have been urged forward by their joint experience of dramatic composition. Although *Osorio* was put aside when it failed to attract a producer, Coleridge was pondering on writing plays again while he was in Malta, and he began to revise *Osorio* soon after his return to England in 1806; in 1813 it was produced at Drury Lane. This renewed acquaintance with the dramatic medium may be linked with the observations on 'dramatic illusion' in 1808, and the preparation of the first series of lectures on Shakespeare given in 1811 and 1812. What is suggested is a reciprocal stimulus between the creative and the critical activity, a situation at all times typical of Coleridge's mind. Again in the years from 1815 to 1818 a similar network can be traced, as he worked on *Zapolya* and hoped for its stage appearance, wrote the *Biographia Literaria*, reviewed *Bertram*, and in 1818 delivered more lectures on Shakespeare which included his argument on the unities and 'willing illusion'.

Links suggested by facts and dates are of little value of course if the creative work itself shows no sign of supporting such connections. But both *Remorse* and *Zapolya* could be described as 'dream-plays', and because of this they leave no doubt that the poet is creatively excited by his sense of a valuable relationship between the worlds of drama and dream. He brings the two together with distinctive imaginative results.

Coleridge as playwright is primarily concerned with the inner history and developing experience of his characters. His people are haunted by the past, and each drama shows their shadowy, distorted, or vivid memories affecting their present behaviour and influencing the course of events. The plays arrive at denouements which throw new light on past and present, yet only confirm the essential nature of the characters as they have previously revealed themselves. The structure and movement of his plays therefore follow the same laws that Coleridge attributes to dream experiences, with the final assessment provided by waking thought. Here again, that is, are many of the features he observes in his study of dream psychology: the ever-present and influential past; the prophetic element in these promptings from earlier experience; the fundamental truth of the dreaming self in what it tells of the daytime personality.

The unity of the plays is to be sought at the level of subjective experience, as the theory of dramatic illusion also advocates. He works in terms of the compressed psychological time-scheme which dreams have taught him: past, present and future all implicit within the moment. From Coleridge's point of view, theory and practice therefore assist each other. Our theatre-state of receptivity will prepare us to recognize the psychological unity in the play, and conversely, the condition of 'illusion' will be more readily and more intensely brought about because the play itself takes us into the autonomous world of mental space and time. So, although *Zapolya* Part II takes place twenty years after Part I, the first part is not an awkwardly dissociated prologue, but the infant memory of the hero Andreas, buried to him but known to us, and dominant throughout Part II as the instinctive force driving him to seek his identity. In *Remorse*, the penetration of a vital past into the present is emblematically given in the motto its hero Alvar uses, describing himself as one who can 'bring the dead to life again' (II.i. 163). Throughout both plays, abundant reference is made to dreams, trances, presentiments, visions, nightmares; in each play also, places of highly significant personal associations are revisited—the forest cavern in *Zapolya*, the seashore in *Remorse*—these scenes being charged with past and present feeling simultaneously. By such devices the propriety of a subjective unity is maintained.

Coleridge invites his audience not merely to enter into the theatrical experience of 'willing illusion', but into a further elaboration of this. When we share in the states of mind of the characters and live with them in their haunted experience, we are none the less still exercising

171

our voluntary consent to do so. Our position is more complex than theirs, for we know the true situation while they are at the mercy of their unwilling illusions. Past and present are misread or half-known by Ordonio or Teresa, but not by the audience. We 'choose to be deceived' as, knowing Alvar to be at their side, we sympathize with Teresa's ignorance of his whereabouts and feel guilt with Ordonio who ordered his death and thinks it accomplished; or as we long with Bethlen the peasant to discover his true identity, knowing him from the first to be 'royal Andreas'. We and they are burdened dreamers; but for us it is a state of responsive double awareness, a waking dream.

Coleridge's ability to permeate his scenes with dream sensation, and to blend external with subjective action for fine dramatic effect is well illustrated by the cavern scene in *Remorse* (IV.i). We are involved in this scene, not merely as witnesses of a crisis in physical conflict but as participants in a psychological ordeal, because of the compelling evocation of dream-terror in the action. Isidore, Ordonio's ex-accomplice, is lured by night to the cavern so that Ordonio may silence him. He explores his surroundings, discovering a deep chasm as his foot plunges over the edge, and in the shock of this he recalls a nightmare of the previous night as one which anticipated this event and promised a disastrous outcome, only averted in the dream because his wife woke him. He tells all this vividly to Ordonio and the night-mare impressions merge with the present situation to heighten the tension most powerfully. The opportunity for a stroke of dramatic irony is splendidly taken by Coleridge as Ordonio, listening to the tale, sees in it a cue for action. As they struggle, he pushes Isidore into the chasm, and so the dream prophecy is fulfilled by a macabre logic, as Ordonio appreciates:

> I have hurl'd him down the chasm! . . .
> He dreamt of it: henceforward let him sleep,
> A dreamless sleep, from which no wife can wake him.
> His dream too is made out . . .   (168–71)

A dream of murder becomes reality: and so Ordonio's whole guilt-ridden history may be summarized. The imagery in his speeches is frequently that of nightmare (e.g. III.ii. 79–82; V.i. 221–2), and here too Coleridge's imaginative judgment shows its quality in this harmony of speech, action, and psychological import. That he set particular store by the interplay of dream and actuality, the idea of a man's destiny being determined by the fate which resides in his own psyche, is proved by a manuscript note which he added to the *Osorio* version of the cavern scene. Where Isidore begins to narrate how 'sorely' his 'last night's sleep' was haunted, Coleridge wrote:

This will be held by many for a mere Tragedy-dream—by many who have never given themselves the trouble to ask themselves from what grounds dreams pleased in Tragedy, and wherefore they have become so common. I believe, however, that in the present case, the whole is here psychologically true and accurate. Prophetical dreams are things of nature, and explicable by that law of the mind in which where dim ideas are connected with vivid feelings, Perception and Imagination insinuate themselves and mix with the forms of Recollection, till the Present appears to exactly correspond with the Past. Whatever is partially like, the Imagination will gradually represent as wholly like—a law of our nature which, when it is perfectly understood, woe to the great city Babylon—to all the superstitions of Men!

And at the end of the scene, he adds another comment on Isidore's fate: 'I think it an important instance how Dreams and Prophecies co-operate to their own completion'. Thus he sees such dramatic scenes as valuable imaginative experiences wherein we approach some of the 'laws of our nature', and central among them, the crucial relationships of past and present, memory and presentiment, especially as these are most freely hinted to us in our dreaming hours.[9]

If *Remorse* offers much evidence for Coleridge's researching mind being alert and actively experimental under the demands of dramatic creation, *Zapolya* in its whole character confirms that he sees the drama as an opportunity for delineating something of the 'varying degress of consciousness' which plague and inspire humanity. Centrally in *Zapolya* we are engaged in the desperate effort of the hero to find out his true name and solve the riddle of his birth. As Bethlen strives to become known to himself as 'royal Andreas', he acts out the human struggle to wake to a more complete consciousness, to make full sense out of the haunting fragments our dreams give us. 'I feel and seek the light I can not see' Bethlen cries (I.i. 324), and the pain of his quest is described as

> ... the ground-swell of a teeming instinct:
> Let it but lift itself to air and sunshine
> And it will find a mirror in the waters
> It now makes boil above it. (I.i. 375–8)

[9] In the light of these theories, Coleridge's excitement at finding St. Michael's Cave in Gibraltar, 'the very model of that which I described in my Tragedy...' can be readily appreciated (2.2045; April 1804).

Again, the scenes in forest and cavern blend geographical location with mental space, and so the drama sustains its psychological unity, keeping that inner harmony which draws in the spectator and renders him susceptible to the experience—and without which *Zapolya* would be no more than a *Bertram*. The play ends in triumphant revelation: 'behold your King!' (IV.i. 346). Instinct is raised to 'air and sunshine', Andreas not only is himself, he recognizes himself and celebrates this victory of literal self-possession. And into this fullness of knowledge the dream life too is integrated, a mastered phase of experience.

We may use Coleridge's own words in the final speech of *Zapolya*, and conclude that the scenes of his plays 'force wisdom on us all', rousing us to a renewed and more exhilarated self-awareness. In this, they take their place with the rest of his work, critical and creative alike. To leave them out of account, or to regard them as peripheral, is an injustice, and this is especially so in the context of Coleridge's investigations into the strange, associated regions of theatrical and dream experience. Here they form an essential link in his bold researches.

15

Byron: The Pilgrim and Don Juan

DOUGLAS GRANT

G OETHE'S opinions on Lord Byron are an excellent preparative:
the adulation of later critics comes to seem like ordinary
praise.

Goethe read *Manfred* with the deepest interest, as one of the
progeny of his own *Faust*. He was generous enough to acknowledge
that Byron had 'made use of the impelling principles in his own way,
for his own purposes, so that no one of them remains the same'.
We find, he went on, in the same place, 'in this tragedy, the quin-
tessence of the most astonishing talent born to be its own tormentor'.
This self-inflicted torment was, in Goethe's explanation, the natural
consequence of Byron's remorse at the outcome of his notorious
Florentine adventure: a guilty wife discovered and murdered by
her husband, who was found dead himself in the street that same
night. 'Lord Byron removed from Florence, and these spirits haunted
him all his life after.' The Florentine lady's were the chilling tones that
sounded when Astarte admonished Manfred, 'Tomorrow ends thine
earthly ills'. His imagination heated by such 'unbounded and
exuberant despair', it was hardly surprising that the poet was
inspired to improve on Hamlet's reflections in Manfred's soliloquy
beginning, 'We are the fools of time and terror'. Byron and Shakespeare: Goethe was always happy to bring them into equal conjunction.

Goethe discussed *Manfred* in *Kunst und Altherthum*, but I have
taken my quotations from the translation included in the notes to

175

Thomas Moore's edition of Byron.[1] Moore quotes Goethe at length, but he at last grows tired of 'this German criticism' and turns with relief to the article on *Manfred* in the commoner pages of *The Edinburgh Review.* He does not let pass unremarked, of course, Goethe's nonsense about a Florentine adventure. Such a tale, he noted, is 'an amusing instance of the disposition so prevalent throughout Europe, to picture Byron as a man of marvels and mysteries, as well in his life as his poetry'. Moore knew uncomfortably well whom Astarte really represented and why all Manfred's frantic urgings could hardly induce her phantom to speak.

Manfred is the first piece in the eleventh volume of Moore's edition of his friend's works. 'In the contents of this Volume,' Moore remarked, introducing it, 'together with the fourth Canto of "Childe Harold", the reader may trace the poetical, as well as personal, history of Lord Byron, from October, 1816, when he left Switzerland, down to the beginning of 1820, by which time he had taken up his residence at Ravenna.' The volume includes, Moore went on, 'some example of almost every kind of poetical composition in which he ever excelled: among others, the first, and perhaps greatest, of his dramatic efforts, and the earliest specimen of his comic narrative'. *Manfred* and *Beppo* are, as Moore suggests, the key pieces, but among the other, longer verses are *The Lament of Tasso*, *Mazeppa*, and the *Ode on Venice*, and among the shorter, the delightful familiar addresses to Murray the publisher and Tom Moore himself. Moore exaggerates the exclusiveness of the eleventh volume. The reader who wishes to follow Byron's history as a man and development as a poet from the time of his residence in the Villa Diodati—a fitter inaugural date than that of his departure from Switzerland—to his removal to Ravenna will need the Third as well as the Fourth Canto of *Childe Harold* and some of the poems in the tenth volume, including among them *The Prisoner of Chillon*. But with this reasonable adjustment, Moore's claim is a fair one; the poems in the eleventh volume enable one to reach the right conclusion about Byron's development in those significant years. The right conclusion must as always be the modern one: Byron grew up, as a man and a poet. The studied posturings and torrential rhetoric of *Childe Harold* and *Manfred* were put aside in favour of the disengaged assurance and conversational realism of *Beppo:* Advance, Don Juan.

[1] *The Works of Lord Byron: With his Letters and Journals, and his Life,* by Thomas Moore, 14 vols., 1832, xi. 71–3 n.

Moore's is the most convenient of the editions of Byron. I am sure that the others list more variants and are better at snapping up allusions—not least, the obvious—but Moore's has the singular merit of its annotations. There are quotations from the poet's letters and journals, of course, but also lengthy passages from the critics of the day, Jeffrey, Scott, Sir Egerton Brydges among them—and Professor Wilson. (The invariable according of his title to Wilson shows how rare an apparition a professor used to be in the purlieus of contemporary letters.) These critics cannot be said to have spoken the last word on Byron's poetry, but there is a pleasure in reading what is always well written and in seeing how the poetry affected these highly intelligent contemporaries—often in ways that would suggest if not a contradictory, a more enlarged reading of the poetry written in the eventful period from 1816 to 1820 than the one usually entertained today; a useful supplement that helps towards settling the ambiguous image of the poet. We cannot pretend that even our critics have given an entirely clear impression of Byron, except for those who discount all that he wrote of length in favour of *Don Juan*.

Take *Manfred*, for example, since we began with it. Goethe extolled it highly, but as he could be supposed to be biased towards a work which drew upon him for inspiration, Professor Wilson's views might pass as the more impartial. *Manfred* would be the poem, Wilson asserted, 'next to "Childe Harold", which we should give to a foreigner to read, that he might know something of Byron'. He can hardly moderate his praise, but, glancing only at his views on the character of the hero, he finds in Manfred, 'more of the self-might of Byron than in all his previous productions. He has therein brought, with wonderful power, metaphysical conceptions into forms'.[2] Goethe himself could have said no more. Jeffrey was nearly as enthusiastic, but more particular than his fellow countryman. He was prepared to be frank when he found fault. He disliked the introduction of 'satirical and political allusions' into the 'Hymn of the Spirits', for example, but he commented enthusiastically on the 'still and delicious witchery in the tranquility and seclusion'[3] of the valley where Manfred calls up the Witch of the Alps. Later in the same scene, he cannot refrain from remarking that 'both the apparition and the dialogue are so managed that the sense of their improbability is swallowed up in that of their beauty'.[4]

[2] *ib*. p. 31 n.
[3] *ib*. p. 29 n.
[4] *ib*. p. 32 n.

A reader of today can only pause in wonder at such enthusiasm. I should have thought that most of us would have found the character of Manfred woefully theatrical and the descriptive verse meretricious, to keep to the matters on which Moore calls up critical support. Manfred would seem to be a blatant expression of the poet himself, in blown conceit, self-justifying and self-pitying, and the descriptions are corrupted by the same affectation.

A good test of the validity of such an unsympathetic judgment would be Byron himself, as he is shown in his letters and journals of the time. The first passage which Jeffrey praises as 'still and delicious witchery'—to let a single instance stand for all—runs as follows:

> It is not noon—the sunbow's rays still arch
> The torrent with the many hues of heaven,
> And roll the sheeted silver's waving column
> O'er the crag's headlong perpendicular,
> And fling its lines of foaming light along,
> And to and fro, like the pale courser's tail,
> The Giant steed, to be bestrode by Death,
> As told in the Apocalypse.

Byron was drawing in these lines on his memory of his visit to the Jungfrau in September 1816. He described in his journal how the sun, playing upon a mountain torrent, the Staubbach, formed 'a *rainbow* of the lower part of all colours, but principally purple and gold . . . The torrent is in shape curving over the rock, like the *tail* of a white horse streaming in the wind, such as it might be conceived would be that of the "*pale* horse" on which *Death* is mounted in the Apocalypse'.[5] In the prose, the image of the water streaming like a horse's tail in the wind strikes the attention of the reader as immediately as it must have come into the poet's own mind, but in the poem it is spoilt by the calculating effect of the deliberate verse.

Byron has not always conveniently given us his prose as a means of checking the sincerity of his verse, but much of the verse written in the first three years of his exile is similar to this passage in *Manfred*. In the third Canto of *Childe Harold* there is a famous stanza (XCIII) in which he describes a thunderstorm over Lake Leman which he witnessed on 13th June, 1816, at midnight.

> Most glorious night!
> Thou wert not sent for slumber! let me be

[5] The first part of this quotation is quoted by Moore in a note to this passage (*ib.* p. 29): the second part is quoted by Leslie A. Marchand, *Byron*, New York (1957), ii. 653.

> A sharer in thy fierce and far delight,—
> A portion of the tempest and of thee!
> How the lit lake shines, a phosphoric sea,
> And the big rain comes dancing to the earth!
> And now again 'tis black,—and now, the glee
> Of the loud hills shakes with its mountain-mirth,
> As if they did rejoice o'er a young earthquake's birth.

The stanza runs well enough, but the scene suddenly loses its reality in the pathetic fallacy at the end . . . and then the eye drops to the note in small print in Moore's edition. This stanza, Sir Walter Scott declares, presents 'a picture of sublime terror, yet of enjoyment, often attempted, but never so well, certainly never better, brought out in poetry'.[6] Sir Walter was clearly not worried by showy rhetoric and pathetic fallacies, and the approval he accorded to this stanza he would have volunteered to most of Byron's poetry at the time.

Scott's exclamations over the poetry, and those of the other critics recruited into the notes by Moore, could be dismissed as instances of the aberrant taste of the age, in its liking for the flashy and luxuriant, but they may also serve as a reminder to us to read more cautiously as we go. Several passages in the longer poems of this time, many stanzas in Cantos Three and Four of *Childe Harold* are demonstrably bad, the diction being inadequate to the sense. A stanza or so before the description of the thunderstorm, Harold apostrophizes the stars, 'which are the poetry of heaven', and continues by describing how the quiet night plunges him in 'thoughts too deep':

> All heaven and earth are still: From the high host
> Of stars, to the lull'd lake and mountain-coast,
> All is concenter'd in a life intense,
> Where not a beam, nor air, nor leaf is lost,
> But hath a part of being, and a sense
> Of that which is of all Creator and defence.

The attention hardly pauses on these lines to unravel the idea from the diction, which progressively weakens as it wavers between its attempt to define pantheism aphoristically and its need to rhyme. But the attention need not pause. The impetuosity of the poet's feelings will in a moment have carried the reader on to the thunderstorms and the sublimities which Sir Walter stands waiting to stress. In a word, *Childe Harold* and the other poems must be read generously, without

[6] *Works.* viii. 175 n.

too scrupulous a care for faults of diction, or too prompt a disposition to put down all mannerisms as faults. 'The bosom which is not touched with it—' urged Sir Egerton Brydges in favour of *The Lament of Tasso*, 'the fancy which is not warmed,—the understanding which is not enlightened and exalted by it, is not fit for human intercourse.'[7] Sir Egerton puts it rather strongly, but his admonition ought to be taken as a practical illustration of Emerson's dictum that there is 'creative reading as well as creative writing'. The comments printed by Moore in his edition, Sir Egerton's among them, suggest that we may have lost the art of reading Byron.

The art may have been lost because we have come to know Byron himself too well. 'No man is a hero to his valet.' The truth of the old adage still holds—in spite of Byron. We have all become Byron's valets. We can follow his movements almost from day to day in Professor Marchand's wonderfully explicit pages, the latest and fullest in the endless series of biographies. We know the dates on which he began to diet. We can untangle his assignations. We can count up his assets in ready cash. We can compare the mood in which he wrote home in the morning with the tone of his spirits as he began to compose the same night. We know everything, including nonsense when we see it—such nonsense as Goethe wrote about, a Florentine amour and assassinations in the dark.

''Tis to create,' runs one of Byron's most famous critical declarations, in the third Canto of *Childe Harold*,

> and in creating live
> A being more intense, that we endow
> With form our fancy, gaining as we give
> The life we image, even as I do now.

All the 'forms' which Byron's fancy imagined during these years—Manfred and Tasso and, of course, the Childe himself—are now taken primarily, on the best psychological theory of compensation, as expressing and assuaging Byron's despair at the sad course of his private life. Everything in the poetry, from motivation to circumstance, must be referred back for explanation to the poet's own character and progress, at the expense of appreciation. It is consequently idle to talk of Manfred or the Childe or any of the other figments as if they were anything but selfish projections of the poet, unreal in any of the senses that reality can normally be credited to

[7] *ib*. xi. 93 n.

characters in literature. The process was beginning to work strongly in 1816, prompted by the scabrous and factual gossip that followed upon the breakdown of the poet's marriage. Byron was distressed by it and protested against it in the Dedication to the fourth Canto of *Childe Harold*. There will be less of the Pilgrim and more of himself in this, the last Canto, he wrote resignedly: 'The fact is, that I had become weary of drawing a line which every one seemed determined not to perceive . . . it was in vain that I asserted, and imagined that I had drawn, a distinction between the author and the pilgrim.' The passage is usually construed as a belated acknowledgement on Byron's part of what had long been obvious, but it is curious that he should have gone on to affirm that his readers' refusal not to confound the poet with his creation had decided him to bring the poem to an end.

Goethe may have wildly sought in the poet's spurious biography for an explanation of Manfred's secret remorse, but in other remarks he showed his usual and more acute understanding. 'I could not', he said in conversation with Eckermann in 1827, 'make use of any man as the representative of the modern poetical era except him, who undoubtedly is the greatest genius of our century. Again, Byron is neither antique nor romantic, but like the present day itself.'[8] Byron as an expression of the 'spirit of the age' may be too obvious an idea to be paraded yet again in these lenten days, but Goethe's observation reinforces the distinction that Byron himself had wearily called attention to in the Dedication to the fourth Canto. Say what we like, Childe Harold is not the man—nor are Manfred and his peers.

I should have thought it impossible for anyone to identify himself with Lord Byron, short of infatuated conceit. We need not go as far as Goethe, who asserted that but for one fault—to be mentioned later—Byron 'would be as great as Shakespeare and the ancients',[9] without acknowledging that the vital play of intelligence in his correspondence and journals—to keep off the suspicious ground of his verse—would as quickly tax our lesser wits beyond endurance as the devasting energy of his private life would have annihilated our strength. We may fervently admire his genius and sympathize with him in his adventures, but, while asking for yet more letters and further private details, that is as far as we can enter into his circum-

[8] *Conversations of Goethe with Eckermann*, Everyman ed. (1935), p. 211.
[9] *ib*. p. 155.

stances. On the contrary, we can identify ourselves with Childe Harold—at least, the whole of Europe once did.

The comments which Moore generously included in his edition tellingly show how closely and passionately Byron's contemporaries felt with his characters—anyone who did not was, in Sir Egerton's bold words, unfit for 'human intercourse'. Why the Childe should be a 'wandering outlaw of his own dark mind' might exactly elude them, as Manfred's particular offence did, mercifully, but the vagueness of these hidden causes allowed them to put on these *persona* as their own and in those disguises to experience the emotions most coveted by the age—the consciousness of individuality, the love of freedom, the pangs of unrequited love, the intoxication of energy, the solemnity of ancient places, the sublimity of mountains: all the turbulence and elevation of one of the most remarkable eras in the European consciousness. They could experience their own time in Byron's poetry and experience it coherently, in memorable verse.

We are grudging in our admiration; Moore's commentators can supplement our nervous tepidity. 'It required some courage to venture on a theme beset with so many dangers,' Jeffrey remarked on the description of Waterloo, but see, he continues, 'with what easy strength he enters upon it, and with how much grace he gradually finds his way back to his own peculiar vein of sentiment and diction.' 'This stanza is very grand, even from its total unadornment,' Brydges exclaims over the stanza that follows two later (XXIII), the one beginning,

> Within a window'd niche of that high hall
> Sate Brunswick's fated chieftain . . .

Prompted by these critics' enthusiasm, we suddenly begin to see what extraordinary achievements such passages are; how brilliantly, in the stanzas on Waterloo, Byron has established the image of the battle, in diction which is individual and idiomatic—a gift to elocution.

The reader travelling through Europe with Childe Harold is conducted to one sacred spot or hallowed relic after another and told what above all else he wants to know: what he ought to see and seeing, ought to feel. 'Clear, placid, Leman,' the Bridge of Sighs, the 'Niobe of nations', 'the dying Gladiator'—they pass in turn, but not separately; they are the successive stages in a continuously developing sensibility, which reflects sublimity upon ordinary experience from its association with the wonders of the present and the glories of the

past. 'There was a sound of revelry by night,' is the beginning of the
passage on Waterloo, describing the ball, a rare occasion, attended
by only the favoured, but the passage ends with the grief of the
bereaved, an emotion that everyone except the callous is called upon
to feel.

> They mourn, but smile at length; and, smiling, mourn:
> The tree will wither long before it fall;
> The hull drives on, though mast and sail be torn;
> The roof-tree sinks, but moulders on the hall
> In massy hoariness; the ruin'd wall
> Stands when its wind-worn battlements are gone;
> The bars survive the captive they enthral;
> The day drags through though storms keep out the sun;
> And thus the heart will break, yet brokenly live on.

Such poetry is translatable—into the facts of everyday life, in spite
of the mysterious affliction of its well-born narrator, and into other
languages, which only use different grammars to express the same
sentiments.

Byron might reasonably complain that Childe Harold was being
confused with his own character, but he himself nakedly intruded his
private affairs into the third Canto by invoking his daughter, Ada,
in the very first stanza and by returning to the same subject at the
conclusion, in a shameless burst of self-pity: 'I have not loved the
world, nor the world me.' Sir Walter Scott seriously rebuked the poet
for luxuriously indulging and dramatizing himself in these stanzas.
Scott was especially alarmed by Byron's notion that he had a claim
to happiness and the world's respect by right of his genius. There is
no 'poetical path' to 'contentment and heart's-ease,' Scott affirmed;
those gifts are awarded regardless of the prerogatives of intellect.
'To narrow our wishes and desires within the scope of our powers of
attainment; to consider our misfortunes, however peculiar in their
character, as our inevitable share of the patrimony in Adam . . . to
stoop, in short, to the realities of life . . . such seem the most obvious
and certain means of keeping or regaining mental tranquillity.'[10]
Scott's words may fall as sadly Christian after the defiant misanthropy
of the Childe, but they help to explain where Manfred and Tasso and
Bonnivard and the Childe himself all fall short of their pretensions
to inclusive experience. 'Were it not for his hypochondriacal negative
turn,' Goethe similarly argued, though more succinctly, 'he would be

[10] *Works*, viii. 185 n.

as great as Shakespeare and the ancients.' After the heroics and extravagances, the sentiments and ardours, of the Childe and Manfred the reader must 'stoop to realities'—realities to which Byron himself stooped when he invented a new character which could not be embarrassingly confounded with himself—Don Juan.

Don Juan is so much to our taste that we have come to neglect the earlier poetry which made Byron famous throughout Europe as the first man of the age—memorable poetry which readers of a century carried in their heads. 'As he stood there in the Coliseum,' Henry James observed about the young man in *Daisy Miller*, illustrating lightly but truly where Byron excelled and where he fell short, 'he began to murmur Byron's famous lines, out of "Manfred"; but before he had finished his quotation he remembered that if nocturnal meditations in the Coliseum are recommended by the poets, they are deprecated by the doctors.' Unfortunately, the habit has become inveterate of reading in poetry only on the strength of 'medical advice'.

16

Keats and 'The Feel of Not to Feel It'

JOHN JONES

In a drear-nighted December,
　　Too happy, happy tree,
Thy branches ne'er remember
　　Their green felicity:
　　The north cannot undo them,
　　With a sleety whistle through them;
　　Nor frozen thawings glue them
　　　　From budding at the prime.

In a drear-nighted December,
　　Too happy, happy brook,
Thy bubblings ne'er remember
　　Apollo's summer look;
　　But with a sweet forgetting,
　　They stay their crystal fretting,
　　Never, never petting
　　　　About the frozen time.

Ah! would 'twere so with many
　　A gentle girl and boy!
But were there ever any
　　Writh'd not at passed joy?
　　The feel of not to feel it,
　　When there is none to heal it,
　　Nor numbed sense to steel it,
　　　　Was never said in rhyme.

DISLIKE of 'the feel of not to feel it' goes back as far as Richard Woodhouse, Keats's contemporary and friend, who transcribed the whole poem three times and also redrafted the

final stanza to get rid of the offending line.[1] The same dislike prompted some unknown person to replace this line by 'to know the change
and feel of it' in a version of the lyric which appeared in two periodicals (the *Gem* and the *Literary Gazette*) in 1829, with Keats eight
years dead; and it can still be traced in H. W. Garrod's definitive
Oxford English Texts edition. In 1939 Garrod printed 'to know the
change and feel it', in the teeth of Keats's autograph—the only one
then known—and Woodhouse's three transcripts. On his side was
nothing that could be ascribed with any confidence to the poet, or
even dated from his lifetime.[2] Nineteen years later, in 1958, came the
second edition of Garrod's admirable book. In the meantime another
autograph had been discovered,[3] and this confirmed 'the feel of not
to feel it' while recording in its margin, in a hand which is certainly
not Keats's, 'to know the change and feel it'. Nevertheless Garrod
persisted in his earlier course.

Woodhouse's objection went deeper than this one line. He wrote
to a friend:

> I plead guilty, even before I am accused, of an utter abhorrence of the
> word 'feel' for feeling (substantively). But Keats seems fond of it and will
> graft it 'in aeternum' on our language. Be it so.[4]

Whatever Woodhouse may have thought, 'feel' is not just a verbal
point; it leads straight to Keats's sensuality. And the truncating of
'feeling' into 'feel' mimics the disquiet of an entire critical tradition
which wants to interpret its way through and out the other side of
this sensual gift of his, but is always having the door slammed in its
face.

Matthew Arnold pronounced that 'a merely sensuous man cannot

---

[1] Woodhouse proposed:

> But in the soul's December
> The Fancy backward strays,
> And sadly doth remember
> The hue of golden days:
> In woe, the thought appalling
> Of bliss—gone past recalling,
> Brings o'er the heart a falling
> Not to be told in rhyme.

[2] Two transcripts give 'to know the change and feel it'. The first (Garrod's 'Hamp-
stead transcript') is probably copied from the *Literary Gazette*. If so, it has no authority.
The other appears in a volume compiled in 1828 by two members of the Keats circle,
J. C. Stephens and Isabella Jane Towers. The *Gazette* and the *Gem*, which printed
independently of each other, must, one admits, have got their copy from somewhere.
Garrod asks (lvii); 'For if Keats himself did not write the *Gazette* version, who did?'
The answer is, we don't know.

[3] By Mr. Alvin Whitley, who announced his find in the *Harvard Library Bulletin*
(1951).

[4] *The Keats Circle* (1948), ed. H. E. Rollins, vol. I, p. 64.

either by promise or by performance be a very great poet', and went on to distinguish between the sensuous Keats and the very great poet who possessed 'intellectual and spiritual passion'.[5] But whereas Arnold's documentation of sensuousness is, as one would expect, convincing, that of spirituality and intellect is negligible—the end of the *Grecian Urn* (where dissatisfaction with that poem begins), the first line of *Endymion* (a proposition which rings hollow and remains unvindicated in rather the same way as Arnold's 'intellectual and spiritual passion'); and otherwise the letters, a scrap of occasional journalism and the prose Preface to *Endymion*. Where has the very great poet got to?

Run-of-the-mill criticism of Keats has largely occupied itself with elaborate yet slovenly revampings of the Arnoldian spirituality and intellect. There is no need to give names. The more interesting work has tried to seize the nettle of Arnold's 'merely sensuous man'. Middleton Murry had an instinct for the Shakespearean solidity, the physical conviction, even the Shakespearean secular sublime, of Keats.[6] Dr. F. R. Leavis based his case for Keats, and against Shelley, on the younger poet's 'grasp of the actual', his certain feel and hold of things.[7] Mr. John Bayley looks straight at the sensual imagination and commends its unmisgiving vulgarity.[8]

But they all run into trouble. Murry on 'ripeness is all', no doubt encouraged at first by a good angel whispering in his ear that ripeness is this poet's master-metaphor, ends by talking as if Keats had actually written *King Lear*. Dr. Leavis saves the Keats who faces facts—the *Nightingale's* last stanza—at the fearful cost of discarding the Keats who burrows into his dream-forest's 'embalmed darkness'. Mr. Bayley allows his keen sense of what is characterful in Keats to determine his judgments about Keats's finished art. So Murry concludes that non-existent Keats is great Keats, Bayley that bad Keats is good Keats, Leavis that a helpless part of Keats is the competent whole of Keats.

The serious task is to dislodge the 'merely' from Arnold's 'merely sensuous man', and then to apprehend a poet whose sensuality is ample enough to contain both the realist and the dreamer—contain them in a few words:

---

[5] *Essays in Criticism*, Second Series.
[6] Especially in his *Keats and Shakespeare*.
[7] 'Keats': in *Revaluation*.
[8] 'Keats and Reality': In *Proceedings of the British Academy*, 1962. 'Unmisgiving' is Leigh Hunt's word, gratefully borrowed and most sensitively deployed by Mr. Bayley.

Ay, in the very temple of Delight
Veil'd Melancholy has her sovran shrine,
    Though seen of none save him whose strenuous tongue
    Can burst Joy's grape against his palate fine;

and in whole poems, like *St. Agnes* and the odes.

Worked out, that would be the whole truth; but now our concern is with one corner of Keats's sensuality, his feel of not to feel. Therefore back to the 'drear-nighted December' lyric and its disputed line.

A strong light falls on this line, especially on 'feel' of one version against 'know' of the other, because it has the important job of declaring what exactly it is that 'was never said in rhyme'. Keats did not lack ordinary good sense. He was aware that knowing a change —loss of youth, love, talents, faith—and responding to it emotionally has very frequently been said in rhyme; this is perhaps the commonest of all lyric themes. Nor should we be quick to assume that the clinching assertion of the poem's final line is a conscious fraud, and that in so far as he means anything he is only saying that knowing and feeling 'the change' has never been expressed perfectly, or well enough; so really his poem is pretty silly.

On the contrary, the presumption must be that his punch-line intention behind 'was never said in rhyme' is genuine. Good intentions do not make good poems, but they do suffice to guarantee the honest force of that 'never' and its direct, unequivocal reference to the line under dispute. Quite simply, he must be taken to mean what he says; and once we do so we see that the strongest reason (textual considerations apart) for preferring 'the feel of not to feel it' is its intrinsic sound sense. Keats, as I say, was not a fool. His feel of not to feel is not a clumsy alternative to the memory of vanished feeling. He has taken the reflection out of remembrance, and has isolated that bereft, self-enfolded state, the pressure of something missing, definite yet featureless, precise but unutterable, perfectly known and conceptually void. We all recognize the experience, it is a feel we all have. This is, and is worthily, what 'was never said in rhyme'.

An artist seldom troubles to remark that a thing has not been done unless that particular possibility enters, however vaguely, within his own aspiration. Moreover it is a sign of greatness in an artist that he should want to do what he alone can do, his ambition springing from insight into the whereabouts of his originality. In this lyric Keats has hit on a persuasive means of presenting his feel as the closed, conceptless circuit which it quintessentially is. The negative form (yet positive too, since the feel of *not* to feel is just as much a Keatsian entity as any other feel) scarcely admits of misinterpretation. That is why it discomposes people. The only way to force open its closed circuit is to rewrite the line—which is what has happened.

By substituting 'know' for 'feel' somebody reintroduced reflective mind into Keats's memory and threw his whole poem out of true. It now revolves round a fatuous contrast between us unlucky men who have intelligence and can remember our lost joy, and trees and streams which have no intelligence and cannot. In fact the poem's root contrast, by no means fatuous, was between the feel of present pain and the feel of absent pleasure. The first belongs to the tree and stream in the grip of winter wind and frost, the second to us. With agreeable wit Keats has allowed himself the mental words 'remember' and 'forgetting' in the first two stanzas where there is no danger he will be misunderstood. We cannot fail to see that rememembering and forgetting is a mere politeness, a poet's courtesy towards his trees and streams. We devalue them accordingly, and in doing this lay ourselves open to the calculated shock of his third and 'human' stanza where the mental words, so far from appearing in full literal force as seems inevitable, are withheld completely and feel dominates.

The same reversal is pursued through the stream's quasi-mental 'fretting' and 'petting', in contrast with the mindless automatism of the human 'writh'd'. The preposition in the line 'writh'd not at passed joy' also merits attention. Woodhouse appends a note to one of his transcripts of the poem: '*Of* in Miss R.'s copy in Keats's handwriting.' One of our two surviving autographs also reads 'of' for 'at', and I wish it were possible to see the other (the location of which is now not known) to ensure that this unobtrusive variant has not been overlooked there. In any case, we know that Keats wrote 'writh'd not of passed joy' at least twice. It is an extraordinary and un-English phrase, but not without its rationale. It is determined by the overall pattern of the human but mind-free third stanza. The snag with 'at', Keats's instinct will have told him, is that it undoes the work of 'writh'd'. On its own 'writh'd' conveys an impression of epileptic helplessness, but when '*at* passed joy' is joined to it the mental taint 'in contemplation of' begins to infiltrate. Replace 'at' by 'of' and the automatism is sustained throughout the line. This is the same 'of' as in 'sick of the palsy' or 'of overeating'.

So Keats hesitated. He may well have judged the 'of' version intolerably freakish. However 'at' does not improve matters much in this direction, while working harm in another. In fairness we should recall that he made no move to publish the poem. It is one of his quirky, half-successful comments on the logic of feel.

Close to 'drear-nighted December' is the *Ode on Indolence* which is a poem about the feel of scarcely to feel, poised on the verge of not to feel:

> Ripe was the drowsy hour;
> The blissful cloud of summer-indolence
>   Benumb'd my eyes; my pulse grew less and less;
> Pain had no sting, and pleasure's wreath no flower:
>   O, why did ye not melt, and leave my sense
>   Unhaunted quite of all but—nothingness?

Again, scarcely to feel is a special and positive feel. This twilight state fascinated Keats. Indolence was a favourite word of his, and in a journal-letter to America he weaves a loose meditation round it and the ode.

> This morning I am in a sort of temper indolent and supremely careless: I long after a stanza or two of Thomson's Castle of Indolence—my passions are all asleep from my having slumbered till nearly eleven and weakened the animal fibre all over me to a delightful sensation about three degrees on this side of faintness—if I had teeth of pearl and the breath of lillies I should call it langour—but as I am I must call it Laziness. In this state of effeminacy the fibres of the brain are relaxed in common with the rest of the body, and to such a happy degree that pleasure has no show of enticement and pain no unbearable frown.[9]

Indirectly the letter reveals why this poem—also unpublished by him —does not deserve a place among the great odes of 1819. It is half raw, tethered to the poet through his present self-scrutiny, damagingly subjective. At the same time the *Ode on Indolence* is too interesting to be dismissed as a failure.

So is the more obviously unsuccessful sonnet *On Visiting the Tomb of Burns*:

> All is cold Beauty; pain is never done:
> For who has mind to relish, Minos-wise,
>   The real of Beauty, free from that dead hue
>   Sickly imagination and sick pride
>   Cast wan upon it?

'This sonnet I have written in a strange mood, half-asleep' writes Keats to his brother Tom,[10] betraying an introspective zeal like that

9 *Letters* (ed. Rollins), vol. II, p. 78.
10 *Letters*, vol. I, p. 309.

which permeates *Indolence*. Once again unpublished by John, the sonnet adds wrong ('cold', 'dead', 'sick') feel to the feel of not to feel and of scarcely to feel. Wrong because of our human failure to 'relish'—Keats's authentic palate-word—the beautiful in the clean simplicity of its own truth. Other things creep in, and we need the wisdom of that divinely-advised legislator, Minos, to keep them out. This is familiar ground. Often Keats's reader encounters a bitter, sickly, sterile taste belonging to beauty which has become thus fouled and tainted:

> all the pleasant hues
> Of heaven and earth had faded: deepest shades
> Were deepest dungeons; heaths and sunny glades
> Were full of pestilent light; our taintless rills
> Seem'd sooty, and o'er-spread with upturn'd gills
> Of dying fish;[11]

and Endymion's goddess asks her mortal lover,

> 'I am pain'd,
> Endymion: woe! woe! is grief contain'd
> In the very deeps of pleasure, my sole life?'[12]

Hers is perhaps the most nagging of all Keats's mature doubts, the point where the love-hate tension between realist and dreamer appears at its creative sharpest. Must human feel always be poisoned by human reflection? Lamia certainly knew how

> To unperplex bliss from its neighbour pain

but her skill has a rather trivial supernatural aura throughout, and Keats's exposition is, *au fond*, repellently comic.

Returning from that uncomfortable poem to 'drear-nighted December' ('drear' belongs within the 'cold', 'sickly' complex), we observe Keats dealing both with non-feel and mis-feel by way of trees and men. Trees are enclosed within present sensation, their good times are not spoilt by anticipation of bad, nor in bad times do they torment themselves with memories of 'their green felicity': theirs is the world of the vale of soul-making letter ('Suppose a rose to have sensation, it blooms on a beautiful morning, it enjoys itself'). But we do torment ourselves and spoil our feel, it is a fact of our humanity. In another famous letter Keats exclaims 'O for a Life of Sensations

[11] *Endymion*, I, 691.
[12] *ib*. II, 822.

rather than of Thoughts!' And at the same time he knows it cannot be so.

In good times, then, the tree has no poisoning fear of trouble ahead. This falls outside the immediate scope of 'drear-nighted December' but is one of the *Nightingale Ode*'s profound implications. The tree is 'too happy'. I want to put my finger on that idiosyncratic 'too', and then place 'too happy, happy tree' alongside 'being too happy in thine happiness' in the ode. What is the force of this happiness, and of the poet's sharing its extremity, its too-ness, with the bird?

The nightingale's joy is revealed by the opening stanza in its singing 'of summer in full-throated ease'. Its good fortune, its objective happiness, is later stated thus:

> Thou wast not born for death, immortal Bird!

The second is linked to the first (note Keats's reminder at 'the voice I hear') by the bird's unspoilt sensation, that is by its mindless and therefore timeless enclosure within the mid-May of the ode. Much has been written about the nightingale's immortality. People want to know what estrangement from death this is that the bird enjoys but which the poem expressly denies to human beings. The answer is, the bird's embalmed feel, its perfect yet living containment within its song of summer. The nightingale is like the bees in *To Autumn* for whom 'warm days will never cease'—like but more so since, in the light of *Autumn's* gentle, insistent naturalism, this persuasion of the bees is a kind of poet's dream, and fragile, whereas the nightingale has truly, invulnerably, no winter within her present feel which is her voice and her life; she does not know death, there she is immortal.

The human poet is not immortal. He reaches out in desire ('And with thee fade'), then in assertion ('for I will fly to thee'), and finally achievement ('Already with thee!'). Nevertheless the union of man and bird is haunted by transience ('this passing night') and by death in whose arms it is perhaps safe (hence 'half in love with easeful Death'); but it cannot be sustained otherwise, as Keats's *tour de force* the repeated 'forlorn' is about to prove. 'Forlorn' turns the song 'plaintive' for the listening poet, it does not touch the bird.

And so 'In a drear-nighted December' is one of the unsuccessful poems which line the road to the *Nightingale's* 'forlorn'. But, of course, 'forlorn' itself is rich in cross-reference to the other odes: the deceived bees of *Autumn*, the bursting of Joy's grape at the end of *Melancholy* (the unburst grape is tasteless and the burst grape is over), the *Psyche*—moth's *Liebestod* when the open window and the blazing torch summon it to love and death, the marvellous turn at the 'little town' stanza followed by 'Cold Pastoral!' in the *Grecian Urn* where Keats casts a glance of tender scepticism at the pleasures of love-making inside a work of art. These are all triumphs of his sensuality, silent removers of the 'merely' from Arnold's 'merely sensuous man', moments when realist confronts dreamer in mis-feel or non-feel (not in 'spiritual and intellectual passion' if words are to know their place), the thing which Madeline enacts in *St. Agnes:*

> Her eyes were open, but she still beheld,
> Now wide awake, the vision of her sleep:
> There was a painful change, that nigh expell'd
> The blisses of her dream. . . .

Once and unforgettably, Keats's 'feel of not to feel' occupies an entire poem, *La Belle Dame sans Merci.* Unlike *St. Agnes* and the odes which are antiphons shared with varying stress between realist and dreamer, *La Belle Dame* is a song sung by the spirit of non-feel, a lyric dilation upon the forlorn experience. The word in the dreary-cold-sick syndrome which *La Belle Dame* in fact prefers is 'wither'.

> O what can ail thee, knight-at-arms,
> Alone and palely loitering?
> The sedge has wither'd from the lake,
> And no birds sing.

Withering is momentarily opposed by ripeness, the master-metaphor of Keats's affirmative sensuality:

> The squirrel's granary is full,
> And the harvest's done—

only to be reasserted in the third stanza:

> I see a lilly on thy brow,
> With anguish moist and fever dew,
> And on thy cheeks a fading rose
> Fast withereth too.

Withering and fading bear down ripeness; so instead of the double force of 'gathering' in *To Autumn*, garnering and departure, fruition and death, the harvest of *La Belle Dame* is just a toneless end—note 'done'—like Wilfred Owen's 'finished fields of autumns that are old'. And for the same reason the narrative heart of the poem ('I met a lady') is uncannily without hope from the start, and the Keatsian tasting sinister ('roots of relish sweet'), and the dream which follows 'on the cold hill side' impossible of ripe fulfilment.

'Cold', repeated in

> And I awoke and found me here,
> On the cold hill's side

joins wither in the forlorn vocabulary, but wither has the last word:

> And this is why I sojourn here,
> Alone and palely loitering,
> Though the sedge has wither'd from the lake,
> And no birds sing.

Not that vocabulary means much, except in its underground connection with the entire not-to-feel pattern, and in its antithetical relation to affirmative feel and ripeness. These associations are the business of all Keats's greatest work, but they run singularly deep in *La Belle Dame* which may help to explain why it took so long to establish itself as a masterpiece. It is the saddest poem he ever wrote, its tune an unresonant white thread whose sterile end is its sterile beginning round again. This is the absolute purity of not to feel, the nature of the land where no birds sing.

17

Shelley's Lyrics

G. M. MATTHEWS

I<small>T</small> is easy to slip into the assumption that 'self-expression' was among the objectives of the early English Romantics. T. S. Eliot may unwittingly have made it easier, by combining a distaste for Romanticism with his principle that 'Poetry is not a turning loose of emotion, but an escape from emotion; it is not the expression of personality, but an escape from personality'; if so, this would be ironical, for it is from the Romantics that his principle derives. When Eliot says: 'the more perfect the artist, the more completely separate in him will be the man who suffers and the mind which creates', he is developing Shelley's view that 'The poet and the man are two different natures';[1] when he affirms, of the poet, that 'emotions which he has never experienced will serve his turn as well as those familiar to him', he is generalizing from Shelley's endeavour in *The Cenci* 'to produce a delineation of passions which I had never participated in'.[2] The word 'self-expression' dates from the nineties, and the idea that an artist wants to express his own 'individuality' in art is alien to the early Romantic poets, all of whom would have repudiated, or did explicitly rule out, any such notion. Shelley would have had difficulty in even making sense of it. Every great poet, he agreed, left the imprint of an individual mind on all his works, but that imprint was the brand of his limitation as much as of his greatness; it was a by-product of his real aims. For an artist to seek, or a critic to praise, 'self-expression' would have seemed absolutely meaningless to him.

[1] *The Letters of Percy Bysshe Shelley*, ed. F. L. Jones, Oxford (1964), II. 310.
[2] *Letters*, II. 189.

This has never deterred critics from assuming not only that the lyrical heart-cry is Shelley's typical utterance, but that he is liable to utter this cry at virtually any moment. Charles Kingsley and F. R. Leavis have recognized even the Catholic murderess Beatrice Cenci as Percy B. Shelley. Turn but a petticoat and start a luminous wing. David Masson decided in 1875 that Shelley's poetry was 'nothing else than an effluence from his personality',[3] and in 1965 the medical psychologist Dr. Eustace Chesser declared that Shelley 'does not even *notice* the existence of the hard, external world which pays no attention to his wishes. His gaze is directed all the time on his own emotional states'.[4] The present essay tries to remove a major obstacle in the way of a more intelligent discussion; and it is first necessary to see in plain figures what Shelley's contribution as a lyrical poet really was.

From *Original Poetry* (1810) to *Hellas* (1822) Shelley published twelve volumes of verse. Seven of these contain no separate lyrics. *Original Poetry* had four 'personal' lyrics,[5] all bearing on Shelley's attachment to Harriet Grove. *Posthumous Fragments of Margaret Nicholson* was artfully-packaged propaganda, and its concluding poem is the only personal one it contains. *Alastor* has ten shorter poems: three addressed to Coleridge, Wordsworth, and Napoleon respectively; two translations; and again one 'personal' lyric, the 'Stanzas.—April 1814', which concern the Boinville-Turner entanglement. *Rosalind and Helen* (1819) has three shorter poems, 'Lines written in the Euganean Hills', 'Hymn to Intellectual Beauty', and 'Ozymandias', the second of which contains a striking autobiographical passage. The 'Euganean Hills' I believe to have even less reference to Shelley himself than Donald Reiman has already ably argued.[6] *Prometheus Unbound* contains nine shorter poems, including the allegorical 'Sensitive Plant';[7] once again, the only lyric with unequivocal personal application is the 'Ode to the West Wind'. A total of seven or eight 'personal' lyrics in twelve volumes of verse, only half of these in the last eleven volumes—a modest ration, one

---

[3] *Wordsworth, Shelley, Keats and other Essays*, p. 129.

[4] *Shelley and Zastrozzi: self-revelation of a neurotic*, p. 29.

[5] By 'personal' lyrics, I intend (*a*) short poems that name names ('What would cure, that would kill me, Jane'), and (*b*) poems that seem recognizably biographical ('Her voice did quiver as we parted'). (*b*) is, however, a very unsafe category.

[6] 'Structure, Symbol, and Theme in "Lines written among the Euganean Hills",' *PMLA*, 77, September 1962, 404–13.

[7] 'There is no justification for the frequent definition of the Sensitive Plant as Shelley saw himself or as a special category of man, such as the Poet ... The Garden ... is the total animate universe as it is experienced by man, the Sensitive Plant.' (E. R. Wassermann, *The Subtler Language*, Baltimore (1959), pp. 257–8).

might think, for a monotonously self-regarding narcissist whose genius was essentially lyrical. This is not quite the full story, of course. Two volumes had 'personal' dedications; Shelley himself called *Epipsychidion* 'an idealized history of my life and feelings'[8] (though nobody can explain the history it records, and it is not a lyric). Two other proposed volumes would have affected the statistics: the early 'Esdaile' collection (at least 57 poems, of which about 23 have direct personal significance), and *Julian and Maddalo*, intended to contain, Shelley said, 'all my saddest verses raked up into one heap'.[9] But these were not published, and after a few unanswered inquiries Shelley seems to have lost interest. *Epipsychidion*, in an anonymous edition of 100 copies, was suppressed by its author within twelve months.[10] Shelley also cancelled a passage intended for the *Adonais* preface 'relating to my private wrongs'.[11] Medwin's story that the poet's self-portrait in *Adonais* was also 'afterwards expunged from it'[12] may be a muddle, but it is a fact that Shelley had enjoined his publisher to make an '*omission*' in the second edition,[13] while the draft proves that the 'frail Form' who comes to mourn Adonais in stanza 31 was almost certainly not, in conception, Shelley himself but some idealized figure born not later than Buonaparte and contrasted with him—perhaps Rousseau.[14]

From *Alastor* onwards, then, Shelley actually published in book form (excluding dedications) four personal or semi-personal poems: 'Stanzas.—April 1814', 'The Euganean Hills', 'Intellectual Beauty', and the 'West Wind'. His ten poems in periodicals were all offered anonymously; of these only 'On a Faded Violet' and possibly 'The Question' might be called 'personal' ('Sunset' and 'Grief' appeared with all the personal parts omitted). *Epipsychidion* was repudiated and suppressed. Four of *Adonais's* 55 stanzas are personal, but allegorized. Some of *Rosalind and Helen* was suggested by a family friendship. This is all. It now seems necessary to ask: how is it that so reticent a poet has gained a reputation for emotional exhibitionism? Shelley's evolution into a lyricist was accidental. Like most

---

[8] *Letters*, II. 434.
[9] *Letters*, II. 246.
[10] *Blackwoods Edinburgh Magazine* II, February 1822, p. 238; Ollier to Mary Shelley, 17 November 1823, *Shelley and Mary* IV. 990–1.
[11] *Letters*, II. 306.
[12] *Conversations of Lord Byron* (1824), p. 314 n.
[13] *Letters*, II. 396.
[14] Some of the relevant stanzas are nos. I-III, XII-XIV, printed on pp. 37–8, 42–3 of *Verse and Prose from the MSS*, ed. Shelley-Rolls and Ingpen, 1934.

poets, he bestowed, over the years, a few[15] complimentary or occasional verses on his intimates, less in the manner of a celebrity dispensing autographs than of an uncle covertly fishing out tips. They were private gifts, and Shelley often kept no copy. 'For Jane & Williams alone to see', he directed on the manuscript of 'The Magnetic Lady', and 'Do not say it is mine to any one', on that of 'Remembrance'; 'The enclosed must on no account be published' ('Letter to Maria Gisborne'); '—if you will tell no one *whose* they are' ('Lines on a Dead Violet'). Later, his widow tried to retrieve everything possible from his worksheets and acquaintances, and was able to publish about 110 short poems and fragments by 1840, when her second edition of the *Poetical Works* appeared. Many of Shelley's best-known lyrics now first emerged: the 'Stanzas in Dejection', 'O world! O life! O time!', 'I fear thy kisses', 'When the lamp is shattered', 'Music when soft voices die', 'With a Guitar, to Jane'. Mary Shelley was right to print all she could find, but it meant salvaging the equivalents of doodles on the telephone-pad, such as 'O Mary dear, that you were here', as well as drafts whose illegibility made them half-incomprehensible, such as 'Rough wind, that moanest loud'. This has not worried the critics much, who have rarely questioned a poem's origins or purpose, being content merely to find it exquisite or shoddy; some, indeed, outdoing Coleridge, profess to be given most pleasure by Shelley when he is not perfectly understandable. Swinburne hailed one half-completed line as 'a thing to thrill the veins and draw tears to the eyes of all men whose ears were not closed against all harmony',[16] and Donald Davie has found another nonsensical fragment manly and wholesome.[17] So Mary Shelley's conscience is partly responsible for the dogma that besides being trivial and self-obsessed, Shelley was negligent of grammar, syntax, and logical structure, with an incapacity to punctuate verging on feeblemindedness.[18]

---

[15] Cold statistics are again helpful. From 1816, Shelley is known to have given one poem to Claire Clairmont, and (probably) to Emilia Viviani; two to the Hunts; three to the Gisbornes; four to his wife; six to Sophia Stacey; and ten to the Williamses—twenty-seven altogether, in six years. Two of these were not lyrics, and five others were commissioned contributions to plays.

[16] *Essays and Studies*, 1876, pp. 229–30.

[17] 'Shelley's Urbanity' (1953), rptd. in *English Romantic Poets*, ed. M. H. Abrams, New York (1960), p. 318.

[18] One experienced modern editor still maintains (*Keats-Shelley Memorial Bulletin* 17, (1966), pp. 20–30) that in a fully representative passage (essentially Prometheus Unbound III. iii. 49–62) Shelley's punctuation corrupts the sense. The reader is given no chance to judge the MS. punctuation for himself (Bod. MS. Shelley e.3, f.2Iv),

Yet although Shelley's negligence is axiomatic, it would not be easy to illustrate by anyone prepared to look into the transmission of his examples. As for self-obsession, Shelley withheld his lyrics from publication for the same reason that Samuel Johnson wrote his private poems in Latin: to keep them private. To treat these intimate verses ('you may read them to Jane, but to no one else,—and yet on second thoughts I had rather you would not') as if they were manifestoes is rather like breaking into a man's bathroom in order to censure his habit of indecent exposure. Still, the reminder that certain poems were printed without Shelley's consent is no defence of their quality. It did not help poor Midas that the secret of his ears was only whispered into a hole in the ground. What that reminder should do is inhibit any pronouncement on a given poem's qualities until the *nature* and *function* of the poem have been inquired into. A straightforward example, not a 'personal' one, is the 'Bridal Song' or 'Epithalamium' of 1821.[19]

Here the reader must first decide which of three 'versions' constitutes the poem. Close consideration will show that neither of the first two versions makes sense; however, as the poet is Shelley, it is perhaps begging the question to suggest that this throws doubt on their integrity. The 'third version' (Hutchinson tells us) derives from Shelley's holograph, and its use as a gloss makes the conjecture a pretty safe one that Versions One and Two represent the foul papers and a Bad Quarto respectively of the authentic Version Three. Nevertheless, one critic has thought it

admirable in its first version. In this first:

> O joy! O fear! what will be done
> In the absence of the sun!

—is as manly and wholesome as Suckling's 'Ballad of a Wedding'. In the last version:

> O joy! O fear! there is not one
> Of us can guess what may be done
> In the absence of the sun . . .

—is just not true. And the familiar tone of 'Come along!' which securely anchors the first version, is merely silly in the others.[20]

---

which in my view is careful, intelligible, and better than Hutchinson's. Bridges's punctilious tinkerings make good sense too, but not quite Shelley's.

[19] *The Complete Poetical Works*, ed. Hutchinson, Oxford (1945), pp. 646–7.

[20] 'Shelley's Urbanity', *loc. cit.* Professor Davie has repudiated this essay (*New Statesman*, 27 November 1964, p. 840). But the dyslogistic passages, I take it, are still part of his faith.

The First Version begins by calling down sleep on the lovers in the middle of begetting a child, and goes on to advocate, among other things, what Lionel Trilling once memorably criticized in the Sexual Behaviour of the American Male ('Haste, swift Hour, and thy flight Oft renew'). Professor Davie's stricture on the Third Version bears hardly on Catullus, whose Epithalamium (62) was Shelley's model. Here is the text of the Third Version:

Boys Sing.

Night! with all thine eyes look down!
    Darkness! weep thy holiest dew!
Never smiled the inconstant moon
    On a pair so true.
Haste, coy hour! and quench all light,
Lest eyes see their own delight!
Haste, swift hour! and thy loved flight
    Oft renew!

Girls Sing.

Fairies, sprites, and angels, keep her!
    Holy stars! permit no wrong!
And return, to wake the sleeper,
    Dawn, ere it be long!
O joy! O fear! there is not one
Of us can guess what may be done
In the absence of the sun:—
    Come along!

Boys.

Oh! linger long, thou envious eastern lamp
    In the damp
        Caves of the deep!

Girls.

Nay, return, Vesper! urge thy lazy car!
    Swift unbar
        The gates of Sleep!

Chorus.

The golden gates of Sleep unbar,
    When Strength and Beauty, met together,
Kindle their image, like a star
    In a sea of glassy weather.
May the purple mist of love
Round them rise, and with them move,
Nourishing each tender gem

> Which, like flowers, will burst from them.
> As the fruit is to the tree
> May their children ever be![21]

In a conventional Epithalamium, the desire and misgiving which both partners feel are polarized on to a reluctant bride, with her mock-modest virgin attendants, and an avid groom, incited by his troop of wanton boys. Catullus's girls ask, 'Hespere, qui caelo fertur crudelior ignis?', to which the boys retort, 'Hespere, qui caelo lucet jucundior ignis?' and later (still addressing Hesperus) comment:

> at libet innuptis ficto te carpere questu.
> quid tum si carpunt tacita quem mente requirunt? (36–7)

which Peter Whigham has rendered:

> for maidens' acts belie their mock complaints,
> affecting aversion
> for what they most desire[22]

Mock-trepidation, 'tender-whimpring-maids',[23] were essential to the ceremony. But the girls' feigned ignorance of what the lovers will do in bed is stressed here for an important reason. This was commissioned work, written for the climactic scene of a play, a wedding-banquet in a 'magnificent apartment' where wealth literally rivals nobility. To compare it with Suckling's mock-turnip 'Ballad of a Wedding' is like comparing a State funeral with Finnegan's wake. The plot is that of Novel IX from the tenth day of the *Decameron*, and concerns a Pavian wife's promise to wait a year, a month, and a day after her husband's departure to the Crusade before remarrying. The time having expired, she unwillingly consents to marry a former suitor; but after the ceremony her consort reappears, the new bridegroom renounces his claim, and the play ends in amity. The girls' declaration, therefore, that not one of them can guess what may be done in the absence of the sun just *is* true: contrary to every expectation, *nothing* will be done—not, at any rate, by those newly licensed to do it. How the 'tone' of a poem can be so confidently criticized without the slightest interest in that poem's provenance or purpose is a mystery darker than Hymen's.

The first line presents in one immediate image the antiphonal unity which structures the poem: the sociable stars are invited to watch

---

[21] Text from Hutchinson, p. 723, with the singular *gate* corrected in line 23.
[22] *The Poems of Catullus*, Penguin Classics 1966, p. 133.
[23] Herrick, 'A Nuptiall Song on Sir Clipseby Crew and his Lady', line 91.

the lovers with the *voyeur* relish of the males who are singing, but also with the bashful, downcast gaze of the bride. The lovers are to be seen and unseen at once, hidden in darkness under the eyes of stars, moon, and one another; for this is a supremely social and an intensely private occasion. The weeping of 'holiest dew' suggests both the modest sanctity of the encounter and its fruitful sensuality;[24] and although the darkness weeps, the moon smiles. These opposites re-echo in the two invocations to the hour of union, a *coy* hour from one viewpoint, moonless 'lest eyes see their own delight' (i.e. lest each is abashed to see his own pleasure mirrored on the other's eyes: a variant of Blake), a *swift* hour from the other viewpoint, transient yet renewable like the moon—and an hour which, after all, both sides want to hasten on. The girls' opening appeal, made jointly to fairies and angels, indicates (like Shelley's word *phryghte* written playfully above the text) just how serious it all really is.

As in Catullus, the verbal dance now brings boys and girls into direct opposition. The planet Venus, whose setting as Hesperus and rising as Phosphorus symbolizes the bedding and rising of a married couple, is besought by the boys to stay hidden so as to lengthen the night, by the girls to return quickly and allow the bride to sleep. Unbarring the gates of sleep—admitting the lovers to their ultimate peace—deftly completes the ceremony whose public end was the shutting of the bedroom door. Finally, both sides drop their feigned postures to join in the traditional invocation for fruitfulness in the marriage: the lovers are to sleep only after duplicating their qualities in a child, as the 'wished starre' of love itself is mirrored in a calm sea. The sea image enters in because it is from across the Mediterranean that 'glassy weather' is even now returning in the person of Adalette's true husband; while the meeting of 'Strength and Beauty' reminds us ironically of the unauthorized union of Mars and Venus, caught in the act by Venus's true husband and exposed to the laughter of the assembled gods. *Golden* gates of sleep and *purple* mist of love sound like poeticisms, but even the make-up matches: these were the colours of the god Hymen, *croceo velatus amictu*, and 'purple' was used atmospherically, in both classical and English epithalamia, of

---

[24] Compare Herrick:

> These precious-pearly-purling tears
> But spring from ceremonious fears . . .
> O! give them [the lovers] active heat
> And moisture, both compleat:
> ('An Epithalamie to Sir Thomas Southwell and his Ladie').

the bliss environing a bridal.[25] The poem is concise, shapely, precisely pointed; mindful of its lineage yet perfectly attuned to its own dramatic purpose. No one would call it an important poem, least of all its author, yet it is almost faultless of its kind, a first-rate piece of craftsmanship.

The kind is not easy to define. It might be called a dramatic imitation into the spirit of which the poet enters with such deceptive wholeness that the pretence—the gap between the playfulness of the role and the absorbed gravity of the manner—constitutes an uncommon sort of poetic wit. A splendid example of this wit is the maligned 'Indian Serenade'. Shelley did not publish this poem either, but the titles of all the existing versions stress that it is *Indian* and for *singing*. It was in fact composed to be sung by Sophia Stacey,[26] and it is a dramatic imitation of an Oriental love-song, not just in atmosphere, the potency of which has always been recognized, but in its entirety. A proper imitation of the mode represented by the following lines required emotional abandonment:

> My cries pierce the heavens!
> My eyes are without sleep!
> Turn to me, Sultana—let me gaze on thy beauty.
>
> Adieu! I go down to the grave.
> If you call me I return.
> My heart is hot as sulphur;—sigh, and it will flame.
>
> Crown of my life! fair light of my eyes!
>   My Sultana! my princess!
> I rub my face against the earth;—I am drown'd in scalding tears—
>   I rave!
> Have you no compassion? Will you not turn to look upon me?[27]

It is a very physical as well as a very evocative poem (five parts of the body are named); its subject is a passionate assignation in which a dream is about to be made flesh and the languishing bodily senses are to be revived by physical love as rain revives the grass. By a hyperbole familiar also in Elizabethan poetry, wind, magnolia-blossom, and birdsong, faint, fail, and die respectively in contiguity with the beloved; then the singer herself capitulates with them ('As

[25] e.g. at the official wedding of Cupid and Psyche in Apuleius, *Met.* VI. xxiv, 'Horae rosis et ceteris floribus purpurabant omnia'.

[26] C. S. Catty, 'Shelley's "I arise from dreams of thee" and Miss Sophia Stacey', *Athenaeum*, 18 April 1908, p. 478.

[27] Turkish lines translated literally in Lady Mary Wortley Montagu's letter of 1 April 1717.

I must die on thine'). Her own person embodies the senses by which she perceives these lesser delights: touch (the wind on the stream), smell (the champaca), hearing (the nightingale); but her senses are ungratified, she is a songless nightingale, a perfume without scent, a wind without motion ('*I* die! *I* faint! *I* fail!'). Her recent love-dream is melting like the champaca's odour, with nothing substantial to take its place. Only the beloved's response will save her, as the effect of *rain* on *grass* lifts the cloying languor of the night; and three lines from the end the loud, anticipatory heartbeats of the lover echo and replace the low breathing of the sleeping winds three lines from the beginning.

The lover in the Turkish poem quoted was a male; Shelley's song could fit either sex, but the draft of line 11, 'the odours of my chaplet fail', shows that his singer is a girl.[28] The title on a manuscript auctioned in 1960, 'The Indian girl's song', confirms what should have been obvious.

This, too, is perfect of its kind. Its imaginative structure is taut and sound, its atmospheric versatility astonishing. Its loving exaggeration, its total absorption in a dramatic pretence, give it some of the qualities of brilliant parody, yet it is no parody. *Craftsmanship* is again the only single word to fit it. As an expression of its author's personality and feelings it is of about the same order as 'Gerontion', or 'Gretchen am Spinnrade'.

A companion piece is 'From the Arabic: An Imitation' (again unpublished) which according to Medwin was 'almost a translation from a translation'[29], in Terrick Hamilton's Arab romance *Antar* (1819–20). But *Antar* is male-orientated, with a hero as stupendously virile as Kilhwch in the *Mabinogion*, whereas Shelley's poem takes the Arab woman's point of view, and amounts to a critique of that novel's values. Such a capacity for adopting the female viewpoint, uncommon in male lyric poets, suggests that others among Shelley's lyrics might repay re-examination. The final stanza of 'Remembrance' ('Swifter far than summer's flight') begins

> Lilies for a bridal bed—
> Roses for a matron's head—

[28] Bod. MS. Shelley adds. e.7, f.153.
> 'The strong aromatic scent of the gold-coloured *Champac* is thought offensive to the bees . . . but their elegant appearance on the black hair of the *Indian* women is mentioned by RUMPHIUS; and both facts have supplied the *Sanscrit* poets with elegant allusions.' (Sir William Jones, *Works*, 1807, V. 129).

[29] *Life of Shelley*, ed. H. B. Forman, Oxford (1913), p. 351.

> Violets for a maiden dead—
> Pansies let *my* flowers be: (Hutchinson p. 718)

Mary Shelley's remorseful letter after Shelley's death has helped to put readers on the wrong track. 'In a little poem of his are these words—*pansies let my flowers* be . . . so I would make myself a locket to wear in eternal memory with the representation of his flower . . .'[30] But in the poem the three flowers, seasons, and birds correspond to three conditions of female life, bride, wife, and spinster; the series, therefore, *cannot* culminate in a male poet. *Pansies*, plainly, are the symbol-flowers of a deserted mistress. One possible way round is to assert that in that case the deserted mistress must be Shelley, in the manner of the character in *Alice* who argued that little girls must be a kind of serpent; alternatively, that although his *personae* are distinct from their creator, their attitudes and verbal habits are not. Both arguments are unpromising. For instance, the lyric post-humously entitled 'Mutability' ('The flower that smiles today Tomorrow dies') has seemed a typical expression of Shelley's disillusioned idealism:

> Whilst skies are blue and bright,
>   Whilst flowers are gay,
> Whilst eyes that change ere night
>   Make glad the day;
> Whilst yet the calm hours creep,
> Dream thou—and from thy sleep
> Then wake to weep. (Hutchinson pp. 640–1)

'Earthly pleasures are delusive—like me, Shelley, you will have a bitter awakening.' But the poem was evidently written for the opening of *Hellas*,[31] to be sung by a favourite slave, who loves him, to the literally sleeping Mahmud before he awakens to find his imperial pleasures slipping from his grasp. This puts the naivety of the sentiment in an unexpected light. Far from voicing a self-pitying bitterness, the poem is really an ironical endorsement, with qualifications, of Mahmud's reversal of fortune. The qualifications arise from the personal loyalty of the slave to her tyrant master, which complicates the irony of the lament and tempers our gladness at his

---

[30] *The Letters of Mary W. Shelley*, ed. F. L. Jones, Norman (1944), I. 176–7.

[31] Bod.MS. Shelley adds.e.7, cover ff.1–2, 154. Compare the song actually adopted in the play:

> '. . . could my prayers avail,
> All my joy should be
> Dead, and I would live to weep,
> So thou mightst win one hour of quiet sleep.' (22–6).

downfall. Something similar was attempted in *Laon and Cythna*, where the only being who showed any love for the deposed Othman was his child by the slave he had violated (V.xxi-xxx).

The dramatic impulse was at least as strong in Shelley as the lyrical, and the two were often inseparable. An especially interesting puzzle is set by yet another posthumous lyric, 'When the lamp is shattered'. Besides a draft, there are two known manuscripts, including one given to Jane Williams (now in the University Library, Glasgow). This is the only one of the nine poems given to her which is without title or dedication at any known stage of its existence, and her copy has one other curious feature. Between the first pair of stanzas and what would have been (if the final stanza were not missing)[32] the second pair, the words *second part* appear, in Shelley's hand. What can this mean?

The draft throws some light. 'When the lamp is shattered' was undoubtedly written for the 'Unfinished Drama' of early 1822, and is closely related to the lyric printed at the opening of that play, in modern editions. In these editions[33] the drama opens 'before the Cavern of the Indian Enchantress', who sings:

> He came like a dream in the dawn of life,
>   He fled like a shadow before its noon;
> He is gone, and my peace is turned to strife,
>   And I wander and wane like the weary moon.
>   O sweet Echo, wake,
>   And for my sake
> Make answer the while my heart shall break!
>
> But my heart has a music which Echo's lips,
>   Though tender and true, yet can answer not,
> And the shadow that moves in the soul's eclipse
>   Can return not the kiss by his now forgot;
>   Sweet lips! he who hath
>   On my desolate path
> Cast the darkness of absence, worse than death!
>   (Hutchinson, pp. 482–3)

All that is known about the 'Unfinished Drama' comes from Mrs. Shelley's headnotes. Undertaken, she says, 'for the amusement of the individuals who composed our intimate society', its plot concerned

---

[32] The final stanza must have existed once, as this text was the source of Medwin's memorial piracy in his *Ahasuerus, the Wanderer* (1823).

[33] Beginning with *The Poetical Works* (1839), IV. 168. The *Posthumous Poems* text has no stage-direction or notes (neither has the draft from which all texts of the play are derived).

an Enchantress on an Indian island who lures a Pirate, 'a man of savage but noble nature', away from his mortal lover. 'A good Spirit, who watches over the Pirate's fate, leads, in a mysterious manner, the lady of his love to the Enchanted Isle. She is accompanied by a Youth, who loves the lady, but whose passion she returns only with a sisterly affection.' The text, some of which is unpublished, does imply a kind of lovers' chain, similar to that in Moschus's Idyl VI, or in *Andromaque*. Diagrammatically it seems to go: Indian girl A, deserted by Pirate lover (or husband) B, leaves admirer E and on a magic island meets (not accompanies) boy C, who himself has been deserted by girl D (the Enchantress?). Presumably B and D began this merry-go-round for the sake of each other, and presumably all would have returned in the end to the original truce-lines.[34] Despite the bittersweet atmosphere of *Faust* and *The Tempest* that haunts the context of 'When the lamp is shattered', and may originate in the poet's own situation, it is ludicrous to treat a song written for private theatricals as if it were the cry of Shelley to his own soul. Not the major love-poets but the minor dramatists, Lyly, Fletcher, and the masque-writers, are in its line of descent.

The notation *second part* could have been intended in a semi-musical sense, of a dialogue in which a second voice takes up and answers the first. The imagery changes abruptly in the 'second part', though both pairs of stanzas share a basic idea: in part one, lamp, cloud, lute, and lips with their 'contents', the hollow heart, the empty cell, the lifeless corpse; in part two, the nest with its winged occupant, the heart as cradle, home, and bier, the raftered eyrie, the naked refuge. Because of the idea common to all these, Professor Pottle's attractive defence of *The light in the dust lies dead*, as meaning that the light reflected from the physical environment (the 'light-in-the-dust') stops shining when the source goes out,[35] seems narrowly to miss the mark. Rather, the light is inseparable from the 'dust' of which the physical lamp is composed, and perishes with it; the glory of the rainbow *is* the cloud, and is 'shed' with the cloud's waterdrops; music and the lute are annihilated together.[36] The heart cannot sing

---

[34] The rehearsals of *Lover's Vows* should warn us that the proposed casting is unlikely to have reflected real alignments, wished or existing. Working backwards from the most tactful final combination we might get: A=Jane Williams, B=Trelawny, C=Edward Williams, D=Mary Shelley, E=Shelley. Shelley, unattached, could thus take the part of the Spirit, fitting in with the role he gave himself in 'With a Guitar. To Jane'.

[35] 'The Case of Shelley' (1952), rptd. in *English Romantic Poets, op. cit.* pp. 302–3.

[36] 'The common observer . . . contends in vain against the persuasion of the grave, that the dead indeed cease to be . . . The organs of sense are destroyed, and the intel-

207

—respond emotionally—when the signal to which it resonates, the spirit of love, is 'mute'; it can only echo, passively, and hollowly the noises of wind and water. All these light-and-dust images are analogues of the 'good Spirit's' lodgement at the earth's centre. He is contained in the reality he energizes, as radiance in the lamp, as music in the lute, as words between the lips:

> Within the silent centre of the earth
> My mansion is; where I have lived insphered
> From the beginning, and around my sleep
> Have woven all the wondrous imagery
> Of this dim spot, which mortals call the world; (15–19)

A cancelled stage-direction hesitates whether to call this Spirit 'Love', but he was evidently to be the Prospero of the island, moving its affairs to their kindliest end.

The whole poem is about the loss of love, and if part one laments that when the physical embodiment is lacking, the essence disappears, part two seems to retort that if the essence is lacking, the physical embodiment disintegrates. It is tempting to guess that the two halves of the poem were intended for the Enchantress and the Lady respectively. This would account for the domestic imagery of the second part, while the ruined cell and the knell for the dead seaman are proper 'currency values' for an Indian Lampedusa on whose shores a pirate-lover has probably been wrecked.

The first word of part two is not *When* but *Where*, so these two lines are a simple inversion: Love leaves the nest where hearts once mingled. It has been asked, In what form are we to imagine Love doing this? To answer, In the form of Love, seems irreverent, but the episode of Cupid and Psyche in Apuleius's *Metamorphoses*, which Shelley much admired, had clearly some influence on this poem.[37] By *first* leaving the nest, the winged form of Love suggests also a fledgling (genuine love is a result as well as a cause of 'mingling').

---

lectual operations dependent on them have perished with their sources . . . When you can discover where the fresh colours of the fading flower abide, or the music of the broken lyre, seek life among the dead.' ('Essay on a Future State', *Essays, Letters from Abroad*, etc. ed. Mrs. Shelley, 1840, I. 234–5).

[37] Cupid and Psyche are happily married, mingling nightly in a love-nest built by Cupid himself, with ivory rafters; Psyche entertains her treacherous sisters with lute and song; a spilt lamp is the cause of Cupid's flight (in Mrs. Tighe's well-known version the lamp shattered: '. . . from her trembling hand extinguished falls the fatal lamp'); he leaves Psyche's bed as a feathered god every morning, and at last deserts it for good; Psyche is then exposed, half-naked, to Venus's mocking laughter and is tormented by the passions of Anxiety and Sorrow; but in the end the lovers are reunited—as no doubt they were in Shelley's play.

This stresses the contrasting images of raven and eagle, because the raven was supposed to evict its young from the nest and abandon them, whereas the eagle is famous for the care it takes of its own young. Golden eagles, as Shelley would know, mate for life, and their nest is permanent, literally cradle, home, and bier.

'The weak one is singled' of course has nothing to do with the sad lot of woman; 'the weak one' is the weak heart, and applies to either sex. The paradoxes (*one* is *singled*, the *weak* one must *endure*), and the pun (*singled*, 'picked on', 'divorced'), lead to the ambiguities of 'To endure what it once possessed', which could have secondary meanings of 'to make indifferent that which is once fascinated', and 'to imprison what it once owned by right', and to the major paradox that 'Love' is now confronted with: why does one who laments 'frailty', transience, choose to nest in 'the frailest of all things', the human heart?

The change of pronoun in the final stanza implies that the speaker has turned to address a human, or superhuman, rival. 'Its passions' (the passions of the heart) will rock *thee*, she says, and reason will only give you clarity without comfort, like the sun in winter. And the epithet *naked* returns to the hint of the fledgling, the product of love's union, not now in voluntary flight but evicted, defenceless, and— perhaps deservedly—laughable.

The parent play is so sketchy that any detailed account of 'When the lamp is shattered' can only be very conjectural. What is essential is to begin with the right questions: what *is* this poem, what was it for? Once the dramatic function is recognized, tone, imagery, emotional mode take on appropriate significances; even if the poem is moving it is not self-expression but artifice, creative play. Shelley's lyrics deserve a fresh—and a more responsible—critical look.

18

What is Kim?

ARNOLD KETTLE

EVERYONE admires *Kim*, but among those who have written about the book there is little agreement. It wonderfully evokes British India—the sights and sounds and smells, the manifold peoples and cultures—there is no dispute about that. But to what end? With what meaning? How, above all, are we to take the reiterated question 'Who is Kim?' reaching its climax in the last pages of the book ' "I am Kim. I am Kim. And what is Kim?" His soul repeated it again and again.' '*Thatt* is the question, as Shakespeare hath said.'

Mr. J. I. M. Stewart says that:

> Kipling came nearest to a successful novel in a book for young people—for we lose contact with *Kim* (1901) when we regard this story of an orphan white boy gone native, and using his native cloak of invisibility to become a peerless Secret Service agent, as other than essentially that.[1]

Mr. Stewart's is, it must be admitted, aesthetically the safe line, for it allows us to respond to the colour and high spirits of the book—its remarkable virtuosity—without being faced with the need to take it seriously. But does it really fill the bill any more satisfactorily than the approach of Mr. Edmund Wilson, which Mr. Stewart is justifiably querying? *Kim*, argues Mr. Wilson,[2] 'deals with the gradual dawning of consciousness that he is really a Sahib' and he finds it hard to respond altogether sympathetically to the book because of Kipling's

---

[1] *Eight Modern Writers* (Vol. XII of *The Oxford History of English Literature* 1964), p. 259.

[2] 'The Kipling that Nobody Read' in *Kipling's Mind and Art*, ed A. Rutherford (1964), p. 29.

failure to measure all the implications of what being a Sahib involves. The trouble with this argument, however plausible in relation to Kipling's outlook as a whole, is that, as far as *Kim* goes, it isn't quite true. Kim *is* conscious of being a Sahib, which in terms of British Indian lingo he indeed is, and his education at Lucknow and with his Secret Service chiefs naturally enough increases such consciousness; but this is scarcely the central subject of the book, and, looking at the novel as a whole, the remarkable thing is how little of a Sahib Kim ends up as. In other words, Mr. Wilson and Mr. Stewart, though in one sense standing at opposite poles critically, both fail to come to terms with the climax and end of the book.

This is not altogether surprising for the end of *Kim* is certainly very odd and I would not wish to suggest any watertight interpretation, a hundred per cent guaranteed. But whereas it is not easy to know exactly how Kipling meant the end of the novel to be taken, it is fairly easy to say what he did not, *could* not from the very nature of the achieved book, intend. Mr. Carrington, for instance, in his valuable biography of Kipling, asserts

> Kim . . . has reached a stage of maturity and must take a decision. No longer a ragamuffin of the bazaars, but a beautiful godlike youth, he must choose between contemplation and action. Is he to follow the Lama or to return to the chains which enslave the Pathan and the Babu to their material duties? . . . Though it is not expressly stated, the reader is left with the assurance that Kim, like Mowgli and like the Brushwood Boy, will find reality in action, not in contemplation.[3]

I do not want to pre-judge the issue which I shall be discussing: but surely this is an untenable argument. If Kipling intended to assure us that Kim will find reality in action as opposed to contemplation, why on earth did he not take steps to do so? If this is the issue and this the choice, nothing would have been easier for Kipling than to have made it clear. Kim has only to murmur a few words to the Babu or to wake before Mahmud goes off and his commitment to them and their Game (in so far as that is what is meant by 'action') will be established. But the words never come. Mahmud and Hurree assume he will come back to them. *We* can only permit ourselves such an assumption if we ignore the whole weight of the final episodes of the book, whose movement in fact is in a contrary direction.

It is the oddness of the ending of the book[4] that reinforces the temp-

[3] Charles Carrington, *Rudyard Kipling* (1955), p. 362.
[4] That Kipling was well aware of the oddness is shown by his own description. 'At last I reported *Kim* finished. "Did *it* stop, or you?" the Father asked. And when I told

tation to see *Kim* as essentially not about Kim but about India. There is a plausible, and indeed fruitful, case for such an emphasis and Mr. Edward Shanks made it when he wrote:

> If, as has been argued, it should be possible to say in a sentence what any real book is *about*, then it must be said that *Kim* is *about* the infinite and joyous variety of India for him who has the eyes to see it and the heart to rejoice in it.[5]

There is a great deal to be said for this approach. It is precisely this sense of the teeming fullness and variegated colour of Indian life that we most remember when we casually recall the book. India is spread out before us, from Ceylon in the sea to the Himalayas that break through the clouds, and the constant journeying of the main characters is like the movement of tiny figures across an enormous map. Not that there is anything *general* about Kipling's picture of India. The human figures are so strongly drawn and so idiosyncratic, their language so rich and various, the colours of the landscape so sharp and the tastes on the tongue so vivid, the sense of the past so pervasive, that there is no danger of a merely geographical—let alone ethnological—survey. There is in fact a strong case for describing *Kim* as being essentially about India the subcontinent rather than about Kim the boy.

For the revelation of the richness and complexity of the Indian scene Kipling has hit upon a series of remarkably effective ploys. The most important, basic indeed to the whole project, is the idea of revealing a whole society and culture through the eyes and experiences of not one, but two central figures, both of whom are at once foreign and yet deeply involved. That Kim is not Indian is obvious and every Western reader immediately grasps its implications. But we do not perhaps recognize so consciously that Teshoo Lama is also '*pardesi*' (a foreigner) speaking a language and practising a religion which to the Indians is in some ways more unfamiliar than the British kinds. The Lama is, of course, Asian and in many respects more at home in the Indian culture than an Englishman, but his strangeness is an important part of his role in the story. T. S. Eliot has spoken perceptively of Kipling's

---

him that it was *It*, he said "Then it oughtn't to be too bad".' Kipling's conviction that it was his *daemon* rather than himself who wrote his books has its own significance and helps to explain why it is so often unsatisfactory to judge his work simply in terms of his known political opinions.

[5] *Rudyard Kipling* (1940), p. 215.

peculiar detachment and remoteness from all environment, a universal foreignness which is the reverse side of his strong feeling for India, for the Empire, for England and for Sussex, a remoteness as of an alarmingly intelligent visitor from another planet. He remains somehow alien and aloof from all with which he identifies himself.[6]

This seems to me to express admirably the effect we get in *Kim*. It is summed up best, perhaps, in the crucial last scene of all in which Kim and the Lama, the non-Indians, are left alone, deeply imbedded in Indian things and nature, yet also isolated, the life of India going on around them, without them, almost in spite of them. But the point one wants to stress about this foreignness of Kim and the Lama is that it gives Kipling, throughout the book, the perfect device for refracting the Indian scene, the perfect 'point of view' for his project; for these two 'experiencing agents' are at once inside and outside what they are experiencing and yet poles apart from one another, so that what they see and feel and respond to in the life around them is recorded in ways which set up for the reader the most revealing and valuable of tensions and insights.

This is one of the reasons why Kipling's own description of the book as 'picaresque' is, though one sees what he means, not very helpful in any attempt to define its quality. *Kim* is picaresque in the sense that its construction seems to be loose and episodic, that it consists of a string of situations rather than of one central 'dramatic' one, and that Kim himself has some of the characteristic attributes of the picaresque hero. But really the use of the word doesn't get us very far. Even the construction is subtler than one might at first suppose. Very few of the chapters end with the ending of an episode: on the contrary, Kipling's sense of continuity and juxtaposition are highly sophisticated. Again, the substitution of two for one single main figure at once undermines (as *Don Quixote* and *Joseph Andrews* long ago demonstrated) the essential simplicity of the picaresque method. And, perhaps most important of all, *Kim* is not in the end —or even, really, at the beginning—an essentially realistic (in the technical sense) account of the adventures of the main figure, or even of two main figures.

There is indeed an important element of truth in the view of Mr. Stewart, that Kim has to be seen as a *Boys Own Paper* hero. Kim is a wonderfully attractive creature, but on the level of surface realism, one can scarcely take him quite seriously. If he is, as I believe, to be

---

[6] *A Choice of Kipling's Verse* (1963), Preface, p. 23.

taken seriously on a level that is more important than surface realism, it is as well to recognize what we are doing.

Kim is a kind of idealized embodiment of what Kipling would have liked an inhabitant of British India to be: above all pettiness and below all theorizing. (If one wishes to be biographical, one can say that he represents perhaps the best of the five-year-old Rudyard Kipling's potential selves). This doesn't sound very complimentary, but it is in fact as good a basis for an artistic creation as any. Kim's progress may be on one level unbelievable (so is Perdita's) but in the important ways it is all right. For the basic imaginative conception of the Little Friend of the All the World corresponds to a real human potential at this point in history and the tendency of idealization is in fact largely offset by the creation of the complementary character of the Lama and the superb and utterly concrete reality of the world which they explore.

Good picaresque literature—the *Lazarillo de Tormes* or, to stretch a point, *Moll Flanders*—gets its effect from the straightforward juxtaposition of an alien or unorthodox or at least irreverent and down-to-earth consciousness upon a social reality which can only marginally absorb it. This sets up a peculiar tension in which a simple but basic irony is brought into play and which historically tends to work well because the irreverence of the picaresque hero in fact bemodies in a crude form some sort of human protest that will burst out later into a respectable philosophy.

Kim, for most of Kipling's novel, has the underdog quality which we associate with the genuine picaresque heroes and which comes out in his unfailing resourcefulness. Like Lazarillo or the Artful Dodger he knows his way around. What limits our response to Kipling's assurance that 'he had known all evil since he could speak' is our sense that Kim himself until the very end tends to escape too easily (partly because he is, after all, as a last resort a sahib) from the *consequences* of the evil he encounters. He has the characteristic of people in pornographic literature (I am not suggesting of course that *Kim* is pornographic) that he does not have to stay till next morning. Until, that is, he establishes a real, long-term relationship with the Lama. All his other relationships, even with Mahbub, whom he is genuinely fond of, are relationships of convenience. That is why we cannot take him as seriously as, say, Huck Finn as a picaresque hero. Yet we *do* take him seriously, on a somewhat different level.

How are we to define that level? Mr. Kinkead Weekes, in what

seems to me much the best consideration of *Kim*,[7] once or twice uses
the word emblematic. Kim sitting on Zam-Zammah ('who hold
Zam-Zammah hold the Punjab') he describes as emblematic, and it
is the right word, indicating Kim's status as going beyond the
casually picaresque. Part of Kim's function in the book, as I have
suggested, is as an agent of discovery, the discovery of India to the
(presumed British) reader: Kipling's not infrequent use of the word
'we' to cover the inhabitants of British India is another facet of this
aspect of the book. But Kim, of course, is much more than a technical
device: he begins, one might say, as the embodiment of a Kiplingesque
ideal; but he finishes as a young man with a nervous breakdown grap-
pling with a real and difficult problem and one highly relevant to his
world and time. Up to the point when, his 'training' finished, Kim
goes to find Teshoo Lama in the temple of the Tirthankers in Benares
his relation to reality is of a kind comparable to that of a Stalky or a
Mowgli, though the reality he touches is far richer and more complex.
Then, when he rejoins the Lama, he at first operates again in the same
way, though on a rather more mature level. But the curing of the Jat's
child is essentially the same kind of exploit as the steering of the Lama
on to the train at Lahore, an exercise in superior technical know-
how. Then comes the episode with the Mahratta on the train. For the
first time Kim's operations as an agent in the Game and his function
as the Lama's *chela* cut directly across one another. The Lama
immediately notices this:

'Oh, *chela*, see how thou art overtaken! Thou didst cure the Kamboh's
child solely to acquire merit. But thou didst put a spell on the Mahratta
with prideful workings—I watched thee—and with side-long glances to
bewilder an old old man and a foolish farmer: whence calamity and
suspicion!'

Kim, with considerable self-control, does not argue but tries to pacify
the old man with the ambiguous admission 'Where I have offended
thee I have done wrong'; but the Lama is too intelligent to accept an
apology which does not go to the roots of the problem:

'It is more, *chela*. Thou hast loosed an Act upon the world, and as a stone
thrown into a pool so spread the consequences thou canst not tell how far.'

From now on the conflict between the Lama's values and those
embodied in the Game cannot be suppressed.

[7] In *Kipling's Mind and Art*, ed. A. Rutherford (1964), pp. 216–34.

'Then all Doing is evil?' Kim replied, lying out under a big tree at the fork of the Doon road, watching the little ants run over his hand. 'To abstain from action is well—except to acquire merit.' 'At the Gates of Learning we were taught that to abstain from action was unbefitting a Sahib. And I am a Sahib.' 'Friend of all the World'—the Lama looked directly at Kim . . . 'To those who follow the Way there is neither black nor white, Hind nor Bhotiyal. We be all souls seeking escape . . .'

The conflict, always implicit, has never before been so uncompromisingly stated. The effect on Kim is to lead him to ask a question which may not at first seem quite relevant:

'I ate thy bread for three years—as thou knowest. [He is referring to the fact that the Lama has paid his school fees at Lucknow.] Holy One, whence came—?'
'There is much wealth, as men count it, in Bhotiyal,' the Lama returned with composure. 'In my own place I have the illusion of honour. I ask for that I need. I am not concerned with the account. That is for my monastery. Ai! The black high seats in the monastery, and the novices all in order!'

And he goes on to reminisce about Tibet. We are not told whether Kim is satisfied by the answer. But it is interesting, and significant, that he should have asked the question at this particular moment.

I think it is clear that there has developed by this point in Kim's mind a clearer comprehension than before of the issues with which he is faced. His question about the source of the Lama's income is, in that context, highly appropriate, for what is emerging is a conflict between two approaches to life: an idealist approach, embodied in the Lama, which sees merit as lying in the rejection of action and the granting of entire precedence to the Idea; and the rather crude materialist approach of Kim, and the participants in the Game, for whom realism is essentially a shrewd awareness of the tactical activity necessary to cope with specific situations. In the earlier sections of the book this conflict, inherent from the very beginning, has largely taken the form of contrast. The Lama is unworldly, Kim precociously worldly. The Lama thinks a prostitute is a nun, Kim knows all about such things. The Lama is vulnerable, Kim tough and protective. Also, balancing the account, Kim is frightened of the cobra, the Lama serenely humane; Kim knowing, the Lama wise. Such contrasts are dramatically effective, injecting their own irony into the narrative; but their deeper implications are not followed up. At the first moment of crisis in their relationship—when Kim is found by the Regiment—the division in his life is glossed over by the

Lama's recognition that 'Education is greatest blessing if of best sorts'. And during the next years Kim is able to lead two separate lives—school and holidays—which never touch, so that the Lama and the Game are kept in different compartments, with the connecting link that experience of the Road is relevant both to the Game and the Search. The period of education over, however, the conflict is bound, somehow or other, to be clarified and fought out.

Kim's question as to where the money came from for his education is, in fact, a very pertinent question. What he is seeking, not perhaps quite consciously, is a chink in the Lama's armour. Is the old man really so indifferent to Doing, to the operation of material reality, as he seems? Is he not perhaps playing some Game of his own? Isn't his indifference, perhaps, a bit of a fraud, a luxury which he can afford because he is, ultimately, materially secure? And Teshoo Lama's reply, simply invoking human need, is so unanswerable that it is not surprising that Kim drops the subject. For the reply does not reject the significance of money, of material activity (a rejection which would have played into the hands of the shrewd realist in Kim) but, rather, puts it in its place. Doing, the Lama's argument implies, is necessary: the question is, where does it lead?

The conflict, which first gains open expression during the episode with the Mahratta, dominates the remainder of the book. Kim manages, as has been remarked, to stage-manage the Lama's return to the Hills in a way which suits the interests of the Game. Once again the contradiction between what he is up to and what the Lama assumes he is doing is side-tracked or temporarily muted. The Lama is happy in the Hills, where the life and air are in harmony with his material needs and habits, and so he thinks less about his Search. But it is clear to the reader that, in dragging the old man into the very jaws of the Game, Kim is building up trouble for himself, and sure enough when the crisis comes it takes a form whose significance cannot be escaped. Superficially, in terms of the tactics of the Game, the events which follow the striking of the Lama have an outcome satisfactory enough. The old man, though badly shaken, survives. The nefarious plans of the Russians are thwarted. Kim can at the same time chalk up a success for himself as secret agent and demonstrate his loyalty and devotion to his Lama. But what has happened in fact makes further compromise impossible. A man cannot indefinitely serve two opposing masters. What the episode brings home to the Lama is not that his defences were inadequate but that material considerations, his love of the Hills, corrupted him and led him to forget the Search.

This is the significance of the return to the Plains, and Kim knows it. That is why Kim's crisis can no longer be put off: it is not simply that he has led the old man into danger, it is that he has led himself to an impasse. His rejection of the advances of the Woman of Shamlegh is relatively straightforward. His Sahib-consciousness helps him out there (though for the reader the episode does not strengthen confidence in the values of Sahibdom). But to the demands now put upon him by the total situation the jaunty self-confidence he can usually muster cannot be adequate. The documents he carries wrapped in oilskin and his sense of responsibility for the Lama now weigh on him almost intolerably and the two burdens pull his mind in opposite directions. When he finally gets rid of the documents to Hurree Babu he literally does not know whether the relief he feels comes from a sense of duty accomplished or burden removed. Kim's crisis is physical, psychological, emotional, moral, all rolled into one. Kipling's sense of the interconnection of all these elements is remarkably shrewd and deep.

The resolution of the impasse, which most readers clearly do not regard as a resolution at all, seems to me beautifully achieved, and I think Mr. Kinkead Weekes's emphasis on the rightness of Lockwood Kipling's final illustration is an excellent piece of criticism. The Pater seems to have understood his son's deeper purposes better than many of his admirers, better perhaps than the author himself.

What Kipling achieves in these last pages—no doubt with the aid of his daemon—is the cutting of a false knot, the clearing away of a false antithesis. Thought and action have been at odds throughout the book. Oversimplifying a little, the Lama has embodied thought, the Idea: Kim has embodied action, Doing. The Search and the Game have been presented—as indeed they are to their adherents— as opposite poles: so that the Search (a concern with values) becomes good but a bit irrelevant and the Game (practical politics) unscrupulous but necessary. And given such an antithesis in practice, since there is no foregoing the claims of necessity, the Game is bound to win, though a niche of respectful but ultimately ineffectual admiration will be reserved for the Lamas of this world. Then, with Kim's breakdown and the Lama's discovery of the River, a double change takes place.

What is Kim?

The change in Kim can only take place when Hurree Babu has taken away the documents, thus bringing to an end the uncompleted adventure in the Hills. It is relief that this episode has been completed, plus admiration for the complex courage of the fearful Babu, that break through Kim's weakness and lethargy and lead to a desire to find a solution of his inner crisis: 'I must get into the world again'. At first he remains frustrated:

All that while he felt, though he could not put it into words, that his soul was out of gear with its surroundings—a cog-wheel unconnected with any machinery, just like the idle cog-wheel of a cheap Beheca sugar-crusher laid by in a corner.

And his soul repeats again and again the cry 'I am Kim. I am Kim and what is Kim?' until suddenly there is a resolution, physical (through tears) and psychological 'and with an almost audible click he felt the wheels of his being lock up anew on the world without'.

This seems to me psychologically an extremely acute and convincing description of emergence from alienation, an emergence begun by a sudden *desire* to emerge, sparked off by an almost casual contact with relevant reality, and continuing through a process in which the physical and mental needs to re-establish contact are inseparably interwoven. Then, the moment of crisis over,

Things that rode meaningless on the eyeball an instant before slid into proper proportion. Roads were meant to be walked upon, houses to be lived in, cattle to be driven, fields to be tilled, and men and women to be talked to. They were all real and true—solidly planted upon the feet—perfectly comprehensible—clay of his cleuay, their more nor less.

And Kim, now lying flat upon the Earth, 'the hopeful dust that holds the seeds of all life' surrenders to her strength, relaxes and sleeps, awaking only after Mahbub, like Hurree, has gone back to the Game and only the Lama is there to help him back to life.

The book then ends with the Lama's account of his discovery of the River. Kim says nothing more except for a few typically down-to-earth comments on the Lama's narrative. The Game is not mentioned. His being a Sahib is not mentioned. The answer to the question 'What is Kim?' is given in terms that make no reference to either. Kim is a man in the world of men, neither more nor less. It is a real world, not an illusion (as the Lama's philosophy would have it), a world of Doing in which action is neither an irrelevance nor an end in itself but a necessary element in the relationship between men and nature, man and man. This is what Kim has come through to. He could not have reached this sense of unity without the help of the Lama, but it is not the Lama's philosophy that he now embraces; he could not have come through without the help of the adherents of the Game, but it is not the rules of the Game that he now submits to. And perhaps the key to the change that has come over Kim lies in the change in the way he formulates his ultimate question. Throughout his life, when critical moments have forced him to pose fundamental problems he has asked 'Who is Kim?' And the question has been accompanied always by a sense of being alone. Now the form of the question is changed from the individualist 'Who?' with its presumption of an answer in terms of some absolute or mystical 'identity', to the more fruitful 'What?' with its possibility of an answer which can begin to resolve the contradictions between the one and the others, between the reality and the idea, between the world of the Game and the world of Teshoo Lama. Kim has escaped from the false antithesis, the choice between action on the one hand and truth on the other, between an amoral materialism and an unworldly idealism. The new materialism to which he advances, and of which the emblem is his sense of identity with the earth and its processes, no longer excludes the human values encompassed in his relationships with the Lama.

No less important—and indeed complementary to the change in Kim—is the change which, in the very last pages of the book, takes place in the Lama. The old man achieves his object and discovers the River to which his Search has led him. But the act of discovery involves a reorientation as significant as Kim's. At the very instant of apparent fulfilment of his quest, when his Soul has escaped from the Wheel of Things and touched the Great Soul, he remembers Kim and, upon this, Soul withdraws itself from the Great Soul.

As the egg from the fish, as the fish from the water, as the water from the cloud, as the cloud from the thick air; so put forth, so leaped out, so drew away, so fumed up the soul of Teshoo Lama from the Great Soul.

'It is only then' as Mr. Kinkead Weekes admirably puts it 'that he sees the River which can cleanse him from a sin still with him; and when one has reached this point any old river will do.' Mr. Kinkead Weekes adds 'The "sin" can only be the element of selfishness in the search for the perfection of self by turning away from others'. That is one way of putting it: another way would be to say that the Lama at this point rids himself of idealism, the illusion that the world itself is an illusion and that any idea—call it the Great Soul or what you will—can have priority over material reality. He sees, in other words, that human relationships and spiritual values have their basis in material reality (this is the significance of the imagery of process through which the Lama expresses himself) and in this way, like Kim, cuts through the false antithesis between truth and action. It is thus that the resolution of the book takes place—not in terms of some new doctrine of salvation, religious or political, but in terms of the acceptance of reality by both Kim and the Lama, an acceptance which will inevitably affect their future actions. What those actions are to be would have involved, of course, another story and one which Kipling never wrote.

A SELECT LIST OF THE
PUBLISHED WRITINGS OF
GEORGE WILSON KNIGHT

Emeritus Professor of
English Literature in
the University of Leeds

Compiled by
John E. Van Domelen

This list was compiled with the support of a grant from the
American Philosophical Society

LIST OF ABBREVIATIONS

W.F. = *The Wheel of Fire*
S.T. = *The Shakespearian Tempest*
C.R. = *The Christian Renaissance*
S.P. = *Shakespearian Production*
S.D. = *The Starlit Dome*
C.L. = *The Crown of Life*
L.P. = *Laureate of Peace*
S.F. = *The Sovereign Flower*
B.S. = *Byron and Shakespeare*
S.R. = *Shakespeare and Religion*
P.A. = *Poets of Action*

1926
1. 'Poetry and Immortality', *The Adelphi*, IV (September), 169–72.

1927
2. 'Brutus and Cassius', *The Adelphi*, IV (March), 555–8. Reprinted in *S.R.*
3. 'Middleton Murry *versus* Goethe', *The Adelphi*, IV (June) 764–6.

4. 'Henry VI and Macbeth', *The New Adelphi*, I (September), 69–73. Reprinted in *S.F.*

1928

5. 'The Principles of Shakespeare Interpretation', *The Shakespeare Review*, I (September), 374–80. Reprinted in *S.F.*
6. 'The Poet and Immortality', *The Shakespeare Review*, I (October), 407–15. Reprinted in *S.R.*

1929

7. MYTH AND MIRACLE. AN ESSAY ON THE MYSTIC SYMBOLISM OF SHAKESPEARE. London: Edward J. Burrow and Co. Reprinted in *C.L.*
8. '*Measure for Measure* and the Gospels', *London Quarterly Review*, CLI (April), 172–85. Reprinted in *W.F.*
9. 'The Style of Othello', *The Fortnightly Review*, CXXV n.s. (1 April), 508–21. Reprinted in *W.F.*
10. 'The Metaphysic of *Troilus and Cressida*', *Dublin Review*, CLXXXV (October), 228–42. Reprinted in *W.F.*
11. 'The Pilgrimage of Hate: an Essay on *Timon of Athens*', *The Churchman*, XLIII n.s. (October), 298–309. Reprinted in *W.F.*
12. 'The Theme of Romantic Friendship in Shakespeare', *The Holborn Review*, XX n.s. (October), 450–60. Reprinted in *S.R.*

1930

13. '*Macbeth* and the Nature of Evil', *The Hibbert Journal*, XXVIII (January), 328–42. Reprinted in *W.F.*
14. 'Shakespeare and Tolstoy', *The Occult Review*, LI (February), 103–7, and LI (March), 177–80. Reprinted in *W.F.*
15. 'Brutus: An Essay in Poetic Interpretation', *The Church Quarterly Review*, CX (April), 40–71. Reprinted in *W.F.*
16. 'The Problem of Hamlet', *The Quest*, XXI (April), 283–93, and XXI (July), 415–24. Reprinted in *W.F.*
17. THE WHEEL OF FIRE. ESSAYS IN INTERPRETATION OF SHAKESPEARE'S SOMBRE TRAGEDIES. London: Oxford University Press. Introduction by T. S. Eliot. Enlarged edition: Methuen and Co. 1949.
18. 'The Love Theme in Amusement, Art and Religion', *The Hibbert Journal*, XXIX (October), 152–8.

1931

19. 'On the Mystic Symbolism of Shakespeare', *The Aryan Path*, II (April), 249–51. Reprinted in Vol. XXXV (October 1964), 456–58. Reprinted in *S.R.*

20. 'The Shakespearian Tempest', *The Symposium*, New York, II (October), 484–506. Expanded in *S.T.*

21. 'Much Ado about Nothing', *Trinity University Review*, Toronto, XLIV (November), 45–7.

22. 'Naturalism and Orthodoxy', *The Canadian Journal of Religious Thought*, VIII (November-December), 364–9.

23. THE IMPERIAL THEME. FURTHER INTERPRETATIONS OF SHAKESPEARE'S TRAGEDIES, INCLUDING THE ROMAN PLAYS. London: Oxford University Press. Reprinted by Methuen and Co. 1951.

1932

24. 'Wordsworth's Vision of Immortality', *University of Toronto Quarterly*, I (No. 2. 1931–2), 216–35. Reprinted in *S.D.*

25. THE SHAKESPEARIAN TEMPEST. London: Oxford University Press. Reprinted by Methuen and Co., 1953, with a 'Chart of Shakespeare's Dramatic Universe.'

1933

26. 'English Literature in the Year 1710', *At the Sign of the Sun*, Sun Alliance Insurance Group, Issue 4 (April), 31–3.

27. THE CHRISTIAN RENAISSANCE WITH INTERPRETATIONS OF DANTE, SHAKESPEARE AND GOETHE AND A NOTE ON T. S. ELIOT. Toronto: The Macmillan Co. of Canada. Revised edition London: Methuen and Co., 1962, with new sub-title: 'With Interpretations of Dante, Shakespeare and Goethe and New Discussions of Oscar Wilde and the Gospel of Thomas'. Appendix on O'Casey's *The Drums of Father Ned*. The note on T. S. Eliot was excluded.

1934

28. 'The Vision of Eros in Jesus and Shakespeare', *The Aryan Path*, V (January), 26–9. Reprinted in *S.R.*

29. 'In Imitation of Swift', *Trinity University Review*, Toronto, XLVI (April), 213–15. This appeared under the same title in *The New English Weekly* (19 July), 324–5.

30. 'Shakespeare and Tolstoy', The English Association Pamphlet 88. London: Oxford University Press. Reprinted in *W.F.* 1949.

1935

31. ' "Kubla Khan": An Interpretation', *Programme*, Oxford, No. 9 (October), 4–9. Reprinted in *S.D.*
32. 'King Lear', *Trinity University Review*, Toronto, XLVIII (December), 67–9.

1936

33. 'A Note on *Henry VIII*', *The Criterion*, XV (January), 228–36. Reprinted in *S.R.*
34. 'The Vision of Jupiter in *Cymbeline*', *Times Literary Supplement* (21 November), 958. Signed article. Expanded in *C.L.*
35. PRINCIPLES OF SHAKESPEARIAN PRODUCTION, WITH SPECIAL REFERENCE TO THE TRAGEDIES. London: Faber and Faber; also Penguin Books 1949. The 1964 (Faber) edition is considerably expanded and contains photographs illustrating the author's acting and productions. This edition is entitled *Shakespearian Production* and contains a new preface. Reissued by Routledge and Kegan Paul, 1968.
36. ATLANTIC CROSSING. AN AUTOBIOGRAPHICAL DESIGN. London: J. M. Dent and Sons.

1939

37. 'Lyly', *Review of English Studies*, XV (April), 146–63.
38. THE BURNING ORACLE. STUDIES IN THE POETRY OF ACTION. London: Oxford University Press. The book's contents variously reissued in *L.P.*, *S.F.* and *P.A.*

1940

39. 'Isaiah in Renaissance Dress', *Trinity University Review*, Toronto, LII (February), 15–16.
40. 'Shakespeare on the Gold Standard', *Saturday Night*, Toronto, (17 February), 6.
41. THIS SCEPTRED ISLE. SHAKESPEARE'S MESSAGE FOR ENGLAND AT WAR. Oxford: Basil Blackwell.

1941

42. 'A New Romanticism', *The Poetry Review*, XXXII (May-June), 163–9. Reprinted in *Hiroshima*, 1946.
43. 'Britain as Dramatic Artist', *Times Literary Supplement*, 5 April, 164, 166. Signed article. Reprinted in *S.F.*

44. 'On Eighteenth Century Nationalism', *English* III (Autumn), 243–6. Reprinted in *Hiroshima*, 1946.
45. THE STARLIT DOME. STUDIES IN THE POETRY OF VISION. London: Oxford University Press. Reprinted by Methuen and Co., 1959, with an Introduction by W. F. Jackson Knight and an Appendix on 'Spiritualism and Poetry'.
46. 'Four Pillars of Wisdom', *The Wind and the Rain*, I (Winter 1941–2), 133–44. Reprinted in *S.R.*

1942

47. An Appreciation of Francis Berry's poem, 'Spain 1939: From Devon', *The Wind and the Rain*, I (Spring), 228–9.
48. CHARIOT OF WRATH. THE MESSAGE OF JOHN MILTON TO DEMOCRACY AT WAR. London: Faber and Faber. Reprinted, condensed, in *P.A.*
49. 'A Great National Poet: England at War. Tennyson's Mystic Imperialism', *Times Literary Supplement*, 10 October, 498, 501. Unsigned article.

1944

50. THE OLIVE AND THE SWORD. London: Oxford University Press. A brief version was published as *This Sceptred Isle* in 1940. In 1958 *The Olive and the Sword* was re-published as 'This Sceptred Isle' in *S.F.* without the first and last sections. The last appears in *S.R.*
51. 'The Road to Samarkand, An Essay on Flecker's *Hassan*', *The Wind and the Rain*, II (Winter), 93–103.

1945

52. THE DYNASTY OF STOWE. London: The Fortune Press.

1946

53. HIROSHIMA. ON PROPHECY AND THE SUN-BOMB. London: Andrew Dakers.

1947

54. THE CROWN OF LIFE. ESSAYS IN INTERPRETATION OF SHAKESPEARE'S FINAL PLAYS. London: Oxford University Press. Incorporates *Myth and Miracle* (1929) as Chapter One. Reprinted by Methuen and Co., 1948.

1948

55. 'The Avenging Mind', *Question*, I (July), 59–77. Reprinted in *S.R.*

56. CHRIST AND NIETZSCHE. AN ESSAY IN POETIC WISDOM. London: Staples Press.

1949

57. 'Drama and the University', *The University of Leeds Review*, I (June), 196–203. Reprinted in *S.P.*, Penguin ed. 1949.

1950

58. 'Masefield's *Tragedy of Nan*', *New Hyperion*, ed. Geoffrey Handley-Taylor. Oxford: G. Ronald.

59. 'The Plays of Lord Byron', *Times Literary Supplement*, 3 February, 80. Signed article.

1952

60. LORD BYRON: CHRISTIAN VIRTUES. London: Routledge and Kegan Paul.

61. 'The Juxon Cups', by R. S. Forman in collaboration with G.W.K., *Notes and Queries*, CXCVII (25 October), 463–7 and CXCVII (22 November), 508–11.

1953

62. 'The Valley of Edirp Gums', *Two Worlds*, No. 3405 (28 February), 3.

63. 'The New Interpretation', *Essays in Criticism*, III (October), 382–95. See also IV (April 1954), 217–22 and IV (October 1954), 430–1.

1954

64. 'Byron's Dramatic Prose', pamphlet based on GWK's Byron Foundation Lecture at the University of Nottingham delivered Friday, 16 October 1953. University of Nottingham: 1954. Reprinted in *P.A.*

65. 'Who Wrote *Don Leon*?' *The Twentieth Century*, CLVI (July), 67–79.

66. THE LAST OF THE INCAS. A PLAY ON THE CONQUEST OF PERU. Published by the author, Leeds.

67. LAUREATE OF PEACE. ON THE GENIUS OF ALEXANDER POPE. London: Routledge and Kegan Paul. Reprinted in 1965 under the title *The Poetry of Pope*.

1955

68. 'The Last of the Incas', *Act: The Drama Magazine*, Act One 1955/Scene One (January), 10–14.
69. '*The Scholar Gypsy*: An Interpretation', *Review of English Studies*, VI n.s. (January), 53–62.
70. THE MUTUAL FLAME. ON SHAKESPEARE'S SONNETS AND THE PHOENIX AND THE TURTLE. London: Methuen and Co.
71. 'Emeritus Professor Bonamy Dobrée, O.B.E.' *The University of Leeds Review*, IV (December), 375–8.

1956

72. 'Spiritualism and Poetry', *Light*, LXXVI (March), 5–9. Reprinted in *S.D.* 1959.
73. 'Colman and *Don Leon*', *The Twentieth Century*, CLIX (June), 562–73.

1957

74. 'Tewkesbury Abbey', *Poetry and Audience*, IV (3 May), 1–2.
75. LORD BYRON'S MARRIAGE. THE EVIDENCE OF ASTERISKS. London: Routledge and Kegan Paul.

1958

76. THE SOVEREIGN FLOWER. ON SHAKESPEARE AS THE POET OF ROYALISM TOGETHER WITH RELATED ESSAYS AND INDEXES TO EARLIER VOLUMES. London: Methuen and Co. The indexes to G.W.K.'s Shakespearian works, compiled by Patricia M. Ball. Principal chapters of *The Olive and the Sword* included.

1959

77. 'Nouvelles Dimensions', *Oeuvres Complètes de Shakespeare*, ed. Evans and Leyris, Paris, V, iii-xviii. Reprinted in *S.R.*
78. 'Shakespeare and Byron's Plays', *Shakespeare-Jahrbuch*, XCV, 82–97.

1960

79. 'John Masefield: An Appreciation', *John Masefield*, *O.M.*, ed. G. Handley-Taylor. London: Cranbrook Tower Press.
80. 'Spiritualism', *Gryphon*, University of Leeds. March, 16–17.

Published Writings of George Wilson Knight

1961

81. 'Acting for a Living', *Gryphon*, March, 29–30.
82. 'Most convincing religious philosophy in existence', *Two Worlds*, No. 3811 (August), 328–30. Reprinted in *C.R.* 1962.
83. 'Lawrence, Joyce and Powys', *Essays in Criticism*, XI (October), 403–17.
84. '*Timon of Athens* and its Dramatic Descendants', *A Review of English Literature*, II (October), 9–18. This later appeared in *Stratford Papers on Shakespeare 1963*, ed. Berners W. Jackson, 99–109; Toronto: W. J. Gage, 1964. Reprinted in *S.R.*

1962

85. IBSEN (*Writers and Critics* series). Edinburgh and London: Oliver and Boyd.
86. THE GOLDEN LABYRINTH. A STUDY OF BRITISH DRAMA. London: Phoenix House. Reissued by Methuen and Co., 1965.
87. 'Byron and Hamlet', *Bulletin of the John Rylands Library* (Manchester), XXXXV (September), 115–47. Reprinted in *B.S.*
88. 'Homage to Powys', *The Yorkshire Post* (6 October), 12.
89. 'Speech at the Dinner Given for Retiring Members of Staff on 18 June 1962', *The University of Leeds Review*, VIII (December), 157–60.

1963

90. '*Owen Glendower*', *A Review of English Literature*, IV (January), 41–52.
91. 'Sight and Sound in Shakespearian Production', *Prompt*, No. 3, 18–20. Reprinted in *S.P.* 1964.
92. 'The Kitchen Sink: On Recent Developments in Drama', *Encounter*, XXI (December), 48–54.

1964

93. 'J. Middleton Murry', *Of Books and Humankind. Essays and Poems Presented to Bonamy Dobrée*, ed. John Butt, 149–63. London: Routledge and Kegan Paul.
94. '*Scrutiny* and Criticism', *Essays in Criticism*, XIV (January), 32–6.
95. THE SATURNIAN QUEST. A CHART OF THE PROSE WORKS OF JOHN COWPER POWYS. London: Methuen and Co.

96. *Shakespearian Production*, enlarged, London: Faber and Faber. See Item 35 above.
97. '*Venus and Adonis*', *Radio Times*, 16 April, 38. Reprinted in *S.R.*
98. 'New Light on Shakespeare's Sonnets', *The Listener*, LXXI (30 April) 715–17. Reprinted in *S.R.*
99. 'Shakespeare and the "Supernatural"', *Light*, LXXXIV (Autumn), 116–23. Reprinted in *S.R.*
100. 'Shakespeare and Theology: A Private Protest', *Essays in Criticism*, XV (January), 95–104. Reprinted in *S.R.*

1966

101. 'T. S. Eliot. Some Literary Impressions', *The Sewanee Review* (January-March), 239–55; republished in *T. S. Eliot: the Man and his Work*, ed. Allen Tate. London: Chatto and Windus, 1967.
102. BYRON AND SHAKESPEARE. London: Routledge and Kegan Paul.
103. 'Symbolism' in *The Reader's Encyclopedia of Shakespeare*, ed. Oscar James Campbell, New York: Thomas Y. Crowell Co. Reprinted in *S.R.*

1967

104. SHAKESPEARE AND RELIGION. ESSAYS OF FORTY YEARS. London: Routledge and Kegan Paul.
105. POETS OF ACTION. London: Methuen and Co. Contains material from *The Burning Oracle* and a condensed version of *Chariot of Wrath*.
106. 'Masefield and Spiritualism', in *Mansions of the Spirit*, ed. George A. Panichas. New York: Hawthorn Books.
107. 'The Duchess of Malfi', *The Malahat Review*, University of Victoria, Canada, 4 (October), 88–113.

1968

108. GOLD-DUST. WITH OTHER POETRY. London: Routledge and Kegan Paul.
109. 'Rupert Brooke', in *Promise of Greatness: the War of 1914–1918*, ed. George A. Panichas. London: Cassell and Co.

Supplementary Items

1. Tape Recordings by G. Wilson Knight. The following tape recordings by Sound Seminars, Cincinnati were published (1968)

by The McGraw-Hill Publishing Company, Maidenhead (England) and New York: 'Shakespeare's Rhetoric'; 'Shakespeare and the English Language'; 'Byron's Rhetoric'.

2. A forthcoming volume by G. Wilson Knight, *Neglected Powers*, to appear probably in 1969, will be a collection of past essays on modern writers, together with new material.

Most of the volumes listed in this bibliography are now published in U.S.A. by Messrs. Barnes and Noble, New York. Exceptions are: *Lord Byron's Marriage*, by The Macmillan Company, New York; *The Christian Renaissance* (1962) and *The Golden Labyrinth*, by Messrs. W. W. Norton and Co., New York; and *Shakespearian Production* (1964), by The Northwestern University Press, Evanston, Illinois.

Reviews, press letters and other minor items have been omitted from this list. A supplement covering these items is likely to appear in the Bulletin of the New York Public Library.

Index